Hot Pants and Spandex Suits

Hot Pants and Spandex Suits

Gender Representation in American Superhero Comic Books

Esther De Dauw

RUTGERS UNIVERSITY PRESS
NEW BRUNSWICK, CAMDEN, AND NEWARK,
NEW JERSEY, AND LONDON

Library of Congress Cataloging-in-Publication Data
Names: De Dauw, Esther, author.
Title: Hot pants and spandex suits: gender representation in American superhero comic books / Esther De Dauw.
Description: New Brunswick: Rutgers University Press, [2021] | Includes bibliographical references and index.
Identifiers: LCCN 2020010829 | ISBN 9781978806030 (paperback) | ISBN 9781978806047 (cloth) | ISBN 9781978806054 (epub) | ISBN 9781978806061 (mobi) | ISBN 9781978806078 (pdf)
Subjects: LCSH: Comic books, strips, etc.—History and criticism. | Superheroes in literature. | Gender identity in literature. | Race awareness in literature. | National characteristics, American, in literature.
Classification: LCC PN6725 .D4 2021 | DDC 741.5/973—dc23
LC record available at https://lccn.loc.gov/2020010829

A British Cataloging-in-Publication record for this book is available from the British Library.

♾ The paper used in this publication meets the requirements of the American National Standard for Information Sciences—Permanence of Paper for Printed Library Materials, ANSI Z39.48-1992.

www.rutgersuniversitypress.org

Manufactured in the United States of America

Contents

Hot Pants and Spandex Suits

Introduction

For almost eighty years, superheroes have been a part of American mass media and, through the increased presence and popularity of superhero films and TV series, are now considered a staple of American culture, exported to international audiences in several different mass media formats. Originally appearing in comic books, superheroes have also appeared in syndicated newspaper strips and radio serials, animated cartoons, TV series, films, and original web content. Most mainstream audiences are accessing the superhero outside of comic book content, through the Marvel Cinematic Universe (MCU) (2008–ongoing), Netflix's series, and the CW Network's TV series.[1] With wide ranges of products serving as superhero merchandise (literally anything you can slap a hero's chevron or face on), superheroes being adopted for various political and social movements, and *Avengers: Endgame* (2019) bringing in a worldwide $2.796 billion at the box office, making it the highest-grossing film of all time, it is safe to say that superheroes are at least as culturally relevant now as when they first took the world by storm.[2] Arguably, with everyday life increasingly saturated with mass media and advertising, superheroes are more present than ever, and, like many other comic scholars, I want to dig into what it is they say about and to us. Situated at the intersection of comic studies, cultural studies, and theories of structural power relations, this book discusses superheroes in their sociohistorical context and determines how they are informed by dominant gender ideology in the American cultural landscape.

A History of the Industry

In this book, I focus mostly on the comics instead of the films or TV series that superheroes appear in, which warrants a brief history of the medium. Despite film and TV's ability to reach a wider audience, the sheer amount of comic titles produced, with roughly seventy-five monthly titles published by Marvel Comics and seventy-three by DC Comics as of this writing, points to comics as being the dominant media format of superheroes. Additionally, TV series and Hollywood movies are considered *adaptations* of the comics, and thus comics remain the primary medium dictating the shape and form of superhero content, even as other media content also influences comics.[3] As the original progenitor of the superhero, the comic book medium and its industry have significantly defined the concept of the superhero.[4] The industry's history was initially documented by fans and expert practitioners, who used labels that Marvel and DC adopted to categorize the different ages of comic book development: Golden Age (1930s–1950s), Silver Age (1950s–1970s), Bronze Age (1970s–1980s), Dark Age (1980s–1990s), and Modern Age (1990s–2010s). Each age is supposedly defined by dominating narrative, formal, or economic trends. While the exact dates of the ages (and the use of this classification) are regularly debated in both fan communities and academia, the industry generally accepts them. Discussing the "extremely articulate critique of that model" by Benjamin Woo, Orion Ussner Kidder writes that Woo "contends that the terms are inherently antithetical to academic rigor."[5] As Kidder states, agreement with this analysis does not preclude the usefulness of these terms, considering its use by the industry, professionals, fans, creators, experts, and the academic field. Recently, the American studies scholar Adrienne Resha provided a compelling argument that we have entered a new stage: the Blue Age of comic books (2010s–ongoing), which is defined by the digitization of comic books and comic book culture's increasingly online presence.[6] When discussing history and comics, these terms are inescapable and will be used in this book when appropriate.

In June 1938, DC published *Action Comics #1* with Superman on the cover for the first time. Comics were a fairly new medium and consisted mostly of collections of reprinted syndicated newspaper strips with few original story lines. Because of the popularity of these collections, publishers began to pay artists and writers for new comic book content, which led to the creation of short comics and, eventually, to the publication of Superman. The immense success of this character launched the superhero genre, which dominated the comic book industry for nearly fifteen years. As Bradford W. Wright explains, "Most comic book titles sold between 200,000 and 400,000 copies per issues," and "each issue of *Action Comics* (featuring one Superman story each) regularly sold about 900,000 copies per months."[7] Following Superman's lead, other publishers jumped on the superhero bandwagon and the market became saturated with other superheroes and imitations, which heralded the Golden Age of Comics. Historically, the Golden Age is defined by the industry's extraordinary output as well as Superman's omnipresence. While there exists, in online boards and fan communities, a nostalgic reverence for Golden Age stories, the quality of the material is often questionable. In Golden Age illustrations, the background is often blank, and there is a lack of detail in objects in the foreground. There is a wooden quality to the characters' bodies, most visible in stoic facial expressions, which can be partly attributed to the low quality of the paper and the cheap printing process that would have blurred any detail in the artist's original composition. Comics were popular with publishers because they were cheap to produce and finished products could be bought cheaply from artist studios or shops. Artists and writers often worked as freelancers and worked together as a studio/shop, which functioned as an assembly line with the writing, drawing, coloring, lettering, and inking of the work divided among contributors. This allowed for the fast production of a fully finished product. The copyright was often transferred to the publisher as part of the sale, with the understanding that the publisher would continue to pay the shop for new issues. Many artists considered comic book work as a way to make money while they worked on their "real art" or until they were contracted to illustrate syndicated newspaper strips, which were more respectable. Both inside and outside the industry, comic books were dismissed as lowbrow mass entertainment. Sold cheaply, they were affordable to the largest demographic in the 1930s: the working poor.

Following the Depression and unprecedented levels of unemployment across the United States, a large part of the population became subject to extreme poverty. The cultural landscape shifted in response, abandoning the "Victorian middle-class axiom" and turning to blue-collar sentiments instead.[8] The middle class shrank while the working class expanded and the working poor and unemployed reached record numbers. Superman was born in this context, with mass media focusing on the common man, who was working-class and beaten down, desperately struggling against the forces of industry and modernization.[9] As Wright writes, "From Depression-era popular culture, there came a passionate celebration of the common man" and his victory over the social forces set against him.[10] Especially science fiction and fantasy offered up avenues of escape by removing the hero from the contemporary modern world, which allowed his masculine abilities to thrive, or by imbuing the hero with abilities that allowed him to conquer the modern world itself. Superman, brought into the world by avid readers of science fiction and fantasy, could bend the world around him for the sake of the disenfranchised and the poor. His creators were young members of the Jewish community, which increasingly rejected the tenets of laissez-faire capitalism in favor of a more social model as their community was disproportionally impacted by the Great Depression and its governmental and municipal budget cuts, as well as segregation and anti-Semitism.[11] As Aldo J. Regalado writes, Superman and the heroes that followed him are rooted in traditional American heroic discourse that sets Anglo-Saxon masculinity within the American context at the top of the racial hierarchy. While Superman set new standards for heroism and created a new image of masculinity, he did so by "redefining the ethnic and class requirements of masculinity in America."[12] Superman created a heroic category that incorporated the working-class man and expanded the concept of whiteness to include non–Anglo-Saxon European. This allowed non–Anglo-Saxon communities to buy into enfranchisement at the cost of punching down, separating themselves from a more easily "recognizable" and identifiable Other, to conform to the dominant order.[13] This "involved masking or de-emphasizing ethnic identity" in favor of an American national identity for white-skinned characters, "embracing models of white masculinity and, to some degree, optimistically championing the social institution of the society they hoped to be a part of."[14] Superman and superheroes like him were often vocal defenders of social justice and the (white) working class, combatting the social evils that created poverty and crime. They functioned as a power fantasy for the economically disenfranchised and the phenotypically white immigrants who found themselves excluded from mainstream society.

This process of breaking open the category of whiteness was accelerated through World War II, as superheroes increasingly fought Nazis, who were portrayed as a European Other. This placed Nazi racism in contrast to American values, such as democracy and freedom, further framing white American identity as a noble and powerful force for good. In this way, American superheroes demonstrated that a (phenotypically) white American identity was the central requirement for powerful masculinity, displacing Anglo-Saxon or Germanic ancestry as a prerequisite for whiteness. As Regalado writes: "Having redefined whiteness in more inclusive terms, American superheroes consolidated these gains for their creators by increasingly resorting to traditional strategies of pitting white masculine heroes against racially defined 'others.' This trend became even more pronounced as the Second World War created opportunities for marrying more inclusive notions of whiteness to a national cause."[15] Essentially, the war provided superhero comics with the opportunity to define white masculinity, elevating the white American above other whites and the racial Other. While this initially sustained a superhero boom, the focus on white men to the exclusion of white women also contributed to the initial, gentle decline in sales in the late 1940s, foreshadowing the 1950s collapse of the superhero genre.[16] As men joined the war, women joined the workforce and increased their independent spending power. Comic books attempted to capitalize on this potential new customer base after the success of Miss Fury and Wonder Woman in 1941 by churning out female copies.[17] However, superhero comics never really recovered. At the end of the war, superhero comic books continued to lose sales while jungle, Western, and crime comics began to flourish. Postwar prosperity ensured that working-class values lost their appeal, and with the rise of capitalist consumer culture, the more social justice–oriented superhero genre could not keep up. Robert Genter writes that "the country transformed from a goods-producing society to a service-centred one and the American worker transformed from the brawny, industrial labourer from the turn-of-the-century into the conformist white-collar worker of the 1950s."[18] In the 1950s, America became increasingly middle class, and without a public eager for a working-class hero, mass media increasingly catered to the middle class and there was no need for a working-class hero. Many superhero titles were canceled.[19]

Not only did comics become less popular due to a changed demographic and competing mass media formats, such as television, but the growing controversy around comic books and their possible link to juvenile crime contributed to declining sales throughout the 1950s. The backlash against comic books heavily rested on the higher- and middle-class understanding of intelligence as the "refinement of aesthetic taste" and fears over the subversive nature of print culture dating back to the nineteenth century.[20] Essentially, highbrow and lowbrow culture is an artificial divide that defines the popular culture of the masses as vulgar and unrefined *because* of its widespread appeal, while highbrow culture is morally superior based on its exclusive availability to the middle or upper class. Intelligence was understood as the ability to identify highbrow aesthetic and entertainment. Comic books embodied lowbrow culture and were increasingly suspect as they "challenged the notions of order, respectability, sobriety, self-control, productivity, and character championed by adherents to the nation's capitalist mainstream."[21] Comics' status as mass media objects also drew criticism from those who feared that consumerism and luxury were corrupting influences that undermined (masculine) virtues at a time when the Cold War required American citizens to remain hardy and vigilant against communist forces. Furthermore, according to Thomas Hine, comic books were extremely popular among young teenagers and children, but contained increasingly violent and disturbing content that was unsuitable for this audience. Because they were so cheap, they were often purchased by children with their own pocket money, without parental oversight, and children often brought comics to school and swapped them.[22] This decreased parental control over the comic book content that children consumed occurred at a time when parents were already wringing their hands at the level of independence that children and teenagers increasingly displayed.[23] Throughout the late 1940s and early 1950s, the comic industry came under fire for corrupting the nation's youth and something had to be done.

As early as 1948, the industry devised self-regulating measures, such as the Comics Code, to deflect criticism. However, this code was ineffectual at curtailing extreme violence through a lack of any consequences for code violations. It did very little to change the industry's output and halt the growing backlash. In 1953, the United States Senate created the Subcommittee on Juvenile Delinquency to examine the extent of juvenile crime and its causes. Many comic book publishers were called on to testify, as well as educators and child professionals, including the child psychologist Dr. Fredric Wertham. While the committee concluded that there was not enough evidence to suggest that comic books directly caused juvenile delinquency, the report heavily implies that they were a contributing factor. Several states attempted to ban comic books, but the bans were defeated in court through constitutional concerns regarding censorship.[24] The situation escalated when Wertham published his book *Seduction of the Innocent* (1954), which is based on his experiences working with criminally convicted children and young people. While his book did not use a scientific method and often misrepresented evidence by not referencing sources, it was very popular. *Seduction of the Innocent* presented compelling anecdotal evidence, and Wertham's genuine concern for children's development clearly shines through. He was particularly concerned with the rampant racism present in all forms of popular culture and its influence over young people's morals and values. He believed in higher regulation for all forms of cultural output instead of allowing economic concerns to dictate the shape of mass media. In other words, he believed that just because crime sells does not mean that it should be sold. Comics, with their hold on the nation's youth and the growing backlash against the medium, were an easy target. Wertham wielded the rhetoric used by Cold War warriors who chastised the nation's lack of moral fortitude, accusing comic books of promoting the kind of depravity that would infect children's minds. While he focused on crime and horror comics as the main source for juvenile crime, he also despised superheroes. He believed they were fascist and taught children, especially young girls, unnatural gender roles.[25] Pressure on the industry increased when schools and church groups organized public comic book burnings and retailers refused to sell comic books.[26] In response, the industry founded the Comics Code Authority (CCA) in 1954 to regulate its output.

The CCA consisted of a main administrator in charge of an expansive team of child care professionals. Publishers were required to pay a membership fee as well as a submission fee for every issue. Each comic would be reviewed, sent back with a list of changes to be made, and issued with the official CCA stamp on completion. Retailers refused to sell comics that did not have the CCA stamp. Some publishers were able to opt out of the CCA without having their comic books boycotted by retail outlets. For example, Dell Comics maintained that its line of education comics had always been beyond reproach and refused to associate its brand with less reputable publishers via the CCA. However, most publishers did not enjoy such a positive reputation and were forced to work with the CCA to get their comics on the shelves. The CCA's approval process could be time-consuming and expensive. Therefore, an extremely strict adherence to the code prevented delays and loss of revenue. Most publishers immediately canceled their horror and crime series, removed any graphic depictions of crime from their detective comics, and eliminated any hints of nudity in their jungle books.[27] The CCA "was tailored to affirm the dictates of suburban home life," middle-class respectability, and the validity of Cold War America's ideological opposition to the USSR, contributing to the creation of increasingly conservative comic books.[28] Within several years, comic books came to be seen as harmless children's entertainment and, as a medium, inherently childish. As Regalado writes, they became "the type of product that could be comfortably dismissed by mature adults with anything higher than lowbrow aesthetic tastes. As such, superhero comic books largely ceased to register as blips on the cultural radars of most social reformers and concerned citizens."[29] Several small publishers perished in this environment, while those that survived returned to the older superhero genre to boost sales.

The late 1950s saw a resurgence of the superhero genre, with a new direction consisting of whimsical what-if narratives, futuristic technology, and a combination of science fiction and fantasy. In this sense, the Silver Age (1950s–1970s) refers to a time when the CCA was initially in control, although the 1960s–1970s saw increasing challenges to its restriction. It is also defined through "its expansion into television and animation, and its expansion of the superhero genre."[30] In terms of gender, the CCA required that men and women fulfill traditional gender roles to fit in with traditional American values. Gay characters were nonexistent or extremely closeted. The code explicitly prohibited the depiction of "illicit sex relations" and "sexual abnormalities."[31] This referred to sexual relations outside of marriage and adultery, which were a staple of pre-code detective and crime comics, as well as homosexuality. While some superheroes have retroactively been identified as gay, such as the Rawhide Kid in *Rawhide Kid* (1955–1957, 1960–1979), no superheroes were openly gay during this time. The CCA also specified that "ridicule of or attack on any religious or racial group is never permissible."[32] Black characters were rare in the Golden Age, and most characters of color at that time were racist stereotypes. Particularly Japanese, Chinese, and other Asian characters were presented as monstrous, an evil racial Other that white America had to defend itself against, reflecting fears about race and yellow peril stereotypes during World War II. While attempting to block racism in comics was a positive step forward for a self-regulating industry, the overzealous application of the code and white fears of discussing racism resulted in non-white characters disappearing from the comic pages altogether.[33] Even narratives that directly engaged with the negative consequences of racism were banned, because they showed racism and people of color being treated poorly by white characters. As a result, racial differences became embodied by white characters who represented a racial Other or characters who had blue, green, or red skin. It was not until the code was less strictly interpreted, owing to the increased liberalization of American society throughout the 1960s, that Black characters reappeared in comic books.

The CCA's control of the industry could not last during the 1960s and 1970s, when changes in America's cultural landscape influenced mass media. The antiwar sentiment and disillusionment with American power and authority made the CCA's insistence on a respectful depiction of authority outdated. With the invention of the first oral contraceptive pill in the 1960s and the rise of second wave feminism, which argued for greater political, financial, and social freedom for women, contemporary attitudes toward sex became less conservative. Simultaneously, the Stonewall riots in 1969 generated a radical gay liberation movement compared with the earlier, more sedate homophile movement. The civil rights movement in the 1960s campaigned to end racial segregation and discrimination against African Americans and secure their citizenship rights through legislation and social awareness. Publishers increasingly pushed the limits of the code, submitting less and less conservative issues, while the CCA increasingly interpreted the code in less conservative ways and stamped its seal of approval on issues that would not have seen the light of day a decade earlier. This led to the creation of characters such as Spider-Man (1962), the Hulk (1962), and Black Panther (1966), who challenged American institutions and pushed back against the more conservative trends in comics.

As Wakanda's representative and king, Black Panther is meant to signify the potential of Black identity outside of white European-American control. In the 1950s, growing resistance to European colonialist expansion led many African nations to seek independence from European governance. According to Adilifu Nama, Black Panther represented "African leaders [who] embodied the hopes of their people and captured the imagination of the anticolonialist movement with their charisma and promise to free Africa from European imperialism."[34] Certainly, Black Panther's resistance to colonial forces taking over Wakanda allows him to function as such a symbol, existing as "an idealized composite of third-world Black revolutionaries and the anticolonialist movement of the 1950s that they represented."[35] However, this representation was not free from racism. As Martin Lund points out, Wakanda is steeped in white stereotypes about Africa.[36] Lund discusses how, in their initial meeting with Black Panther and their first visit to Wakanda in 1966, even the Fantastic Four realize that Wakanda seems to consist almost entirely out of colonial narratives and Hollywood imagery. Wakanda is surrounded by a "primitive" and "undeveloped" jungle that "recalls notions about the African continent as nature-rich but underdeveloped '*terra nullius*, that is, vacant land,' ripe for white interference."[37] The insistence on Wakanda's technological developments, implying a Western view of progress as automatically taking similar routes as Western nations, does not negate the representation of Wakanda as exotic, barbaric, and undeveloped or culturally unsophisticated.

The 1960s also saw the rise of organized comic book fandom, when Julius Schwartz, the editor in chief for DC comics, added full addresses in the letter columns at the back of comic books, which allowed comic book fans to communicate with each other.[38] Once communication was established, the publication of homemade, small-scale fan magazines (fanzines) distributed through the postal system created a thriving fan culture that discussed all aspects of superhero comic book production. This included social issues and how they were handled in comics as well as the CCA and censorship. Fanzines became social spaces where the community shared their enthusiasm for the medium and for specific characters, recounting stories of visiting flea market to find old issues of favorite characters.[39] Fan communities, who fondly discussed old superheroes they had read as children in the 1940s, imbued these 1940s superheroes with new meaning, which Schwartz capitalized on by reviving old superheroes that had gone out of publication. Fan activity was heavily encouraged by Marvel and DC, which used these communities as free market research and advertisement, as fanzines provided a direct pipeline to their customer bases and allowed them to cultivate brand loyalty.[40] This direct interaction between fans and the industry created loyal fans, not just to companies but also to artists and writers, who were able to use their popularity as a bargaining tool to increase their pay, negotiate royalty payments, and maintain greater (although still limited) control over their intellectual property. However, it became increasingly clear that the stories fans wanted to read could not be published in the CCA's controlled market.

Mainstream media's lack of interest in comics, combined with the increasing push against the CCA's limits by fans, led to the code's rewrite in 1970. This ushered in the Bronze Age (1970s–1980s), where female characters could wear more revealing clothing and implied sexual contact was permitted. However, it still prohibited "violations of good taste or decency," which was sufficiently vague enough to leave its application open to interpretation.[41] The "Marriage and Sex" section stipulated that "sex perversions or any inference to the same," which was code for homosexuality, "was strictly forbidden."[42] The code effectively prevented comics from engaging openly with queer characters, and, as a result, Marvel's Chris Claremont and John Byrne created a "subtle" gay character in 1979 called Northstar, a member of Alpha Flight, the Canadian superhero team.[43] His civilian identity was Jean-Paul Beaubier, a French Canadian Olympic skier, who was never seen dating women because he was too focused on his career to commit to a relationship. During the 1980s, Northstar contracted a mysterious illness, which resulted in a hacking cough and limited healing/recovery abilities, which was rumored to be AIDS. However, the story line was squashed by Carl Potts, the editor of the *Alpha Flight* comics, as AIDS was still considered to be a "gay disease" and supposedly would have outed Northstar as gay to the general audience. Instead, his illness became the result of a cosmic disturbance interfering with his mutant powers.[44] The new code did not update its previous restrictions on religion or race, but these rules were now interpreted less conservatively, which allowed for the rise of Black superheroes. John Stewart as the Green Lantern (1971) and Luke Cage as Power Man (1972) were the first attempts to create Black superheroes who resembled real-life minorities. However, these superheroes were still written mostly by white writers, depicted by white artists, and under the control of white editors. As Derek Lackaff and Michael Sales write, these characters were not as progressive as Black readers may have hoped for: "In the 1970s, these attempts to introduce Black faces left many Black comic book readers unsatisfied. Black characters were often given a heavy-handed stigma that immediately marked them as the 'racial' character, especially with their names, Black Panther, Black Lightning, The Black Racer, Brother Voodoo, Black Goliath, Black Vulcan, Black Spider."[45] Black superheroes suffered from tokenism and being "marked" as the single Black superhero. These stereotypes persisted throughout the 1980s and 1990s, although they became increasingly diluted because of growing social awareness.

Throughout the Bronze Age, comics also became more violent, especially toward female characters. While the CCA did state that rape or sexual assault "shall never be shown or suggested," physical violence against female characters continued to rise.[46] Often attributed to the backlash against feminist gains, mass media in the 1980s American landscape increasingly depicted violence against women.[47] On the one hand, it did this by creating "strong" female action heroes who could physically enter combat and go toe-to-toe with any male character as a move toward feminism. On the other hand, it also increasingly killed and mutilated women in action and horror films. The 1980s saw the publication of comics such as *Batman: The Dark Knight Returns* (1986), by Frank Miller; *Watchmen* (1986–1987), by Alan Moore and David Gibbons; and *Batman: The Killing Joke* (1988), by Alan Moore and Brian Bolland. These works contained high levels of violence against women, as well as antiestablishment sentiments, which would have made them unpublishable only twenty years earlier, but which the increased normalization of violence and sexual imagery in the American mass media of the 1970s and 1980s allowed. These publications are often considered the first products of the Dark

Age of Comics (1980s–1990s), and the impact they had on the industry was substantial. They contributed to the growing cultural notion that comics had to be more realistic, which meant gritty and dark compared with the more camp, fantastical variety of the Silver and Bronze Ages, and should be marketed to adults to elevate the medium.[48] This contributed to the still-popular notion that books involving violence and sexual trauma are inherently more artistic, that they speak to the human experience in a way that happier or less traumatic books cannot, and that these texts are worthier of study than camp or silly narratives. While, increasingly, new comic scholars are strongly criticizing this understanding of dark comics, it is an attitude that disappointingly continues to exist in the industry, among both fans and comic scholarship.

Throughout the Dark Age, the relationship between fans and creators shifted again as older fans entered the industry as creators and professionals. This hastened the demise of the CCA as fans-turned-creators made the more radical comics they had wanted to read as teenagers in the 1960s and 1970s. Furthermore, the fan culture's investment in documenting comic history and tracking continuity seeped into the industry, which began to streamline continuity and published books and guides on comic book ages. The sale of these was facilitated through the emergence of the direct market: small, independent comic book shops run by fans who sold not only comics but also all comic-related paraphernalia.[49] This weakened the CCA's power, as a main incentive for companies such as Marvel and DC to adhere to it lay in retailers' refusal to sell comics lacking the CCA seal of approval. Specialty shops, however, did not ban non-CCA comic books. These shops also narrowed the demographic of comic book fans. As Carolyn Cocca writes, the "increasing number of specialized comic shops, higher sticker prices due to higher paper costs, suburbanization, a royalty system and a focus on high sales of superhero comics and merchandise tended to concentrate the comic fan base—it seemed to be mostly male, white and older"; and as these shops were run by this fan base, "many also fostered exclusionary cultures that deterred new and/or demographically different readers."[50] Essentially, comic book shops allowed comic book creators to cater to their fans' wishes more directly, and with the shop functioning as a gatekeeping mechanism, these wishes resulted in sexier and more violent comics catering to straight, white men.

In 1989, the CCA updated the code to reflect the increased acceptability of adult themes in comics and had fewer restrictions on homosexuality, sex, and race. The "Characterizations" section stated that

> character portrayals will be carefully crafted and show sensitivity to national, ethnic, religious, sexual and socioeconomic orientations. If it is dramatically appropriate for one character to demean another because of his or her sex, ethnicity, religion, sexual preference, political orientation, socioeconomic status or disabilities, the demeaning words or actions will be clearly shown to be wrong or ignorant in the course of the story. Stories depicting characters subject to physical, mental, or emotional problems or with economic disadvantages

> should never assign ultimate responsibility for these conditions to the character themselves. Heroes should be role models and should reflect the prevailing social attitudes.[51]

While this version of the code seems to clearly promote equality and positive representation of minorities, its reference to "prevailing social attitudes" still leaves a loophole subject to personal and subjective interpretation.[52] Certainly, the characters produced during this time fell into what was then considered positive representation, with non-white, nonstraight, nonmale characters acting "normal," which is a concept rife with preconceived notions about what people should be and maintains the status quo through the perpetuation and exaltation of normative behaviors. The "Attire and Sexuality" section quoted "decency" and "good taste" when referencing adult sexual relationships and made no specific mention concerning the depiction of homosexuality.[53] As a result, in 1992, Northstar finally came out of the closet, although his sexuality was barely ever mentioned again or alluded to in subsequent publications. Gareth Schott, in his excellent analysis of the character, writes that "while Northstar was initially held up as a gay icon, his impact quickly faded with fewer appearances, some as only a secondary character. Northstar did resurface, only to be killed, resurrected, brainwashed, saved and then cured."[54] Northstar's progressive potential was lost as he never seemed to rise above tokenism. Instead, his "subtle" sexuality is exemplary of how, for most of comic book history, gay superheroes were invisible (to a straight audience). The 1989 code makes no separate mention for race or racism. Most Black characters introduced in the 1970s disappeared by the late 1980s as blaxploitation's popularity plummeted. Other ethnic minority superheroes were even slower to appear, and again, comics interacted with their heritage in a way that either (1) was rife with socially acceptable stereotypes, (2) lumped individual cultures together in a racist potluck of "it is all the same," or (3) whitewashed ethnic minority cultures.

At the beginning of the Modern Age (1990s–2010s), DC and Marvel increasingly began to publish issues or titles without the CCA seal of approval.[55] With the rise of the direct market, comics were increasingly seen as a popular medium with a large customer base, and Marvel and DC attempted to capitalize on the collector mind-set through the production of variant covers, special editions, and shocking story lines that generated attention even in the mainstream media, such as the death of Superman (1992). Outraged by the commercialization of the comic medium, many fans left the community and the backlash caused a massive drop in sales. The inflation of limited edition and special issues attracted not only collectors but also buyers, with an eye to save and resell the issues when they became more valuable. This contributed to the dismantling of comic shop communities. The direct market collapsed, with many small and local comic book shops closing and Marvel even declaring bankruptcy in 1996.[56] By the early 2000s, DC and Marvel were desperate to regain a customer base and were willing to take risks to do so: the CCA was disregarded entirely. In theory, comics were now allowed to include any kind of material they wanted. However, it was not through comics that superheroes became relevant again. Instead, superheroes became culturally relevant for children through cartoons, such as the DC Animated Universe (1992–2006), and through films for adults, such as *Blade* (1998), *Hulk* (2003), *Daredevil* (2003), and *Elektra* (2003). While these films are now often lambasted by fans as poorly written and acted, they were moderate commercial successes at the time. Comic book sales slowly started to rise again, but even without the CCA, most superheroes were still straight, white, and male.

While female characters had seen some increase in numbers in previous ages, only a few superheroes came out as gay, and, at the time of writing, gay superheroes remain low in number. Some gay superheroes have had their sexuality confirmed by editors or authors but have not openly stated or acted on their sexuality in any publication, such as Catman from Gail Simone's *Secret Six* (2005–2006, 2008–2011).[57] Those who are openly gay are either in a relationship or perpetually single. In 2006, Batwoman was marketed as DC's first openly lesbian superhero to hold her own titular comic and was explicitly framed as DC's high-profile lesbian character, intended to be part of DC's regular lineup and slotted to join the planned *Justice League* comic before it was turned into a miniseries. In 2007, Renee Montoya, an established lesbian character in the DC universe, resigned from the Gotham City Police Department (GCPD) after being outed at work and took over the superhero name "Question" from Vic Savage. At the start of the Blue Age, the New 52 reboot also introduced new gay characters, such as Bunker (team member of the Teen Titans), and Gravity Kid and Power Boy (members of the Legion Academy), but these new gay superheroes have received very little media attention, have not appeared in many publications, and have no merchandise. The reboot also impacted Renee Montoya's story line as she appeared once again as a member of the GCPD instead of a superhero in 2015.

In 2012, Northstar received considerable media attention when Marvel announced his marriage to his long-term partner, Kyle Jinadu, in order to celebrate New York's legalization of gay marriage in 2011. The wedding received an extraordinary amount of publicity from Marvel, which promoted it with the tagline "Save the Date" as the event of the year.[58] This kind of attention raised a few questions. Would a marriage between two heterosexual characters draw the same sort of attention? The wedding between Superman and Lois Lane in 1996 certainly did, but that was a relationship with sixty years of history.[59] If most heterosexual couples would not receive this kind of attention, the attention that Marvel's gay wedding received can be read as a celebration of progressive values or an attempt to cash in on current events, targeting a new potential audience. Marvel was eager to present the wedding as a representation of how comics were becoming more progressive and in-tune with contemporary morals and values.[60] Another long-term romantic couple in the Marvel universe are Wiccan and Hulkling, two members of the Young Avengers superhero team who became engaged in 2012. In 2015, in one of the more convoluted story lines detailed in *All New X-Men* (2012–ongoing), the original X-Men team from the 1960s travels to the future (current times) and the young, 1960s-era Jean Grey discovers that the 1960s-era Ice Man is gay by reading his mind. The team discusses how the Ice Man who lives in current times never came out or even seemed to realize that he was gay, which means that Jean's discovery has potentially altered 1960s-era Ice Man's future. However, the comic does not address Jean's violation of Ice Man's privacy and the potential dangers of outing someone without their permission or consent. It seems that in the 2010s, gay superheroes are simultaneously losing and gaining ground.

In addition to an increase in gay characters, the Blue Age has also seen more Black characters join the ranks of the superhero community, such as Batwing (2011) and Miles Morales as Spider-Man (2011). However, these superheroes of color, no matter their strength or weaknesses, often take a backseat to white superheroes. As Albert S. Fu explains, "Despite the creation of numerous heroes of colour, it is still the Caucasian-'looking' aliens (Superman), mutants (most of the X-Men) and talented humans (Batman) that are *mainstream* heroes."[61] Black superheroes are still less popular and less well known, often sidelined in favor of white superheroes. Often, they do not have merchandise that provides greater cultural dissemination, and when they do, it is often because they are paired with a white character or have inherited a legacy name that allows their merchandise to cross race boundaries. When superheroes are lifted from the comic book pages to star in TV series and films, non-Black characters of color are often whitewashed. For example, the white Elizabeth Olsen was cast to play the Romani Scarlet Witch in *Avengers: Age of Ultron* (2015), and although Dr. Strange had been drawn as racially ambiguous for decades, the white Benedict Cumberbatch was cast to play him in *Doctor Strange* (2016). While comics have a long history of rhetorically promoting acceptance and tolerance, they have failed to represent gender or racial equality through character creation and narrative drive, with recent years seeing both progress and decline, especially as superheroes re-entered the mainstream through "superhero blockbuster films, downloadable television shows, and trade paperbacks available in bookstores."[62] At the end of the Modern Age and the start of the Blue Age of Comics, superheroes were no longer contained to comics and the comic book shop.

While the emergence of the comic book shop allowed for gatekeepers to tightly control the social spaces in which comic fans gathered, the demise of small, local comic book shops and the appearance of the internet have opened up social fandom spaces. As Resha identified in her coinage of the term the "Blue Age of Comic Books," the introduction of digitally available comic books is a considerable game changer. She argues that the Blue Age of Comics began in the 2010s, following the debut of comics retailer ComiXology in 2007, and is defined through the increased popularity of digital publication. This includes the use of "digital readers, guided reading technologies and social media."[63] Digital comics, remediated through digital readers, phone or laptop screens, and diverse modes of reading, allow for further capitalizations on newer and younger audiences. Resha writes: "Comics Publishers must simultaneously appeal to an aging, homogenous group of traditional comics readers and to a younger, heterogeneous group of potential readers that is inclusive of women, people of color, and people with disabilities."[64] If we consider white men to be the historical main audience of comic books, and both mainstream culture and comic book publishers indicate that they are, potential new readers present a possibly new demographic hungry for more diverse representation and who are slowly coming into their spending power. Digital comics allow for further reach and distribution, as fans do not rely on their local comic book shop to carry their preferred titles, and destabilize the collector culture that has defined fan culture for several decades. Digital comic platforms displace the gatekeepers of the fan community and allow this space to be opened up to nontraditional readers. As the Silver Age saw the advent of fan communities, so does the Blue Age become defined through the vibrant online fan engagement via social media.

The increased use of online spaces has created an online culture where expressions of appreciation of any given work are primarily through the fan's interaction with the community and engagement with the source material by transforming it instead of both collecting original source material and being able to remember every detail about it in order to provide fan credentials to gatekeepers. While fans initially used online blogs provided by corporations, such as Livejournal or Dreamwidth, they eventually created the Archive of Our Own website, often referred to as AO3, to protect fanworks from exploitation and deletion by corporations as well as possible lawsuits from the owners of the original content. Recently, in 2019, AO3 won the Hugo Award for Best Related Works, highlighting the importance of fanworks and the archive built to house them.[65] Of course, the AO3 online space is not superhero specific and caters to fans of any and all kinds of content, but it highlights how the media industries' engagement with fans is increasingly becoming more important in order to gauge "cultural capital," which is increasingly replacing ratings or sales numbers as the measure of content's success. If fan engagement is becoming the new metric, Marvel's and DC's strategies of slowly catering to more diverse and younger audiences as they come into their spending power are sound. However, in the background there remains a vocal subsection of fans who protest the injection of progressive politics into comics and who "defeminised" *Avengers: Endgame* (2019) by editing out all the "feminine" and "gay" moments.[66]

It is difficult to predict what the future of comics will look like. Certainly, at the time of writing, efforts are made to diversify comic books, such as including more characters of color, characters with disabilities, and characters who are part of the LGBTQIA+ spectrum.[67] There are attempts to bring in more diverse creative teams so that authentic stories can be written for these new characters and allow them to bond with the audience. Of course, with greater visibility, with increased awareness and inclusion, comes a backlash. Some fans who want their comics to remain "politics-free"—as in, filled with what they perceive to be nonpolitical and "normal" identities such as straight, white men—are increasingly resisting these attempts. It is important, then, to understand that there are also many comics that superficially challenge the status quo while actively reinscribing the status quo's gender roles and associated norms and values in order to cater to both groups.

A History of Scholarship

Initially, much of comic book research was preoccupied with justificatory strategies attempting to legitimize the medium as a source of research and with documenting comic book history. As discussed by Hannah Miodrag, this research was jump-started by nonacademic practitioner-theorists or experts whose work, although seminal, is increasingly scrutinized for a lack of theoretical sophistication.[68] However, much of this initial work has provided valuable insights and starting points for the incredible increase in academically rigorous and critically informed scholarship being produced in the past two decades. Furthermore, early studies provided key insights into the comic book industry, the development of comic book fan communities, and the relationship among content creators, editors, the content itself, and the fans, although this work was sometimes too eager to take the artists' opinions of their own work at face value. While comic scholarship has seen a rise in scholars connecting comics to sociohistorical developments and academic theory, practitioner-theorists and other nonacademic experts in the field are also presenting increasingly complex work. Historically, most academic writing about gender and superheroes has focused on (the lack of) female characters and their performance of gender while few male superhero characters have been subject to gender analysis. Writing on male superheroes that does include a discussion of masculinity often focuses on the superheroes' heroic performance in relation to that of their female counterparts, especially female characters' (lack of) dress, agency, or unrealistic and sexualized bodily proportions. There has been a significant focus on the superhero's body as a representation of the masculine ideal. According to Aaron Taylor, the superhero body, or superbody, is of special interest as it is a "culturally produced body that could potentially defy all traditional and normalizing readings. These are bodies beyond limits—perhaps without limits."[69] Such bodies could signify and project gender in new, unique ways, potentially transcending established markers and creating new identities beyond the scope of traditional gender roles. The question is: Do comics actually take this opportunity, or do they remain trapped in the hegemony's consumption and restructuring of radical deviation from the norm? Comics themselves are often considered to be masculine objects: stories about men made by men for other men, containing a script of normative masculine behavior and identity. Carol A. Stabile writes that "the superhero is first and foremost a man, because only men are understood to be protectors in US culture and only men have the balls to lead," which is an attitude perpetuated by comics.[70]

Regarding the superhero as a masculine concept has caused some academic research to focus on conceptualizing the female superhero as separate from *the* superhero. In her article "The Body Unbound: Empowered, Heroism and Body

Image," Ruth J. Beerman draws a distinction between female superheroes and superheroines. According to Beerman, the differences exist in the way the roles themselves are gendered: "Female superheroes are characters like a male character, but who simply happen to be women, serving more as a sidekick or supporting character to the lead, male superhero (such as Supergirl)."[71] Supergirl is classified as a female superhero because she exists as a distaff version of Superman, a copy of him in girl form. Superheroines, by comparison, have their own identities, infused with femininity and womanhood, apart from a male superhero, such as Wonder Woman.[72] While such classification can be a useful tool to discuss female characters and their representations of acceptable femininity, separating sidekicks, supportive characters, or (initially) distaff characters from "real" superheroes plays into cultural notions that the sidekick or helper roles are more feminine, less masculine, and less worthy of recognition (or scholarship). A lack of what Beerman calls superheroines and an abundance of female sidekicks or distaff characters (compared with the nonexistence of male copies of female characters or female lead characters) is obviously concerning in terms of representation, but it is equally dubious to dismiss sidekicks or distaff characters because they perform superheroism in a different way from male superheroes. Furthermore, such categories make it difficult to discuss the evolution of distaff characters into legacy names, where many different characters assume a specific moniker and motif, or distaff characters who go on to attain a larger cultural significance than the male character they were originally based on, such as Captain Marvel.

Traditionally, female superheroes have always had different kinds of powers compared with male superheroes. Comics emphasize the need for physical strength and the ability to participate in physical combat, which female superheroes typically do not do, which frames their powers as weaker than those of their male counterparts. Mike Madrid writes that female superheroes "in comic books have historically been given weaker powers."[73] But how is "weaker" defined? Assuming that it refers to physical strength, it means that comics have fallen into the trap of valuing physical strength over other abilities, no matter their actual effectiveness in combat.[74] Most female characters do not look as physically powerful as male characters do, adding to the interpretation of female bodies as weaker and less resilient than male bodies. For instance, despite their great physical capabilities, Supergirl and Wonder Woman rarely have the sculpted musculature that male superheroes often have. It would break with the fragile feminine stereotype to see them as physically powerful, and providing female characters with nonphysical powers adds to the preservation of female superheroes' traditional feminine beauty. Madrid writes that a female superhero "will look like a supermodel if she possesses what is known as 'strike a pose and point' powers. For as mighty as the X-Men's Storm is, she strikes a pose, extends a hand, unleashes a lightning bolt, and looks great. Just like posing for a picture in *Vogue*."[75] Female superheroes can be powerful as long as they are still glamorous, beautiful, and sexy in the heat of combat. While comics create strong and powerful female characters, sometimes in a clear attempt to gain a larger female audience by promoting "progressive" politics, they often fail to present female characters as active subjects by depicting them as sexual objects even while the female superhero pays lip service to equality.

Superheroes often suffer from what is referred to in gaming culture or video game scholarship as "ludonarrative dissonance," which is used to refer to some games' conflict between the game's narrative as told through the story and the narrative told through the game play.[76] Similarly, comics often create a dissonance through what the characters say versus what the character development or narrative implies. In comics, superheroes often have explicitly articulated mission statements that advocate equality, freedom, and peace. Stories focusing on superhero teams such as the X-Men are often understood as endorsing diversity and socially liberal attitudes with "*Uncanny X-Men* are driven by a metaphor and message—that of tolerance and acceptance," as Neil Shyminsky writes.[77] However, those ideals are often undermined through the genre's requirement of violence and action, character development or design, and the narratives' plotlines. After all, how can a comic promote the idea of equality when its female or Black or Black female characters are sidelined, violated, and killed off while the white male protagonists never die or always come back from the dead?

Simultaneously, comics have often been dismissed as being childish, or sexist and racist by mainstream popular culture, adding to comic scholarship's previous preoccupation with defending the genre as worthy of academic study. With the MCU's popularity, there is a growing backlash against Marvel and DC for racist and sexist portrayals in comics, films, and TV, as evidenced by articles such as "The Superhero Diversity Problem," by Julianna Aucoin.[78] In terms of sexism, the two most common tropes associated with female characters in comics identified by fans and nonacademic experts, or practitioner-theorists, are fridge-ing and the Brokeback Pose. Fridge-ing, derived from the phrase "women in refrigerators," refers to the way female characters are often killed to further the main male character's plot or character development. Comic writer Gail Simone first coined the term in response to *Green Lantern #54* (1994), where the main character returns from a mission and finds his girlfriend's mutilated corpse stuffed in the fridge. In 1999, Simone used the term as the name for her website, which lists names of "fridged" female characters.[79] While some fans argued that violently killing women was not a sexist trend because characters who die usually come back from the dead, John Bartol, in an article posted on Simone's website, pointed out that characters returning from the dead are usually male and coined the term "dead men defrosting."[80] Fridge-ing also applies to Black characters who are killed to further the white characters' plot and emotional development. For example, in 2016, the Black superhero War Machine was killed in Marvel's *Civil War II*, and his death becomes a source of conflict between the white female Captain Marvel and the white male Iron Man. The comic consistently highlights the anguish Captain Marvel and Iron Man experience at War Machine's death, as well as their struggle to grieve and move on. This relegates War Machine's death to a plot device as the conflict between Captain Marvel and Iron Man escalates into a title-spanning, universe-wide event.

The second trope is the Brokeback Pose, a term used to identify a common pose for female characters that highlights both their buttocks and their breasts. Often, the only way a real person could achieve such a pose would be through a broken spine, hence the name. This trope was first identified by female fans in online communities in 2012, resulting in several articles discussing the phenomenon on websites such as The Beat and TheGeekTwins, which have significant followings.[81] Although the first Brokeback Pose ever published has yet to be identified, the trend seems to occur as far back as the beginning of the Bronze Age, when sexualized images of female characters became acceptable again. While not all the poses identified as Brokeback are extreme enough that the character's back would have to be broken to achieve them, all of them are clearly uncomfortable. In her analysis of "24 titles/144 issues/14,599 panels," Carolyn Cocca found that "almost every issue contains sexually objectifying portrayals of women."[82] Responses from the industry and other fans who claim that there is nothing sexist about such poses led to the creation of the Hawkeye Initiative in December 2012. The Hawkeye Initiative is a collaboration between several fan artists and artists working in the industry who redraw Brokeback Poses with superhero Clint Barton, also known as Hawkeye. Drawn with a male character, the poses become obviously physically impossible and ridiculous, highlighting both the sexism of such poses and the way they have been normalized and made invisible when applied to female characters.[83] Female superheroes can be powerful, but only if they are sex objects and conform to other "traditionally feminine" characteristics, preferably in service to a male character's story line or the male character's gaze. As Cocca writes in her book *Superwomen: Gender, Power and Presentation*:

> In short, while there are a number of popular, strong, complex, female superheroes, in general what we see is underrepresentation, domestication, sexualisation, and heteronormativity. That is, there are far fewer women than men, the women are portrayed as interested in romance or as less-powerful adjuncts to male characters, the women are shown in skimpy clothing and in poses that accentuate their curves while the male characters are portrayed as athletic and action-oriented, and both women and men are almost always portrayed as very different from one another and interested only in opposite-sex romance and sex.[84]

Increasing the amount of female characters is not enough. They need to appear in narratives that support them and challenge the status quo.

Academics such as Gareth Schott, Rob Lendrum, and Ramzi Fawaz have focused on the development of gay characters in comics, pointing out that gay superheroes still perpetuate stereotypes or function as token characters. Both Schott and Fawaz, as well as Kara Kvaran, discuss Northstar as the token gay man and briefly touch on the Rawhide Kid as an example of stereotypes used to imply a character is gay without openly stating so in the text. Kvaran believes that superheroes who openly state their homosexuality in the text allow for more realistic interpretation and that, despite their limitations, their inclusion is a good sign of social progress in American culture.[85] Historically, gay characters have been invisible in comics and openly gay superheroes have been present only in recent years, suggesting increased liberal attitudes toward gender and sexuality in American society. However, most academic scholarship is limited to either the ways in which characters are positive representations or the ways in which these characters remain token characters who fail to challenge stereotypes. Instead, this book focuses on the representation of specific gay characters, such as Billy (Wiccan), Teddy (Hulkling), and Batwoman, and analyzes how their positive representation fails to challenge stereotypes and fits into a discourse that heteronormalizes gay people, challenging how we understand "positive" representation.

The academic research on Black superheroes has been in a similar vein to the work on gay characters, identifying positive representation versus negative stereotyping. Other academic work has focused on excavating and identifying forgotten Black superheroes who inspired or impacted the industry at the time of their publication but were forgotten or buried later on. Much work has been done on identifying the cultural and historical significance of Black superheroes, artists, and authors in a field that is still dominated by white men. This includes, but is not limited to, important work such as Sheena Howard and Ronald L. Jackson III's *Black Comics: Politics of Race and Representation*, Adilifu Nama's *Super Black: American Pop Culture and Black Superheroes*, and Deborah Elizabeth Whaley's *Black Women in Sequence: Re-inking Comics, Graphic Novels and Anime*. Much of this academic research agrees that the industry and superhero comics are struggling with unpacking institutionalized racism. It seems incongruent that narratives traditionally focused on fighting evil, including social evils such as racism, would struggle to represent racial equality or nonracist narratives. Discussing this discrepancy, Marc Singer analyzed *The Legion of Superheroes* comic series (1958–1994), focusing on the issues produced during the Silver Age.[86] The Legion was an intergalactic superhero team, defending the entire galaxy from evil, and prided itself on its refusal to discriminate against any race. However, Singer notes that "the Legion's supposed racial diversity was mitigated—if not virtually negated—by the fact that, of all the races represented in the comic, only one group existed in real life: the white characters who comprised the bulk of the Legion."[87] Humans and aliens were white characters, while characters of color were blue, green, or purple, and "by locating [racial diversity] in protean characters who serve as free-floating signifiers for the racial 'other' without representing any real-world race," *The Legion of Superheroes* never addresses the white supremacy inherent in American culture, nor does it tackle any real racial issues.[88] Instead, it "perfectly illustrates the contradictory treatment of race in many superhero comics: . . . *Legion* ultimately erases all racial and sexual differences with the very same characters that it claims analogize our world's diversity."[89] The comic preached diversity and acceptance of the racial Other but never represented racial diversity in any meaningful way, supporting an ideology of equality without compromising the privilege of white hegemony. This tendency to use white characters as imaginary aliens or minorities that in no way resemble any real-world ethnicities continues to plague the comic book world.

The most well-known version of "superhero comics [representing] every fantastic race possible, as means of ignoring real ones," is the *X-Men* comics.[90] The first issue of the *X-Men* came out in September 1963, and its original team consisted of five mutant team members: Cyclops, Marvel Girl, Angel, Beast, and leader Charles Xavier. While later iterations of the group included characters such as Storm (an African American woman) and Kitty Pryde (a Jewish woman), all of the original characters were white and the bulk of the team has always been composed of white characters. They represent the mutant community, a racial minority often victimized by discriminatory rhetoric and violent assault. This has led many critics, and a large part of the audience, to read *X-Men* comics as analogies for the experiences of racial minorities or LGBTQIA+ minorities. The X-Men's "anti-oppressive message can be applied to any person or peoples suffering from one or another form of oppression in a hegemonic political system," including the "victims of racist, sexist or homophobic violence."[91] While an argument can be made that *X-Men* comics promote racial equality because they encourage identification and sympathy with oppressed minorities, Shyminsky points out that "within a genre whose creators and readers are nearly uniformly white males, the X-Men *actually* solicit identification from a similarly young, white and male leadership, allowing these readers to misidentify themselves as 'other'" and leading comics to "not only [fail] to adequately *redress* issues of inequality—it actually *reinforces* inequality."[92] Because the X-Men are generally young, white males, the comic fails to identify the oppressive hegemony as white and patriarchal while concealing how young, white people can be complicit in its construction. It allows the reader to recognize that the treatment of minorities is unfair on an intellectual level and through this recognition identify themselves as progressive without needing to commit to any self-reflection that would unpack internalized racism, sexism, homophobia, or ableism. The *X-Men* comics inadvertently encourage their readership to interpret the dismantling of white male privilege as oppression, which perpetuates the white male hegemony.

Historically, comics have been written by white, straight, able-bodied, and cisgender men. When that group has been expanded, it has most often included white women first. As Cocca writes, "Dominant groups have been telling not only their own stories but the stories of those whom they have marginalized as well: whites telling the stories of people of color, men telling the stories of women, heterosexuals telling stories of queers, nondisabled people telling stories of disabled people. . . . Often their lack of authenticity means they're not only inaccurate, but harmful."[93] This book investigates the way that these representations are harmful, and how and why they are constructed as such within their sociohistorical context.

The Theory, the Methods, and the Framework

This book provides an analysis of the evolution of the representation of gender and race through superhero case studies to excavate the superhero's promotion of dominant cultural values, specifically conservative and mainstream gender roles as they are determined through the intersection of gender, sexuality, and race. By unpicking the dominant reading of superheroes through the sociocultural context, this book examines how dominant gender roles are reproduced and reinscribed and how these roles might be resisted.

Discussing Karen Barad's concept of intra-action, Nikka Lykke describes American culture as subsisting of subcultures that "interpenetrate and mutually transform each other" within a dominant hegemony.[94] Cultural norms and values that determine acceptable gender roles, sex presentation, racial relations, and so on are influenced by popular media, the increasing relevance of online cultures (memes, vines, TikToks, etc.), corporate concerns (based on economic trends), executive decisions, and artists or creators. All of these influences are themselves influenced by each other and cultural norms and values. This process of influence and intra-action constructs a dominant hegemony that exists as a cultural norm that is both invisible and culturally exalted. Similar to Gilles Deleuze and Felix Guattari's concept of "folding in," intra-action considers subcultures and dominant hegemony to be continuously interacting as the dominant cultural order folds in or absorbs radical, subcultural elements and purges them of their most politically resistant aspects. Through this process, hegemonic-resistant cultural signifiers become part of the hegemony and reinscribe dominant norms and values. Similarly, "media forms, such as film, TV, and advertising are notorious for the ways in which they adopt and absorb oppositional points of view or modes of expression, reframing them in ways that are beneficial to big business and the ruling corporate class."[95] Dominant cultural values, including mass media, consume subcultures and spit them back out in more palatable and normalized formats so that they can be repackaged and resold to mainstream audiences. America, as a country of 326 million people, inevitably produces diverse communities and subcultures, but the existence of a dominant cultural narrative that actively works to present the idea of a cohesive and naturally uniform population cannot be ignored. Many cultural and political clashes occur over what the dominant narrative says about what it means to be a "normal" or "everyday" American. The dominant cultural narrative consistently pressures subcultures to confirm to its norms and values, presenting compliance and "normalcy" as a route toward respectability and acceptance. While many subcultures respond to and resist these pressures, the dominant cultural narrative co-opts these modes of resistance and sells them back to its audience. Superheroes and comics are also subject to these cultural forces and influences.

Media content can be made with the intention of producing readings that challenge or critique the status quo. Superheroes are multiauthored and transmedial products, while comics are collaborative works of art, created by people with their own agendas and outside pressures. While the approach to comics as collaborative art does away with the illusion of the isolated genius, toiling away in the attic, the focus on the collaborators' personal motivations paradoxically prioritizes human individuality over structural influences of power hierarchies. It eliminates the idea of the collaborative team themselves as influenced by structural power hierarchies and how the dominant cultural narrative constructs, and is constructed by, individuals. In addition to considering the collaborative nature of comic books and their superheroes, it is also necessary to consider a "production of culture" perspective when analyzing comics, as argued for by Casey Brienza's article "Producing Comics Culture: A Sociological Approach to the Study of Comics." This prioritizes the context in which comics are produced, taking the production of cultural objects as fundamentally influenced by the power structures within that culture and its interaction with the dominant cultural narrative. This ties into Roland Barthes's prioritization of the text as the only accessible site of meaning, which the author has no control over once it is in possession of the reader.[96] However, as Stuller writes, "Sex and gender do not and should not define us or what we do, but a combination of nature and nurture colors our lives regardless. Who we are influences the stories we tell and the stories we want to hear."[97] While the dominant cultural context in which we live influences us as individuals, it is possible for individual creators to be well versed and conscious of narrative and subcultural codes due to their own position within society. Therefore, they may be able to offer alternatives that provide resistant readings.

Through media content, advertisements, and all the other myriad ways in which a culture passes on its values to its people, the audience is also subject to these cultural influences. Shaped (in part) by the cultural landscape, audiences often produce a dominant reading of any given text, depending on their specific sociocultural and political context. This does not negate the existence of alternative readings created by other audiences, who might exist in different sociocultural contexts. In turn, alternative readings do not negate the existence of a dominant reading, but automatically imply the existence of the dominant reading. As Bonnie Dow writes, "Resistance or opposition assumes that the viewer 'gets' the preferred meaning of the text . . . prior to resisting."[98] Readings that interpret a text in opposition to a dominant or hegemonic reading require the reader to already be well versed in codes of resistance.[99] However, due to intra-action, these codes are co-opted and regurgitated by the hegemonic order's folding-in mechanism and lose their power. To get an alternate reading, you first need to understand and unpick the dominant reading.

This process of folding in covers all the norms and values within a culture, including the understanding of gender and race. Judith Butler writes that gender is "the repeated stylization of the body, a set of repeated acts in a highly regulatory frame that congeals over time to produce the appearance of substance, of a natural sort of being."[100] Gender is not biologically defined but is constructed by culture and its discourse, which frames itself as based on "natural," biological sex. Additionally, Michel Foucault considers that society's "hold on sex is maintained through language, or rather through the acts of discourse that creates from the very fact that it is articulated, a rule of law."[101] Sex is the biological body, and gender discourse claims that this biological body is the foundation for a "natural" gender binary. Through culture, language becomes layered with additional meanings and connotations based on cultural values; this is what is referred to as discourse. When language is used to discuss sex and gender, this discourse sets the boundaries of the bodies' existence as all the bodies that break the preset boundaries are considered unnatural. Butler, when discussing Foucault, further extrapolates "that disciplinary discourse manages and makes use of [individuals, but] it also actively constitutes them."[102] Discourse constructs biological bodies because it is impossible to access the body outside of discourse. Therefore, any description of the body generates our understanding of that body and, thus, the body *itself* as there is no body that can be accessed outside of that understanding or language. The body constructed through language is then taken as the object that defines culture's gender roles and stereotypes, but actually, it is not possible to distinguish between the two. As Butler writes, "Identity is performatively constituted by the very 'expressions' that are said to be its result." Gender is created through the performance of socially acceptable behavioral patterns and which in turn continually produces these socially acceptable behavioral patterns. Butler writes that biological sex does not create "social meanings as additive properties, but rather is *replaced* by the social meanings it takes on."[103] Natural gender roles that determine social functions due to biological imperatives do not exist; they are culturally constructed gender roles interpreted as biologically determined by the dominant hegemonic order. For women, this includes a submissive role, attributes of gentleness and kindness, a soft and nurturing creature. For men, this includes the active role, attributes of strength and power, and the ability to protect and defend the feminine due to an inherent violent nature. For both, these roles are considered immutable and cannot be altered.

The idea that violence is inherently masculine is part of the American hegemony. Raewyn Connell states that, while there are several different forms of masculinity present in the American cultural landscape, one version of masculinity is "culturally exalted."[104] This form of masculinity is hegemonic, which "can be defined as the configuration of gender practice which embodies the currently accepted answer to the problem of the legitimacy of patriarchy, which guarantees (or is taken to guarantee) the dominant position of men and the subordination of women."[105] The masculine ideal legitimizes the existence of the patriarchy by providing a rationale for conservative gender roles that consider women to be weaker and more submissive than men. The dominant configuration of masculinity in the American landscape is increasingly infused with hypermasculinity, a concept first described in the social sciences by Donald L. Mosher and Mark Sorkin in 1984. Hypermasculinity is understood as "a gender-based ideology of exaggerated beliefs about what it is to be a man."[106] This ideology contains "four inter-related beliefs, namely toughness as emotional self-control, violence as manly, danger as exciting and calloused attitudes toward women and sex."[107] The four elements that construct hypermasculinity are considered to "reflect a man's desire to appear powerful and to be dominant in interactions with men, women and the environment," especially the way violence is used as "an acceptable expression of masculine power and dominance."[108] This positions hypermasculinity as the source of violence in interpersonal relationships, especially toward women, as well as dangerous driving and other risk-taking behavior that men statistically engage in more than women. These same attributes are also considered part of toxic masculinity, a reformulation of hypermasculinity read as specifically damaging to men themselves through the panicked or compulsive rejection of anything that is vaguely constructed as "feminine." For example, toxic masculinity highlights the way the lack of emotional freedom damages men's ability to understand, express, and fulfill their emotional needs, leading to higher suicide rates among men compared with women.[109] These conservative gender roles form the hegemonic ideal of what men and women should be, or what their natural, biological identities are. However, these gender roles also intersect with other demographics, such as heterosexuality and whiteness.

Within the American patriarchy, heterosexuality is also considered to be rooted in the biological body, through the gender binary, which creates complementary gender roles. It is the dominant man that requires a submissive woman to bear his children. The concept of heterosexuality is both constructed by and continuously perpetuating the gender binary, as it requires the existence of opposite genders. The idea that the gender binary and heterosexuality are the biological or natural norm is expressed through the term "heteronormativity." It is a system of beliefs that structurally privileges heterosexuality over any other forms of sexual attraction. In order to maintain those beliefs and those structures, the dominant hegemony folds in any challenges or threats in the form of non-heteronormative sexuality. This is referred to as homonormativity, as coined by Lisa Duggan, which is a form of "politics that does not contest dominant or heteronormative assumptions and institutions but upholds and sustains them while promising the possibility of a demobilized gay constituency and a privatized, depoliticized gay culture anchored in domesticity and consumption."[110] Homonormativity upholds heteronormativity by incorporating acceptable forms of gay identity into the hegemony instead of challenging the hegemony. Jasbir K. Puar further builds on this concept, considering homonormativity as the simulation of heteronormativity accessed through white, middle-class privilege, generated further through homonormative Islamophobia in the wake of the terrorist attack on September 11, 2001. This is a process "whereby homonormative and queer gay men can enact forms of national, racial, or other belongings, by contributing to a collective vilification of Muslims."[111] Homonationalism, as Puar defines it, is a process whereby nationalism is conflated with Islamophobia and terrorism with Islam, which ensures that the white American, middle-class gay community can access certain forms of citizenship by "siding" against terrorism and Islam. This homonormative Islamophobia in turn generates heteronormativity as the civil rights this community is given access to are connected to the production of the nuclear family, such as adoption and marriage, which benefits the maintenance of heteronormativity.

It is not only the rejection of Islam and a performance of nationalism that can provide temporary access to privileged spaces. A recent phenomenon in extreme right-wing online communities, referred to as the pink-washing of white nationalism, is the performance of whiteness by people on the LGBTQIA+ spectrum through the rejection or harassment of people of color.[112] This provides (temporary) acceptance in extreme-right circles and allows white LGBTQIA+ people to (temporarily) evade persecution. Of course, there is nothing new about racial bribes, which are the mechanism by which the dominant hegemonic order convinces white people that they have more in common with each other than with working-class, gay, or disabled people of color. The racial bribe persuades white communities to punch down on communities of color and, therefore, buy their way into privilege. Karla Martin writes that "Whiteness is often centred as the norm, as the unspoken standard that everyone else should conform to and be judged by."[113] Framed as the norm, behavior that does not fit white behavioral patterns is marked as deviant or excessive and becomes the excuse to bar non-white people from white spaces. As discussed in *Unhooking from Whiteness* (2013), the dominant white hegemony "is the privileging of ideas, interests, values, beliefs, assumptions, images and norms associated with Whites."[114] whiteness is a set of behaviors and interests that are not only associated with the white community and its hegemony but also serve that white community at the cost of racial minorities' oppression. It is behavior that is committed to maintaining the hegemony. Black characters who act white or are written to promote respectability politics further normalize the idea that whiteness is a natural, biological norm that non-white people violate.

The dominant cultural narrative favors bodies that are white, able-bodied, heterosexual, and gender conforming. In turn, it discriminates against bodies that do not fit these ideals in specific ways depending on the nature of the nonconforming body. As mass media consistently regurgitates this dominant cultural narrative, its audience is consistently bombarded by the message that these bodies are wrong, unnatural, and suspicious. While it is easy to dismiss the messages in entertainment as merely entertainment, it is important to understand that one of mass media's functions is to disseminate and reaffirm the dominant cultural values and ideology of a society. As Dawn Heinecken writes: "The media are seen as major instruments of cultural expression."[115] Therefore, they wield considerable power over their audience and over the members of any given culture. As superheroes are increasingly present within all forms of mass media, the ideology or scripts that they present are also increasingly powerful. This book aims to place superhero comic books in their sociohistorical context to unravel the dominant power hierarchies that they reproduce or challenge.

The Main Act

To analyze the representation of gender and race in comics, I focus on several specific superheroes and chart the developments and changes of these characters' gender performances and their intersection with race and sexuality over time. Therefore, these case studies were selected based on their publication record and cultural or historical significance. They needed to have been published as a comic book character from their inception, preferably beginning in the early days of superhero comic books, by one of the big two: Marvel and DC, which have been powerful players throughout the industry's history and currently dominate the market. Additionally, the characters should have appeared in print consistently since their inception, preferably in titular comics but otherwise in group/ensemble or crossover titles.[116] Cultural or historical significance refers to superheroes who have had a long-lasting impact on the industry, who were the first of their kind and generated imitations and copies, or who have gained acclaim to such an extent that even non–comic book readers would be able to identify them. This includes superheroes such as Superman, Wonder Woman, Captain America, and Iron Man, who each have impressive publication records and are easily identifiable by mainstream audiences. Supergirl may be a less obvious choice, due to gaps in her publication records and being recognizable mostly due to Superman's success, but she has enjoyed a consistent following and, as Superman's distaff character, has offered valuable insights into how characters with similar or identical powers are treated differently based on gender.

The selection for gay characters was hindered by there being very few characters on the LGBTQIA+ spectrum and none from the early days of superhero comics, aside from characters who were retroactively identified as gay. There have been lesbian characters in superhero comics since 1987 (Maggie Sawyer), and the first with superpowers was Mystique in the *Uncanny X-Men* comics in 1990. However, Mystique is a villain or antihero and, therefore, not a superhero. The first openly lesbian superhero was DC's revamped Batwoman in 2006. Explicitly marketed as DC's flagship lesbian character, Batwoman was the most logical choice despite her comparatively short publication history—although a character with the same name was published as early as 1956. The first openly gay male character was Marvel's Northstar, first published in 1979, who came out as gay in 1992. However, due to Northstar's low cultural impact and sporadic publication history, as discussed by Gareth Schott, he was not selected for this study.[117] The next most well-known gay superheroes would have been Midnighter or Apollo, but they were not published by Marvel or DC and their series, *The Authority*, was not aimed at mainstream (comic book) audiences.[118] Therefore, I have selected Hulkling and Wiccan, who have enjoyed medium levels of popularity (initially among young readers), have appeared in publication fairly consistently, and have been key players in some story lines that have impacted the Marvel comic book universe at large.

The Falcon, as the first Black American superhero, was the first obvious choice to discuss Black male superheroes. Luke Cage, as the first Black character with a solo titular comic without the word "Black" in his superhero name, and with a considerable cultural standing, was also a clear choice. Another logical choice would have been Black Panther, who was the first Black superhero published by Marvel in 1966. However, Black Panther was initially only a guest character and did not have his own titular comic until 1977, which was later than both the Falcon's partnership with Captain America (1969) and Luke Cage's solo title (1972). Therefore, the Falcon and Luke Cage were prioritized. For the last two case studies, Storm and Kamala Khan were selected. Storm is the first Black female superhero who led a superhero team. Her cultural significance should not be underestimated, and omitting her from the book would have been a grievous oversight. There were several other candidates to accompany Storm in the book (e.g., Vixen, Nubia, Monica Rambeau, Misty Knight). All of these had limited publication runs and not always had a titular comic. Additionally, in terms of cultural capital, Kamala Khan as Ms. Marvel outpaced them all. Kamala's sudden and immense success, as documented by Carolyn Cocca and Adrienne Resha, and her speedy incorporation into the Marvel universe through team-ups with the Avengers, Wolverine, and Miles Morales as Spider-Man made her inclusion both obvious and crucial. Each case study will be discussed one by one; grouped by gender, sexuality, and race per chapter; and arranged in chronological order by publication date within chapters.

Chapter 1, "White Superheroes and Masculinity," maps out how the ideal "biological" masculinity perpetuated in comics is closely tied to notions of whiteness, American nationality, and technological and scientific advancement. The first section, "The Phallic Body: Superman and the Underwear of Power," analyzes Superman as the original embodiment of the superhero concept. Appearing in a wide variety of mass media formats, Superman is one of the most well-known and identifiable characters in modern culture. The stylized chevron on his chest has become a logo that denotes his character and mythos. Every reboot of his origin story has maintained the same basic elements, the consistency of which, as well as his fixed appearance and supporting cast, has turned him into an icon. Since his first publication in 1938, he has never been out of print, representing a continuum of the male body in mass media. Focusing on class, American national identity, and the status of the immigrant, this section analyzes Superman's masculinity and the visual elements that contribute to his gender construction. The second section, "Man-Made Anatomy: Captain America's and Iron Man's Artificial Superbodies," discusses Captain America and Iron Man. In 1941, nine months before America entered World War II, Steve Rogers became Captain America. While Superman could not fight on the front lines, Captain America was part of a military squad on the European front, engaging Nazi enemies on super-secret missions. Dressed in the colors and motifs of the American flag, he fought as the living embodiment of America itself, encoding and perpetuating ideals of masculinity in the process. Widespread American cultural beliefs concerning the military, masculinity, and scientific and technological developments intersect in Captain America's origin story. The same can be said for Iron Man, who literally embodies technological innovation through his robotic suit. This section teases out different forms of masculine embodiment, specifically in light of Captain America's and Iron Man's artificially constructed bodies. In terms of masculinity, comics promote conservative gender role behavior, which limits their ability to present antihegemonic narratives.

Chapter 2, "The White Female Body," examines the femininity represented by female superheroes outside of the fridge-ing phenomenon and the Brokeback trope, focusing on the female physical combatant. Female superheroes, by their very existence, complicate the traditional masculine warrior ideal as exclusively masculine and are often depicted in ways that diminish that complexity to reduce the challenge they pose to traditional gender roles. The first section, "The Female Warrior: Wonder Woman as the American Female Soldier," focuses on Wonder Woman, who, while not the very first female superhero, was the first to reach a large audience.[119] As a female soldier and physical combatant, Wonder Woman was designed as a celebration of femininity. She has been in print continually since her creation in 1941 and has a significant presence in popular culture. In the second section, "Barbie Dolls and Porn Stars: Supergirl and the Plasticization of the Female Body," the analysis of Supergirl offers a discussion of the way male and female superheroes' design differs. Discussing the 1950s' KleenTeen and the increasing sexualization of young girls, this section formulates a theory of bodily plasticity required for the construction of the female body.

Chapter 3, "Gay Characters and Social Progress," analyzes the intersection of gender and homosexual identity. The first section, "The Rise of Homonormativity: Wiccan and Hulkling," discusses how Marvel introduced a young gay couple in the contradictory cultural context of post-9/11 America and how they engage with the forces of homonormativity and homonationalism. Billy and Teddy in the *Young Avengers* represent the performance of heteronormative gender roles in gay relationships in media as a route to social acceptance, or low-risk engagement with LGBTQIA+ representation by the producers of mass media. The second section, "Externalizing the Queer: Batwoman and Her Monstrous Doubles," identifies Batwoman as a Gothic lesbian. She is consistently doubled and cast as the Other, through her romantic relationship, her twin sister, and her villains. The section analyzes Batwoman's performance of the homo/heteronormative and her gender transgressions, leading to monstrous transformation and Doubles.

Chapter 4, "Legacy, Community, and the Superhero of Color," focuses on intersectionality and the presentation of race by superheroes of color, who are forced to exist within a white-as-norm culture. The first section, "Seeking the Black Male Superhero in the Falcon, the Black Captain America, and Luke Cage," discusses Kenneth Ghee's concept of the culture-bound hero as the only true hero of color. Ghee seeks to locate a Black superhero who presents an antiracist narrative through his or her loyalty to the Black community while fighting the white oppressive hegemony. It analyzes the Falcon's performance of heroism, masculinity, and Blackness in the context of his partnership with the white Captain America, and investigates Luke Cage's blaxploitation roots in light of Luke's relationship with his community and how that develops alongside the increasing visibility of the incarceration epidemic of overpoliced African American communities. The second section, "Womanhood and Community: Storm and Ms. Marvel's Intersectionality," discusses Storm's existence as the only Black character in a team of white people, who are taken to serve as a racial allegory. It discusses Storm's intersectional identity and the dismissal of this complex identity by the communities she seeks to belong to. Additionally, it also discusses Ms. Marvel in relation to her community and her mentor, Captain Marvel. It analyzes how community-focused narratives can present antiracist narratives and how understanding intersectional identities is fundamental to the construction of such narratives.

These case studies set out the ways that superhero comic books have engaged with dominant cultural ideology and how that ideology has been perpetuated or challenged. At the moment, American society is both increasingly conservative and liberal, with opposing forces in mass media and politics contributing to the disappearance of the moderate, facilitated in part by the rise of neoliberalism.[120] Its confluence of progressive rhetoric, conservative politics, and free economics has created a society that increasingly views itself as progressive even while its cultural and societal forces are increasingly conservative and work to de-radicalize progressive opposition through the late stage capitalism's folding-in mechanism. Considering that resistance is increasingly co-opted and resold in a consumer-good package, can superheroes provide codes or methods of resistance? Investigating the ways in which superheroes reinscribe and challenge conservative gender roles along lines of race and sexuality, this book excavates how the dominant American cultural narrative imagines men and women as superheroes and what that means.

CHAPTER 1

White Superheroes and Masculinity

This chapter analyzes the white male superhero and the representations of white masculinity in American superhero comic books by discussing three well-known male superheroes: Superman, Captain America, and Iron Man. The ideal masculinity promoted by superhero comic books is constructed through the cultural significance of what it means to be American as it was established during World War II and the Cold War. It incorporates elements of hegemonic masculinity, such as military power, institutionalized whiteness, and scientific discovery. Superheroes use this construction of masculinity to function as power fantasies compensating for the cyclical idea of masculinity in a state of crisis. The sociocultural context of superhero masculinity is key as it engages with masculinity's fundamental tenets and a cultural panic about a lack of masculinity that occurs with every paradigm shift within wider American culture, which is facilitated and accelerated by popular culture and mass media.

The Phallic Body: Superman and the Underwear of Power

In 1938, following the Depression and President Roosevelt's New Deal, Superman was born. As discussed in the introduction, the cultural landscape of the 1930s was filled with celebrations of the common man and working-class heroes. According to Bradford W. Wright, Superman initially "championed social reform and government assistance to the poor," which "sometimes led him into conflict with the legal and political establishment," especially corrupt local government officials.[1] Created by Jerry Siegel and Joe Shuster, sons of first-generation immigrant parents, and written for an American audience made up of immigrants and their descendants, Superman was a power fantasy of the disenfranchised attempting to gain access to dominant social strata through qualities provided by their old-world heritage. Through his phenotypically white appearance, Superman opened up the concept of whiteness by replacing the requirement of Anglo-Saxon or Germanic heritage with white passing, and so all phenotypically white appearances were folded into privileged, American spaces. Superman actively worked to combat growing anti-Semitism or anti-immigration stances by emphasizing the American melting pot as fundamental to the American national identity. He also represented the impoverished populace, resembling the physicality of the working class created through backbreaking manual labor with large arms, shoulders, and chest. His civilian identity as a journalist, which did not require formal education or qualifications, also framed him as aligned with the working class as journalists often wrote in defense of the working class and in favor of public reform.[2] In his identity as Clark Kent, the journalist, Superman had a good excuse to investigate the social problems of Metropolis while advocating for policies that would benefit the working class. Moreover, it left Clark's educational background vague, avoiding any implication that our hero might not be working class.

For much of the Golden Age (1930s–1950s), Superman's body is big but lacks detail.[3] His muscle definition is nearly invisible in the early comics with only vague outlines underneath his uniform, mostly pectorals and quadriceps. Superman's physical powers seem to stem from his wide chest, round shoulders, and beefy upper arms, implying that big muscles are synonymous with strength and capability. His body exudes a moral strength associated with the honest working man, which fits his origins as the common man's hero. Throughout the years, Superman's general appearance has remained relatively unchanged, allowing the image of his costume, appearance, and chest chevron to become fixed. Looking back on his first appearance in *Action Comics #1* (1938), he is still recognizable to a modern audience. On the cover there is a man in a blue bodysuit, red underwear, boots, and cape, with an *S* chevron on his chest. There is little detail in the background to distract from the central figure: Superman holding a car aloft and crashing it into an embankment. Two of the three other figures are fleeing the scene while the third seems to be cowering in place. Considering the class tensions at the time and Superman's common-man origins, it is significant that Superman is depicted smashing a car, a luxury item not many could afford in the 1930s, which would become an important symbol of status and masculinity.[4]

Superman's status as a working-class champion changed in the early 1950s, when, increasingly, white men worked in middle-class white-collar office jobs. During this postwar peacetime, superheroes lost their appeal, but mystery, horror, and Western comics became extremely popular. To appeal to a changed audience, superheroes had to change as well. With education becoming more available as a means to and result of social mobility, cultural values began to incorporate the idea that education could contribute to a white man's masculinity, which became less defined by physical prowess. Instead, masculinity was increasingly understood as being defined by a white man's ability to survive in a corporate environment, providing for his family while attaining professional success as a marker of status. Initially, this created anxiety about "the feminizing effects of a new and growing sector of the economy—the white collar worker, the organization and advertising man—who sat at a desk all day, physically inactive and under great stress," as Anne Fausto-Sterling writes.[5] This anxiety was compounded, as Clark Davis discusses, by the fact that the middle class struggled to find a familiar construct of masculinity in corporate culture. Instead of the familiar concept of the middle-class American man, who was self-employed, the middle-class man was increasingly employed by other middle-class men, much as the working class had been. With society turning toward white, middle-class cultural values, the new reality of men in the workplace had to be reconciled with old-fashioned constructions of middle-class masculinity.[6] Corporate culture quickly developed its own definition of white, middle-class masculinity. Instead of self-employment, "advancement up the corporate ladder had become a legitimate route to the attainment of virtuous manhood."[7] Corporations claimed their employees required specific male attributes, and climbing the corporate ladder became a sign of superior masculinity over weaker, less masculine men. This narrative also functioned as a gatekeeping mechanism to exclude women and men of color. For those men who failed to achieve corporate success, the construction of acceptable middle-class masculinity remained a problem. Because they were denied advancement or promotion, their masculinity had to be affirmed by something else. Davis writes how masculinity "increasingly centred on activities outside the workplace."[8] Middle-class men were encouraged to use their leisure time to indulge in activities such as fishing, hunting, and sports to affirm their masculinity as well as harden the body softened from sitting behind a desk all day. In art and advertisement, the "typical" man became less physically imposing in the shoulders, with a slimmer and more trim physique sustained by good, old-fashioned American hobbies instead of manual labor.

Following this cultural shift, Superman also became a figure of middle-class masculinity. Clark Kent became an educated, middle-class son of working-class parents, symbolizing the potential of social mobility for the white working class in the 1950s. As a journalist, he was now required to possess formal education and qualifications. Instead of fighting for social programs and reform, Superman fought to preserve the status quo. His fight for truth and justice became "truth, justice and the American way," highlighting Superman's loyalty to America during the Cold War and alleviating any anxieties around his immigrant status.[9] Despite consistent anxieties toward immigrants in conservative circles, the immigrant experience is one of the fundamental elements of American identity. According to Gary Engle, "All Americans have an immediate sense of their origins elsewhere."[10] While new immigrants struggle with the conflicting needs of assimilation and the preservation of their heritage, Superman represents the idealization of white immigrants using their non-American heritage to become successful while internalizing American values. As Danny Fingeroth points out, Superman's powers were "actually only attained because he came to Earth—on Krypton, he and his people had none."[11] Superman's Kryptonian physiology is powered by the Milky Way's yellow sun, resulting in superpowers. But those powers only exist *because* he came to America. He is the American Dream made flesh.

In the 1950s, Superman's newfound allegiance to America replaced his peace mission to benefit the entire world. This loyalty can remain unquestioned because there is no apparent impulse for Superman to abandon America and return to Krypton. He knows little of its culture and has no tangible connection to it, such as relatives who have remained there. He grew up without a Kryptonian community and, as an adult, defends Earth against other Kryptonians trying to settle there, preventing the establishment of a potential community to which he can belong. When other Kryptonians appear, either Superman arranges for them to become integrated like him (e.g., Supergirl) or they are subject to suspicion. Lori Maguire points out that the "preoccupation with Krypton at this time and the villains that Superman faced from there" hint at the cultural anxiety about outside threats during the Cold War.[12] Kryptonian culture increasingly served as an allegory for the Soviet Union, presented as anti-American: cold and heartless. Luckily, Superman always defeats Kryptonian elements threatening the status quo and re-establishes America's moral and cultural superiority. Engle considers forsaking the past in favor of current loyalties to be a part of the American cultural consciousness: "Thus the American identity is ordered around the psychological experience of forsaking or losing the past for the opportunity of reinventing oneself in the future. This makes the orphan a potent symbol of the American character. Orphans aren't merely free to reinvent themselves. They are obliged to do so."[13] Being both an immigrant and an orphan, Superman must completely reinvent himself. Furthering Superman's alienation from Kryptonian culture, the 1950s established an American family for him. John and Martha Kent, Superman's adoptive parents, became important characters, which "firmly [entrenched] Superman in the small town family environs of Smallville."[14] A new kid-sister archetype was added in the form of Supergirl as well as various pets (including Krypto the super dog), and an entire new comic was devoted to Superman's adventures as a young boy (the 1949–1977 *Superboy* comics) to make him seem more human and all-American. The *Superboy* comic "transformed the once-mysterious, hardboiled, violently individualistic champion of the oppressed into a well-mannered, helpful, respectful, and obedient citizen."[15] Isolated from Kryptonian culture and immersed or adopted into American culture, Superman is encouraged by his human father to use his Kryptonian abilities in service to humankind. Superman's new background and his clear rejection of Kryptonian culture firmly cast him as an upstanding American citizen, which is made possible through his phenotypically white appearance.

During the Cold War era, which overlaps with comics' Silver Age (1950s–1970s), Superman increasingly fought to protect America from threatening outside forces, such as hostile aliens serving as a metaphor for communism and nuclear armament.[16] During this time, Superman's powers increased, reflecting the growth of American strength and the increasing paranoia of possible outside threats. Paul R. Kohl writes that "Superman emerged from the era of the Second World War with new powers, much as his home country did."[17] Reflecting popular American sentiments about America's position in the world, Superman had seemingly become all-powerful. However, with Superman's new powers came a new threat: kryptonite, an element toxic to Superman. As Kohl says, initially,

Superman "could not fly, only leap and a bursting shell *could* penetrate his skin. A *deus ex machina* weakness was not necessary for a character that was not yet all-powerful."[18] Symbolizing the superpowered United States of America, Superman can be threatened only by kryptonite. As pieces of Krypton's planetary core subjected to cosmic radiation, which makes it toxic to Superman, kryptonite is part of Superman's home world haunting him and his adopted country. This would become a striking theme throughout the 1950s, reflecting American fears about the Cold War and the Red Scare in the form of immigrants or American-born individuals with foreign loyalties penetrating American society and destroying it from within.

Superman's increase in power and abilities in the Silver Age was accompanied by an increasingly slimmer body, compared with his body in the Golden Age, while his muscle definition increased. His abdominal muscles tend to have more detail while his shoulders are less comically round. His chest remains the focus of his strength, wide and with defined pectoral muscles, but his waist has narrowed and he looks less stocky. Instead of the working-class physique from the Golden Age, Superman possesses the less muscly, white middle-class body that sits behind a desk, with occasional outdoor exercise providing a wholesome American physique. While Superman never needs to exercise, his body is always portrayed as extremely fit and muscular.[19]

Historically, Western culture has been fascinated with muscular bodies, as evidenced by the persistent popularity of the warrior of the classical world, the strong man circus figure, and eventually the bodybuilder, which became a popular figure as the action hero in the 1980s. Like that of the bodybuilding hero, Superman's muscle definition increased during the Bronze Age (1970s–1980s) and the Dark Age (1980s–1990s). Panels from those periods demonstrate an increased focus on details in general, partly because of innovations in printing techniques and digital art. The rise of the bodybuilding action hero also coincides with the rise of the establishment villain, who works within institutionalized bodies of power in the United States. During the 1950s, at the height of power of the Comics Code Authority (CCA), as discussed in the introduction, such villains were impossible due to the CCA's demand that American authorities always be portrayed respectfully to avoid fostering mistrust between youths and authority. The 1980s, however, allowed for a less patriotic Superman who reflected society's increasing questioning of American values and its government. While Superman continued to uphold American values throughout the 1990s and 2000s, he officially refused to accept American citizenship in 2011 and declared himself a citizen of the world. However, Clark Kent remains an American citizen. Initially, Clark Kent was simply a foil, a weakling disguise, but over the years Superman became a public role with Clark Kent increasingly serving as the "real" person. As Clark Kent states in the television series *Lois & Clark: The New Adventures of Superman* (1993–1997), "Superman is what I can do. Clark is who I am."[20] In the industry and fan communities there is an ongoing debate considering which of the two identities is "real" or if Clark/Superman's true identity is a mix of the two. But, as Randy Duncan points

Figure 1.1. Modern Superman. *Source*: Scott Snyder et al., *Superman Unchained #5* (New York: DC Comics, 2014). © 2014 DC Comics.

out: "In all versions, he is Clark Kent before he creates the identity of Superman. In all versions the moral examples and guidance of Jonathan and Martha Kent mould his character."[21] Even if Clark Kent is not the "real" identity, he is a vital part of the Superman comics and his rural, small-town upbringing in the American Midwest marks him as quintessentially American. His renunciation of American citizenship merely pays lip service to an international audience. Time and again, Superman's American nationality is a fundamental part of the white middle-class masculinity he constructs, which is also informed by his possession of the ultimate masculine body. Increasingly, this body is drawn with an absurd and fetishist amount of musculature, as demonstrated by figure 1.1.

The Modern Age (1990s–ongoing) has made voyeuristically detailed comic art, like figure 1.1, taken from *Superman Unchained #5* (2014), ubiquitous. This figure reflects the most recent updates to Superman's look and advances in digital art in contemporary times, culminating in wide, background-heavy splash panels and close-ups.[22] In figure 1.1, which is a full-page spread in the actual comic, Superman's muscular definition is remarkably detailed. Despite the skintight appearance of the suit, it looks bulkier and sturdier compared with previous iterations. At all times, the whole of the suit can retract into the S chevron, easily hidden underneath his civilian clothing, reflecting audiences' awareness of increasingly sophisticated technology. In *Superman: He'l on Earth* (2013), Superman calls it "kryptonian battle armor" and discusses how it reacts to only Kryptonian DNA.[23] Its thin black lines give the impression of interlocking armored panels. The high collar, with red piping, is reminiscent of a formal marine uniform collar. As such, the suit has been significantly militarized in appearance, reflecting post-9/11 American media's preoccupation with American technological superiority in the face of terrorism. The usual underwear worn over his tights has been reimagined as a belt pointing to his crotch: a sudden deviation from what has become a staple of the genre. Popular culture is filled with characters who signal their desire to be or "dress up" as a superhero by wearing underwear over tights. What used to be a reference to the strong man's costume has become a superhero reference, identified as the "Underwear of Power" trope by fans.[24] For years, few artists deviated from this trope, especially in regard to the Superman costume. In fact, when the creative team for the Superman film *Man of Steel* (2013) revealed their new costume design in a preview, some fans expressed outrage at the replacement of the traditional underwear with the belt. The question asked here is, What does the Underwear of Power do that makes it so important? Aside from being a conventional staple, it fulfills an important function in the construction of Superman's masculinity.

Superman's masculinity is partially constructed through the voyeuristic depiction of his body in his skintight costume. Aaron Taylor suggests that the superbody, with its bulging muscles and endlessly, panel after panel, reproduced physicality, is fetishized. There is an unmistakable element of spectacle inherent in drawing and producing such detailed musculature: a process that "undermines the virility of male superheroes."[25] According to Taylor, it is the element of spectacle, the invitation to *gaze* upon the body, that is emasculating as "the reader is invited to ogle the bodies of these men in much the same way as the bodies of the women."[26] Being reduced to an object the audience is encouraged only to look at instead of a subject the audience is encouraged to identify or sympathize with is dehumanizing. He identifies the sexualization of male characters as a force that denies male superheroes a powerful, autonomous sexuality because "In a fictional universe in which any part of the anatomy has the potential to be super-powered, the superpenis is still strictly taboo."[27] Taylor claims that the male superhero is castrated, which reinforces his emasculation and sexualization, reducing him to the objectified state of many female characters. The fetishization and dehumanizing impulse of the voyeuristic gaze endangers the authority of the superhero.

While it is true that being reduced to a sexual object is dehumanizing, the lack of a superpenis does not contribute to the emasculation of the male superhero as there is no explicit drawing of the superpenis for the exact reason Taylor puts forward in his essay: to be drawn explicitly and sexually is dehumanizing and undermines the authority of the superhero. If drawing a character with exaggerated physical features in voyeuristic close-ups is emasculating, adding a penis in the same detail would prevent this emasculating sexualization only if you consider the penis to always be read as a source of power instead of a source of sex. Rather, drawing a character's genitals lends itself to voyeuristic, sexual, objectifying, and dehumanizing readings. Furthermore, there is no need to draw the superpenis, because it is inescapably present through its absence. The reader's eyes are consistently drawn toward the crotch, because the skintight bodysuit of the hero tends to be one single color, except for the chevron and the underwear. The Underwear of Power consistently frames the crotch and the penis to make drawing an actual bulge unnecessary. Drawing a penis would further reduce the superhero to a sex object and sabotage the superbody's purpose: to inspire subject desire in the reader. The male superhero is not drawn as a sexual object but as a powerful subject, even accounting for the eroticism present in voyeuristic close-ups. Adding a penis would undermine that carefully navigated difference. Taking into account that the main target audience of comics still consists of heterosexual, white, male teenagers and young adults and that, in general, the audience American mass media caters to is white, heterosexual, and male because of male-as-norm culture, drawing a superpenis would imply a homoerotic subtext. By only implying the existence of the superpenis, superhero comics can deflect such homoerotic interpretations. The absence of the superpenis is a refusal to portray the superhero in a sexualized manner and dehumanize him. Peter Lehman writes that this silence on and refusal to engage with the male body as sexual is "a symptom of homophobia: this subject, the silence seems to say, can be of interest only to gay men."[28] When the main audience is believed to consist of straight men, homoerotic implications must be eliminated to prevent the alienation of the straight audience, who could not possibly be interested in the male body as a body that is sexually available.

The absence of the bulge, but the presence of the underwear, can then be understood as a way for the superpenis to be simultaneously present and absent to safeguard the hero's masculinity. In this manner, the underwear functions as a visual representation of the "no homo" response. The phrase "no homo" was first coined in the hip-hop industry, where it was used for straight audience affirmation. According to Joshua R. Brown, the "no homo" response "functions to negate a supposed misconception or misconstrued reading. . . . In saying something that the speaker might think will be understood as 'homosexual', the added 'no homo' disqualifies such a misunderstanding for the audience."[29] In other words, the "no homo" response is a linguistic tool used by men to distance themselves from homosexuality. When men in an established, straight, and male social group behave in a manner that the group's understanding of gender roles considers gay or feminine, the "no homo" response quickly reframes that behavior as masculine by denying any homosexual intention.[30] This equates masculinity with heterosexuality. As Brown points out, "The problem is not necessarily that you commit a sexual transgression, but that you have committed a gender transgression."[31] The group's construction of masculinity depends on its maintenance of heterosexuality, which means members of the group define masculinity and homosexuality as mutually exclusive. Homosexual individuals or social groups are identified as the nonmasculine Other, implying that gay men are not real men. The widely adopted use of "no homo" by American popular culture at large indicates that these beliefs concerning masculinity and heterosexuality are present in mainstream American culture. Through the Underwear of Power, Superman also perpetuates the idea that homosexuality and masculinity are mutually exclusive.

The construction of masculinity as fundamentally incompatible with homosexuality is enforced through consistent identification of (groups of) men as nonmasculine by male groups attempting to assert their masculinity. In *On Language and Sexual Politics*, Deborah Cameron analyzes conversations between men and finds that an important part of masculine discourse is the identification of other men as gay, meaning "failing to measure up to the groups' standard of masculinity."[32] By identifying others as homosexual, they reaffirm their own heterosexual masculinity. Cameron observes how young men "are compelled, paradoxically, to talk about men's bodies as a way of demonstrating their own total lack of sexual interest in those bodies."[33] Men are encouraged to look at men in order to define masculinity as what it is not: homosexual. The group's identification of themselves as masculine depends on warding off the homosexual, as if it could infect their heterosexual group and render them all nonmasculine. Of course, looking and gazing inevitably imply interest, and "no homo" is used to ward off the suspicion that the speaker looked sexually instead of analytically. Thus, "no homo" serves to normalize or heterosexualize gazing at male bodies to avoid homosexual panic. Brown asserts that "Given the frequency of the phrase, it has become ritualized as a sort of incantation, protecting the speaker from interpretations of their own words."[34] For comics, the Underwear of Power has become a ritualized incantation to protect the audience from homosexual panic at appreciating heavily detailed masculine musculature. However, as Taylor's essay confirms, it *is* possible to read the male superhero as sexually charged. As a visual medium, comics demand that both the artists and the audience engage with men's bodies. Conforming to American ideas about masculinity and sexual interest, these artists and their audiences also have to demonstrate "a total lack of sexual interest in those bodies" to ensure that this depiction is never interpreted as sexually attractive.[35] Covering up the superpenis is a visual ritual to prevent it from dominating the page and sexualizing the superhero. The artist portrays the masculine body in lavish detail as a demonstration of the superhero's masculine physique and power while the covered penis attempts to prohibit a homoerotic interpretation of the image. The underwear and detail-less bulge (if there is a bulge at all) frame the male body as nonhomosexual.

Covering up the superpenis serves to protect not only the masculinity of the superhero but also the masculinity of the audience due to penis anxiety. According to Lehman, in contemporary American society, people "are asked either to be in awe of the powerful spectacle of phallic male sexuality or to feel pity for, be ashamed of, or laugh at its vulnerable, failed opposite."[36] The penis is either the superpenis or the micropenis. The real biological penis is always the micropenis as the superpenis is not a physical, material thing. It is a phallus. Stephen Frosh writes that the phallus is "that which is taken to be the sign of difference, privileging one sex over the other, producing divergent subjectivities," which is culturally defined.[37] The phallus is not the biological penis but everything that a culture or society has deemed masculine and justifies masculinity's superiority or dominance over everything that is non-masculine or feminine. Masculinity is understood to be rooted in the penis as a "natural" and "biologically determined" rationalization of the oppression of femininity and those groups of men who do not possess the cultural masculine ideal. Because the ultimate masculine signifier has been conflated with the image of the penis, the phallus exists as an enlarged penis that symbolizes the domination of the environment. The biological penis cannot achieve such mastery and becomes irrelevant when compared with its cultural counterpart, except as an image that can smash the phallic illusion and castrate its supposed owner. Displaying a hard penis may achieve the effect of the phallus, but it also contains the possibility of its destruction through the specter of the soft, biological penis. Being confronted with Superman's bulge would create anxiety in the (assumed male) audience, no matter the size of the bulge. If the reader interprets the bulge as too small, it would indicate that Superman is in possession of the micropenis, which would undermine Superman's phallic effect and destroy his potential as a powerful subject fantasy. If the reader reads the bulge as too big, Superman would be in possession of the superpenis and, because of the phallus binary, identify the reader as possessing the micropenis, which creates penis anxiety. The Underwear of Power masks the bulge, simultaneously emphasizing the presence of the penis while rendering it invisible, making Superman safe for male consumption.[38]

However, in the past two decades, new superhero designs and old superhero redesigns such as Batman and Superman have not included the Underwear of Power, even though most merchandise consistently depicts these heroes with their underwear. Instead, many superheroes now have a belt, moving away from "gimmicky" costumes toward more "realistic" depictions of the superhero. For example, a non-superpowered hero like Batman needs a utility belt to store his equipment. But why would Superman need one? If it is a question of practicality, does the advantage of limited storage space weigh up against the risk of having a part of his costume easily grabbed while grappling with a villain? The Underwear of Power is considered old-fashioned, but its effect is crucial to the success of male superhero characters and the belt has a similar effect. It both draws and deflects attention away from the crotch.

Reconsider the image of the modern Superman (figure 1.1). With the audience looking up at Superman, the crotch towers over the reader, and yet it is the chest that undoubtedly dominates the image.[39] Even as the crotch is at the center of the page, its Ken-doll-like appearance redirects the reader to the overwhelmingly large chest. The use of yellow in the *S* chevron in a panel dominated by blue and red also draws the reader's eye toward the chest. The image clearly demonstrates how the male superhero body conforms to an inverted triangle: the immense chest dipping into a slim waist, with no bulge to disturb the clean, geometrical lines. Superman's overwhelming and dominating power, his phallus, is not found in the crotch but in the chest, which becomes the site of all male power. In *The Male Body: A New Look at Men in Public and in Private*, Susan Bordo discusses how "in classical Western art, the convention has been to represent the heroic body as muscular, but the actual penis as rather small."[40] Minimizing and covering up the penis in Western art originated in Descartes's dualist discourse, which placed nature opposite culture: animal versus man and the body versus the mind. The penis was considered to be part of nature and the body. Covering it up was interpreted as a move toward reason, linking rationality with masculinity as opposed to femininity, which is rooted in the womb, the cause of hysteria. Inclusion of the biological penis was unnecessary as the chest functioned as a phallus and became the site of power and intelligence, providing dominance over other, weaker biological bodies. The Underwear of Power, combined with the increasingly detailed muscular definition of the chest, ensures that the superhero conforms to that model. The belt is another step in that direction as the bulge becomes less visible without a brightly colored cloth to draw attention to it. The penis, although present, becomes invisible and the chest is always huge and hard, impenetrable and masculine.[41] The superhero possesses an inverted triangle body shape, which creates the image of the ultimate masculine body. Superman's superpowers and masculinity are obviously inherent and natural, through his Kryptonian ancestry, but even when male superheroes have powers that originate outside the masculine body, the narrative will frame these powers as a discovery or reflection of intrinsic, biological masculinity. The masculine must always project the illusion of being natural or innate, especially when it is artificially constructed, as evidenced through Captain America and Iron Man.

Man-Made Anatomy: Captain America's and Iron Man's Artificial Superbodies

Captain America entered the world in 1941 and left it in 1949, when World War II was over and American audiences lost their appetite for wartime stories. The *Captain America* comics focused on Steve Rogers, a sickly young art student rejected from the army because of his poor health. Eventually, the army selects him for Project Rebirth, an experimental procedure intended to produce a supersoldier. The creator of the procedure is murdered, leaving Steve as the only supersoldier. He is sent to the front as part of a regular army battalion and has to hide his identity as Captain America from his fellow soldiers. In 1953, Marvel attempted to revive the character in *Captain America: Commie Smasher!*, which was canceled in 1954. In later years, the series became an embarrassment because of its low quality and Red Scare pandering. In 1972, when the continuity established in the new *Captain America* series (1964–2014) began to clash extensively with the events of the 1950s series, Marvel retconned the universe. Supposedly, during the 1950s, several people had operated as Captain America. The most famous operative, William Burnside, had his name legally changed and underwent cosmetic surgery to look and sound like Steve. He injected himself with the superserum, but without the stabilizing effects of the radiation treatment, Burnside became paranoid and fanatically racist, which retroactively explained away the attitudes prevalent in *Captain America: Commie Smasher!* In the meantime, the original Captain America, Steve Rogers, was recast as a "man out of time." During his final mission, Steve crashed his ship into the Arctic and went into suspended animation, waking up twenty years later in *Tales of Suspense #59* (1964) and *The Avengers #4* (1964). Steve continued to appear as Captain America in *Tales of Suspense* (1959–1968) and *Captain America* until 2014, when he temporarily retired and Sam Wilson took over the Captain America title. In 2016, Steve returned as Captain America in *Captain America: Steve Rogers* (2016–2017) and *Captain America* (2017–ongoing). Steve has also appeared in numerous special event comics, special editions, limited series, and extensive appearances in ensemble comics.

Recast as a man out of time, Steve kept his World War II origins, which allow him to function as a positive symbol of America's moral superiority and power. World War II, as Jason Dittmer writes, "has long served as a touchstone for Americans seeking to ground an identity of both power and innocence during periods in which American power has been tainted or delegitimized (such as the post-Vietnam era)."[42] In the American cultural landscape, World War II is the good war. It was a time when American power was used to support values propagated as quintessentially American, such as democracy and freedom. Fighting the Nazis, whose atrocious crimes against humanity made them the go-to villains for decades, Steve does not exist in any moral "gray" spaces.[43] Captain America's association with World War II allows him to embody all those virtues and identifies Steve Rogers as the real Captain America, while others who lack Steve's moral rectitude are dismissed as imposters. In fact, Steve's moral superiority and, by extension, heroic masculinity are often framed as the qualities that made him Captain America, instead of the serum, as other recipients of the serum never transformed into a hero. This includes not only Burnside but also characters such as the Anti-Cap, a volunteer for the navy's supersoldier program in the early 2000s, whose existing mental health problems were exacerbated by the process. These consistent failures to re-create the serum despite scientific advancements within the Marvel universe prompt the question: Is it that the serum has never been correctly reproduced, or is there something specific about Steve Rogers that made the serum work?[44] The comics themselves often imply the latter, and the 2011 film *Captain America: The First Avenger* establishes that the serum only magnifies what already exists on the inside. Burnside, a product of McCarthyism, became excessively violent and paranoid. The Anti-Cap's mental health issues, as well as untreated emotional and psychological trauma, increased significantly.[45] Steve, who grew up during the recession and has a strong sense of duty, became the perfect American soldier. Despite his frail and "unmanly" stature, Steve attempted to volunteer for the army multiple times. When that failed, he willingly submitted himself to horrendous scientific experiments that could have killed him. He is portrayed as daring, determined, and heroic. In other words, the narrative implies that he already possessed all the qualities associated with American warrior masculinity. He only required a superbody to match, which was provided by the military and its scientific advancements.

Figures 1.2 and 1.3 were taken from *Captain America: Reborn* (2011), which reiterates Steve's 1940s origin story, coinciding with the promotion and marketing for the 2011 film.[46] Figure 1.2 depicts Steve Rogers before he was injected with the superserum. It is cut from a medium-size panel and displays Steve's pre-serum body as small and ill defined, especially compared with figure 1.3, which is a cropped full-page spread. The pre-serum panel is saturated with brown, a muted color. Steve's body seems ready to fade into the background. His arms and legs are very thin, much like his waist. The leanness of his belly can be attributed to malnourishment. However, a closer analysis reveals that even pre-serum Steve's body has well-defined musculature: his pectorals are so pronounced that they cover his sternum, and his rib cage is covered by a layer of fat (because we cannot see any definition of his individual ribs). Steve's body, demonstrating his physical weakness, nonetheless has potential for muscularity, hinting at the innate masculinity the serum will uncover. While figure 1.3 is one of the many full-page spreads demonstrating Captain America's massive physique throughout the *Captain America: Reborn* volume, pre-serum Steve is never drawn in such a dominating way. The use of the full-page spread immediately after only medium- and small-size panels of pre-serum Steve's diminutive body only reinforces how puny pre-serum Steve looks compared with Captain America's powerful and masculine physique. Figure 1.3 has a vibrant blue color, and the lightning bolt in the background adds to the sense of power, glinting of Captain America's muscles. He has a powerful, active stance that adds dynamism. The group of muscles on the left of his abs do not actually exist in the human body, and his abs are so large that they cover his belly button, which was pronounced in figure 1.2. His face is smaller than his pectorals, and he is so large that he would not be able to touch his own armpits. Like other male superheroes, Steve has a powerful, muscular masculine body.

The superserum not only made Steve bigger but also empowered and masculinized him, a narrative popular in the American cultural landscape of the 1940s that presented the war as a way to reinvigorate men. Following the widespread poverty of the Depression, a significant number of men were rejected from the first draft in the 1940s due to poor health following prolonged malnourishment and physical neglect. Subsequent drafts redefined medical standards while public

Figure 1.2. Pre-serum Steve. *Source*: Ed Brubaker et al., *Captain America: Reborn* (TPB) (New York: Marvel Comics, 2011). © 2011 Marvel Comics.

awareness campaigns admonished citizens to take care of their health by taking the right kind of supplements and doing men's work. The military instituted training methods geared toward beefing up the male body and, as Christina Jarvis documents, boasted that "basic training not only increased muscle tone and overall strength, but also contributed to greater stamina and better cardiovascular fitness."[47] Captain America fits into this 1940s narrative about male bodies in the military and the use of scientific advancements, such as x-rays, vitamin supplements, and protein potions, to improve bodily health. The promotion of soldiers'

Figure 1.3. Post-serum Steve. *Source*: Ed Brubaker et al., *Captain America: Reborn* (TPB) (New York: Marvel Comics, 2011). © 2011 Marvel Comics.

increased strength and the economic growth that occurred through households doubling their income with men entering the military and women entering the workplace "contributed to the sense that World War II had reinvigorated and masculinized the nation."[48] Similarly, Steve is masculinized by the military and scientific advancements. In the 2011 retelling of Steve's origin story, the masculine transformation in figure 1.3 is underlined through the focus on Steve's crotch, which is in the center of the page and has a prominent bulge, unlike most other drawings of superheroes. The lightning, aside from conveying power, is also a frame guiding the reader's gaze toward the bulge. The only noticeable figure in the background is at crotch level. Steve's whole body seems to curve toward his crotch, as does the rest of the room, including the Tesla coil behind him. The added string detail to his boxer shorts, missing from pre-serum Steve's boxers, also serves to draw in the reader's gaze. And yet, the chest still unquestionably dominates the page through its sheer size, symbolizing Steve's masculinity and warrior potential. The link between empowerment and the military, popular in 1940s propaganda, has remained part of American military masculinity, as evidenced by the 1980s recruitment slogan "Be All You Can Be," which lasted until the early 2000s.[49] Throughout the 1940s, the cultural understanding of masculinity increasingly revolved around the muscular body produced through military service. While the 1950s' corporate masculinity and the 1960s' rise of counterculture masculinity challenged this fixation on masculinity, the deeply rooted connection between masculinity and physical fitness or muscularity remained part of conventional masculinity. The gains of feminism in the 1970s and 1980s exacerbated the idea that masculinity was in crisis, and part of the backlash against these gains was an increased focus on extreme physicality and muscularity as a route to masculinity through the glorification of bodybuilding in mainstream culture.

The bodybuilder action hero made popular in the 1980s, such as Sylvester Stallone in *Rambo: First Blood* (1982) and Arnold Schwarzenegger in *The Terminator* (1985), contributed to the kind of body superheroes are now expected to have. According to Harrison G. Pope Jr., Katherine A. Phillips, and Roberto Olivardia in *The Adonis Complex*, a bodybuilder's physique "is characterized by well-developed chest and arm muscles, with wide shoulders tapering down to a narrow waist."[50] The bodybuilder has the inverted triangle body shape superheroes also have. In *Spectacular Bodies*, Yvonne Tasker writes that the bodybuilder is always "clearly marked as *manufactured*."[51] It is carefully, consciously constructed instead of naturally occurring because, as *The Adonis Complex* states, "the male body simply cannot exceed a certain level of muscularity without the help of steroids or other chemicals."[52] Without steroids, or a superserum, a body like that of the bodybuilder or the superhero is simply not possible. Steroids, used in cycles and at high dosages, combined with any kind of workout schedule, change the body drastically in the space of a few weeks. *The Adonis Complex* describes this body as simultaneously visible and invisible: "Steroids have created athletes, actors and models bigger and stronger than any ordinary man, and the media have promulgated their images everywhere. These images have glorified the steroid-pumped body, portraying it as a model of health, athletic prowess, hard work and dedication—while almost never admitting that it was a product of dangerous chemicals."[53] The steroid body is increasingly present within American culture, but remains invisible because the media unquestioningly presents these bodies as the result of hard work. While the body itself is visible, the context is invisible and the body becomes a "normal" body instead of a "steroid" body. The message is: this is simply what real men look like. Captain America follows this tradition, as

Dittmer points out: "While the 'super-soldier serum' is responsible for his physique, the success of Captain America in crime fighting is clearly attributed to his hard work. . . . Indeed, *Captain America* comics are laced with images of the Captain practicing his acrobatic maneuvers or lifting weights. While the drugs given to him by the U.S. government may have advantaged his start, his continued success is scripted as attributable to his continued hard work."[54] Even though the audience knows that Steve's body is artificially produced, the narrative implies that his innate masculinity has made this transformation possible, while his continued hard work maintains it. The discipline and self-control required for this hard body are also a sign of superior masculinity. Here is where cultural ideas about the malleability of human bodies and technology intersect. The artificially created body, which brings out innate and natural masculinity, allows Steve to maintain his masculine body by lifting weights and working out. The comics maintain a contradictory duality: Steve as a technological product requires maintenance to keep his artificially constructed masculine body in mint condition, but as a natural body is also sustained through his innate masculinity's capacity for hard work and self-discipline.

Captain America embodies a masculinity that is both innate (masculine virtue) and artificially created (superserum enhanced body) and is gained by joining the military, the ultimate signifier of American hegemony. According to Aaron Belkin, for some individuals "military service certifies one's competence, trustworthiness or authenticity" and represents "beliefs, practices and attributes which enable individuals to legitimize their claim to authority by associating themselves with the military."[55] Military masculinity is associated with authority and validated masculinity consisting of bravery, strength, and loyalty to one's country. Steve's desire to join the military demonstrates his need to affirm his innate masculinity in the face of his nonmasculine (and weak) body. His eventual rank of captain and subsequent masculine body only prove his status, which also proves his quintessential American exceptionality. As Belkin states, "Military masculinity is often portrayed as a central element of the American melting pot, a site where citizens come together, become soldiers and defend the nation as to minimize foreign threat."[56] In the cultural imagination, the military is viewed as an access route to authentic American identity, which rests on American (white, masculine) exceptionalism.[57] Steve's position within the military and his ascension to superhero status as Captain America allow him to participate in American exceptionalism and even embody it.

Steve, as Captain America, dresses in the colors and motifs of the American flag, as seen in figure 1.4, and wearing America's symbols positions him as the exemplary nationalist superhero.[58] Dittmer defines the nationalist superhero as a hero who "explicitly identifies himself or herself as a representative and defender of a specific nation-state, often through his or her name, uniform and mission."[59] The star on Steve's chest functions as a chevron, explicitly linking Steve's superhero identity to American nationalism, rooted in the phallic chest. The link with American nationalism strengthens Steve's performance of masculinity through

Figure 1.4. Captain America full uniform. *Source*: Rick Remender et al., *Captain America #16* (New York: Marvel Comics, 2012). © 2013 Marvel Comics.

the gendered divide between nation and state, which reflects cultural gender roles. Dittmer writes that in "gendered reading of national security culture, it is the 'soft' feminine nation that is to be protected by the 'hard' masculine state."[60] The soft feminine nation, the homestead where the women and children reside, needs to be protected by the state, the masculine institutions built and maintained by men such as the government and the military. The nation/state divide mirrors the gender dynamics present in the ideal of the nuclear family and the masculine ideal of the warrior: the masculine father/husband/warrior who protects the female mother/wife/civilian. The nation/state divide, in the American context, inevitably also perpetuates colonialist thinking where the nonnative, white man conquers the feminized native land by removing the racial Other, which is nonmasculine and, thus, feminized, which also protects white women. According to Belkin, this protection of the feminine co-exists with the annihilation of the feminine within the warrior: "Femininity is coded as an arbitrary, fictional construction which represents weakness, subordination, emotionalism, dependency and disloyalty. These traits are framed as dangerous aspects of the unmasculine that warriors must reject at all costs if they are to acquire enough strength to defend national security."[61] In the gender binary, the nonmasculine is the feminine and therefore must be eliminated in case it corrupts the masculine, even as masculinity itself is privileged within the heteropatriarchy based on its ability to protect femininity.

As a nationalist superhero, Steve embodies the ultimate warrior, and both the protection and destruction of women are central to that identity. The tension between these two contradictory impulses is present in the *Captain America* comics through the contrast between female villains and female allies. The female villain is often a femme fatale who attempts to seduce the hero. While they inevitably fail, such women must be destroyed.[62] The female allies are either female superheroes, or support characters who share the superhero's commitment to his duty, or the civilian girlfriend. While, as good women, these female characters deserve protection, to be protected means to be removed from the narrative. To prevent these women from being used against the hero, they must be rejected and eliminated. Therefore, despite the protection of the "good" feminine as key to warrior masculinity, Steve often exists in isolation from the feminine. He tends to work in male-dominated teams, such as the Avengers, or in team-ups with Bucky Barnes or Sam Wilson. Like many superheroes, Steve is also continually single or in on-again-off-again relationships with women to support "hetero-heroism" in comics, which Dittmer defines as "the role of the nationalist superhero's body in [representing] the relationship between masculinities and heterosexual domesticity."[63] As a superhero embodying the white, male American ideal, he has to embody the conflation of white masculinity and heterosexuality as well as the idealization of the family unit where the mother provides domesticity and the father provides protection from the outside world. Steve is often shown longing for the nuclear family and yet is always single because of "his inability to fulfil his girlfriend's emotional needs because of his intense devotion to duty and the obviously never-ending requirements of that job."[64] Because Steve is the embodiment of the perfect soldier, he can never stop being that soldier. While he protects the homestead, he will never be able to leave the front lines and return to that homestead, preventing domestication by any female partner. He chases the dream of heterosexual domesticity but never achieves it. He simultaneously provides protection of the female while maintaining a masculinity devoid of the feminine.

The destruction of the feminine is required not only in warrior masculinity and the military institution but also in scientific discovery, which are all inextricably linked in the figure of Captain America. During World War II and the ensuing decades, the United States coupled the demands of military defense to scientific advancement, with the federal government providing most of the funding for scientific research.[65] As Brian Easlea writes, this connection between the military and scientific innovation already existed in scientific discourse itself, which consistently used military language and metaphors, specifically the masculine conquest of the feminine.[66] It reproduced the gendered nation/state discourse, where nature is represented as the feminine nation and scientific discovery as the masculine institutions built on the conquest of the nation. Steve's masculinization, symbolizing the masculinization of America itself, represents the conquest of the weak and female body/nation/nature by the strong and male mind/state/scientific progress.

The construction of masculinity requiring the elimination of the feminine and scientific advancement's obsession with conquering the feminine are fueled by the masculine desire to control feminine procreative power. Building from some of Phyllis Chesler's work, Easlea goes on to theorize that, in scientific discourse, creation must be expressed in masculine terms, using aggression and destruction. For instance, Robert Oppenheimer was dubbed "the father of the atomic bomb," and successful bomb tests were coded in terms of delivering baby boys, such as the July 1945 confirmation that "Doctor has just returned most enthusiastic and confident that the little boy is as husky as his big brother."[67] Technology as masculine procreation can be traced back to womb envy, a concept in psychoanalysis developed by Melanie Klein and Karen Horney.[68] Womb envy is the envy of women's procreative ability and, theoretically, causes cultural sentiments that favor men. For example, the idea that the public sphere is masculine and equating the cerebral with the male while reducing the female to her (procreative) biology as set out in Descartes's dualist discourse. Another consequence would be that men are pushed to compensate for their lack of biological procreativity and "have to create other things outside themselves to compete with the potent symbol and actuality of women's biological and emotional creativity."[69] By excluding the female, scientific and technological discourse can be framed as a male enterprise: a masculine way of procreating.[70] Jacqueline Stevens connects womb envy to the creation of the phallus as a cultural signification for male virility and power. She frames the phallus as "compensatory masculine myths about phallic power and even birth-giving abilities."[71] Connecting the phallus to birth-giving abilities provides another insight into the importance of the penis bulge in the blue panel from *Captain America: Reborn*. It marks him as a virile male product of masculine procreation. Mark Moss further theorizes this idea of technology as male procreation and states that "Whether on the inside with electronics or on the outside with design, technology is a surrogate for biological creation. Technology, in most of its manifestations, is what a man can do."[72] What women can do is a faulty, biological process, which must be improved by superior male creations given life through dedication, determination, and masculine power. The creation of the white, American supersoldier with an innate superior masculinity is framed as the product of American men's ingenuity, the American military institution, scientific procreation, and the elimination or conquest of the female. Captain America's artificial body brings all these strands together.

One of the most artificial bodies in superhero comics is the body of Iron Man, and the cultural forces that helped construct it are very similar to those embodied by Captain America, despite the twenty years between their creation. Tony Stark's superhero persona, Iron Man, first appeared in *Tales of Suspense #39* in 1963, during the Cold War and its reconstruction of middle-class masculinity. As a genius, rich industrialist, Tony becomes Iron Man after he is captured by insurgents who command him to build weapons for them. He promises he will, but instead of using the material they provide to build weapons, he uses it to create the Iron Man suit and escapes. Using his suit, he fights crime and international villains. Initially, most of his enemies were explicitly communist, and Tony functioned as a justification for capitalist ideology following the 1950s era of cultural conservatism and capitalist enterprise. As a rich business owner who looked after his workers, Tony validated capitalist ideology as the superior and more dignified system compared with the exploitative communist system. Tony also embodied some of the cultural fears surrounding masculinity and the status of the "self-made man" in an increasingly corporate and consumer-focused society. As mentioned previously, the 1950s' rise of corporate middle-class masculinity struggled to reconcile traditional ideas of middle-class masculinity as self-employed. As Michael Kimmel writes: "The central characteristic of being self-made was that the proving ground was the public sphere, especially the workplace. And the workplace was a man's world (and a native-born white man's world at that). If manhood could be proved, it had to be proved in the eyes of other men."[73] The most prominent feature of the self-made man was his success in the free market, proving his masculinity to other men who had access to the public and professional sphere. Tony proved that, even in the 1960s, when corporate culture had become the norm, it was still possible for the white self-made man to make his fortune in America. Tony perpetuated the American Dream of hard work as an automatic gateway to wealth. His genius and technological innovations were part of this capitalist construct, connecting progress and innovation to the free market, which in turn funded Tony's scientific research. Therefore, Tony did not confirm to the usual relationship between scientists and the United States government, which funded most technological progress at the time.

Throughout the twentieth century, scientific development in the Western world was increasingly funded by the military. This decreased the ability of the scientific community to discuss research across borders or even projects within the same institutions as rising geopolitical tensions increased the need for secrecy. Members of the scientific community increasingly worried about the future of the field, including a lack of research dissemination and the possible violent real-life applications of their work. Even before World War II, scientists expressed concerns about the motives behind military funding, and many struggled to reconcile their own progressive, liberal beliefs with the death and destruction their work caused. In the

1950s, with McCarthyism and the Red Scare, refusal to participate in weapons projects could result in accusations of un-Americanism and communist sympathies, which further strengthened the government's control over scientific work.[74] Tony, as an entrepreneur, free from the constraints or demands of funding and regulation, exists in opposition to the government and its insistence on complete control over scientific discourse. As Robert Genter writes, "One of the main narrative threads of *Iron Man* concerns Stark's continuing problems with military officials who are trying to control his research and who begin questioning his loyalty."[75] This further contributed to Tony's function as the capitalist superhero who heroically resists government intervention and promotes neoliberalist capitalism. During most of the comics, Tony's wealth protects him from government control and allows him to continue his work, even when he turns away from weapons manufacture toward consumer goods production in more recent comics.

By the 1960s, technological advancement had given birth to consumer culture, with new technological products aimed at housewives to help them produce cleaner and better homes. Simultaneously, consumer culture urged men to amass greater wealth in order to purchase more things for the home and prove their manhood through the acquisition of status symbols. However, wealth and consumer culture increasingly created anxiety about the condition of white masculinity in America. Raised in comfort and affluence instead of the strenuous conditions of the past, so said the cultural narrative, prevented white boys from becoming hard, masculine citizens strong enough to withstand the tide of communism. K. A. Cuordileone writes that people were "increasingly struggling with the fear that Americans were growing too soft and self-indulgent next to their hard-driving, self-denying Spartan enemies in the U.S.S.R."[76] Cultural anxiety about the soft man was rooted in anxiety about the corrupting power of femininity in two forms: affluence in the form of luxury and the domineering mother. Moss writes that manhood can be questioned over "worry over decadence, and importantly, the subsuming of hardiness in favour of luxury."[77] Luxury, like femininity, is seen as corrosive, infecting the hardiness required to construct masculinity.[78] Children who grew up in luxury would not have the necessary experiences to become hard men. Children were also corrupted by the excessive feminine influence of the mother.[79] The domestic sphere was seen as female, and the authority the mother wielded in the home became a source of anxiety. Many mothers, whose influence was considered too powerful, were diagnosed with Momism, a supposedly severe pathological condition that caused mothers to "make psychological wrecks of their own children—*particularly boys*."[80] Mass media claimed that Momism prevailed among white, middle-class women who were full-time mothers and homemakers and failed in their femininity by not being content with their place in the home. Momistic mothers created weak, neurotic, and soft men who would be susceptible to homosexual and communist influences. Both the fear of excess and the fear of undue motherly influence on male children should have been dissolved through the concept of togetherness. Cuordileone discusses how the 1950s encouraged a return to the home, a cultural sentiment called "togetherness" urging married couples to do everything together to create a stable home. This would give men the opportunity to teach their sons how to be men and masculinize the domestic sphere to counter the corrosive power of wealth and femininity. However, the rise of corporate culture required men to prove their masculinity through their careers and/or masculine hobbies, and men were driven out of the home. In the cultural narrative, child rearing remained women's business, and this was framed as both natural and a source of anxiety.

Tony simultaneously represented those fears and laid them to rest. He inherited his company and a large family fortune from his parents, placing him in the old-world, upper-class society even while calling to mind images of hardworking, family-owned businesses. The later retcon of Tony inheriting the business from his father, instead of starting it himself, undercuts the narrative of Tony as the self-made man, but this is compensated for by highlighting that Tony is the one who put the company on the map. He took this national, somewhat successful business and made it a Fortune 500 company. At the same time, he grew up in the affluence and comfort of the upper-middle-class home, ruled by the mother, both the American Dream and its nightmarish Double. Representing the fear of weak masculinity fostered in such homes, pre–Iron Man Tony Stark was described as a playboy who drank too much and partied too hard. While the precise context of the Cold War has faded from the narrative, fears of weak masculinity in light of a "feminized" society, with luxury and coddling mothers, are still current. In post-9/11 culture, many of the anxieties and fears present in Cold War culture have returned, including the panic about a crisis in masculinity caused by luxury, excess, and femininity.[81] In the *Iron Man* movie franchise, particularly the first film (released in 2008), luxury and femininity are used to portray pre–Iron Man Tony Stark as lacking in masculinity, which underlines the power masculinity of Iron Man by contrast. When he is kidnapped, cut off from his wealth, and given only the equipment necessary to build weapons for his captors, Tony finally has the harsh environment needed to cultivate a superior masculinity. In these hardening conditions, he is able to construct a powerful body and he literally becomes the self-made man. The creation of the Iron Man is a transformation from soft and inadequate masculinity to hard and superior masculinity. The suit exists as an artificial, self-constructed, hard body. Iron Man functions as the perfect analogy for the way that modern society frames the relationship between innate masculinity and technology's role in bringing it to the surface as a fundamental requirement for superior masculinity.

In the cultural domain, the hard, artificial body is most recognizable through the action figure, which the Iron Man suit resembles. *The Adonis Complex* documents the changes in bodily dimensions for action figures, as representations for ideal body types, over the past thirty years. Figure 1.5 depicts three versions of an action figure. From left to right, they are the G.I. Joe action figures released in 1964, 1974, and 1991. The musculature of the chest becomes increasingly detailed, with the 1991 version appearing dehydrated considering how pronounced the muscles are. After 1964, the waist shrinks and the chest, shoulders, and biceps

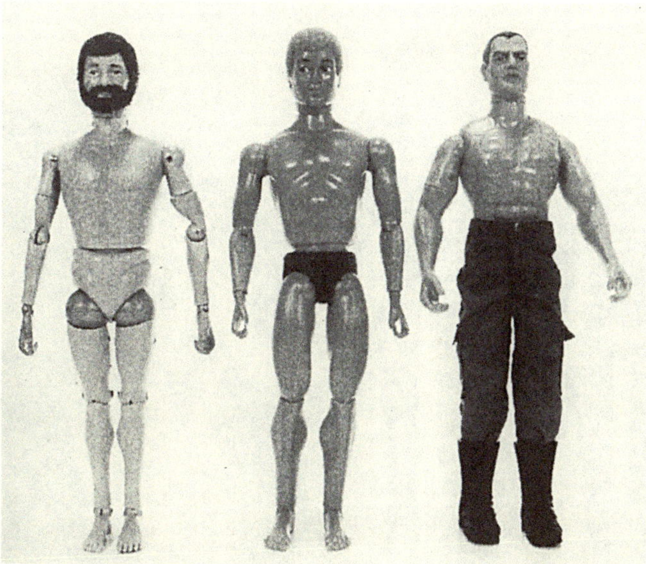

Figure 1.5. The evolution of G.I. Joe, 1964–1991. *Source*: Harrison G. Pope Jr., Katherine A. Phillips, and Roberto Olivardia, *The Adonis Complex: How to Identify, Treat and Prevent Body Obsession in Men and Boys* (New York: Simon & Schuster, 2002), 42. © 2002 Captured Moments.

expand. The G.I. Joe figures released in the 1990s exemplify this evolution, as seen in figure 1.6.[82]

In figure 1.6, the action figure on the far right, produced mid-1990s, is obscenely large. While most of the other G.I. Joe figures are at least a reasonable size (if not reasonably muscled), the last G.I. Joe does not have a body any man could reasonably be expected to possess. In fact, *The Adonis Complex* concludes that, if he were life-size, "he would have a 55-inch chest and 27-inch bicep. His bicep, in other words, is almost as big as his waist—and bigger than that of most competition bodybuilders."[83] As discussed previously, certain body sizes and shapes cannot be achieved without chemical intervention. The implications of these changes in body size promoted to young children are immense as "the ideal male body has evolved in only about thirty years from a normal and reasonably attainable figure . . . to a hugely muscular figure that we believe no man could attain without massive doses of steroids."[84] In only thirty years, the ideal male body changed to resemble that of the bodybuilding action hero. This body, while promoted as the result of masculine perseverance and discipline (the male conquest over the unruly, excessive female-created natural body), is actually the product of unhealthy and dangerous chemicals. Pope, Phillips, and Olivardia explain this obsession with muscularity through the theory of threatened masculinity: "Women can enter formerly all-male military schools, join formerly all-male clubs, and win elective offices once held almost exclusively by men. Women have become less dependent upon men for money, power, and self-esteem. What,

Figure 1.6. The evolution of G.I. Joe, 1990s. *Source*: Harrison G. Pope Jr., Katherine A. Phillips, and Roberto Olivardia, *The Adonis Complex: How to Identify, Treat and Prevent Body Obsession in Men and Boys* (New York: Simon & Schuster, 2002), 42. © 2002 Captured Moments.

then, do men have left to distinguish themselves, to mark their masculinity? One of the few attributes left, one of the few grounds on which women can never match men, is muscularity. Therefore, we hypothesize that the body is growing in relative importance as a defining feature of masculinity."[85] Because the measure of masculinity depends on competition with other men and the elimination of the feminine, women's penetration into formerly all-male spaces forces men to compete with women. Through bodybuilding, specifically the creation of large and lavishly detailed musculature, men attempt to create an exclusively all-male space where they can safely compete against each other. Comparing the evolution of the G.I. Joe action figure with the evolution of the Iron Man suit, it becomes clear that the Iron Man also documents these changes and perpetuates the link between hardness and masculinity.

Figure 1.7 is a modern rendering of the suit as it first appeared in 1963 and embodies the very beginning of Stark's development as Iron Man.[86] Figure 1.8 is from 1983, displaying a significant shift away from the original design when the bodybuilding action hero became popular.[87] Figure 1.9 is from 2013, one of the most recent iterations of the suit.[88] The 1963 suit is the largest, and there is no significant difference in size between the 1983 model and the 2013 model. This seems to contradict the evolution documented in *The Adonis Complex*, but a close examination of the torso shapes reveals an increase in chest size, with a decrease in waist size, creating the inverted triangle shape caused by bodybuilding and steroid

Figure 1.7. Original Iron Man. *Source*: Warren Ellis et al., *Iron Man: Extremis* (TPB) (New York: Marvel Comics, 2013). © 1963 Marvel Comics.

use. The 1983 and 2013 models have this familiar shape, reflected even further in the triangle shape of the 2013 chest chevron. The 1963 version lacks this shape as it predates the bodybuilding action hero made popular in the 1980s. Not only are the sizes of the suits important, but their designs also speak to their purpose, which is infused with meaning about masculinity. As demonstrated through the discussion of Easlea's, Moss's, Klein's, and Horney's work, masculinity and technology are closely linked, and the Iron Man suit embodies this.

The original suit is made completely out of metal, because of the limited resources available at the time of its production, and is mostly a faceless monolith. Judging

Figure 1.8. 1980s Iron Man. *Source*: Catherine Saunders et al., *Marvel: Year by Year, a Visual Chronicle* (New York: Dorling Kindersley, 2013). © 1983 Marvel Comics.

from the joints and the size of the panels, the suit has little flexibility. It is large and powerful, but crude. The suit was built to break Tony out of his cage. It did not require anything besides raw power. As the symbol of Tony's transformation into hard masculinity, this suit underlines the strength gained during his escape. The second design, from 1983, is more futuristic. It is sleeker—aside from its pointy shoulder pads in line with the 1980s' space-age fashion, which further accentuate the inverted triangle torso shape. The most immediate and notable differences from the 1963 design are its shape and the amount of detail in musculature, similar to the development in action figures documented in *The Adonis Complex*. It seems unnec-

Figure 1.9. Modern Iron Man. *Source*: Warren Ellis et al., *Iron Man: Extremis* (TPB) (New York: Marvel Comics, 2013). © 2013 Marvel Comics.

essary for a suit made of metal to have a sculpted chest and oblique muscles. The 1983 suit looks as though it has been poured onto Tony's chest and subsequently hardened into the shape of his muscular body. The 2013 model, while similar to the 1983 model, has a more exaggerated triangle shape and looks much harder. The texture resembles the look of a steel or iron alloy, with a more robotic appearance. The shoulder pads have been rounded out, adding bulk in the shoulders, while the smaller, interlocking panels give it more flexibility compared with the 1963 and 1983 models. The level of detail has increased again, as the joint mechanisms are clearly visible in the gauntlet, elbow joints, and kneepads. The details of the technological elements stand in for muscular definition. The suit seems perfectly capable of flexing its muscles. The level of detail in technological embodiment as a metaphor for musculature strengthens the link between technology and masculinity, specifically, the male body. The ultimate masculine body has transcended human limitations. Instead of using technology to improve on the human body, as with Captain America, an entirely new body can be constructed: harder, more powerful, and more masculine than ever. Like robots and cyborgs, the suit has no real racial markers, but it nonetheless functions as a white body. In white-as-norm culture, whiteness is considered the neutral, nonracial norm, and even without genitalia or beard growth, the suit is clearly male. Functioning as the powerful, hard body that houses the brain of the white man inside it, the suit embodies white masculinity and its link to science, power, and aggression.

The production of technology is connected to the idea of the white, self-made man. Moss discusses how the self-made man engages in processes of self-modification, where "Autonomy and making something different with one's hands are also significant."[89] Self-modification through technological means is fundamental to the construction of the self-made man's masculinity because it involves the creation of and by the male. Moss states that "A specific version of the American entrepreneur and the self-made man is often focused on technology. More specifically, it lingers around the appropriation of different kinds of technology in order to harness some kind of power."[90] Moss links technology, masculinity, and consumerism. It is the appropriation of technology and its creation that harnesses power and masculinity. Throughout the years, the Iron Man suit has changed significantly and becomes more sophisticated and elaborate, corresponding to scientific advancement and cultural discourse's dissemination of it. Reinventing the suit allows Tony to continually reconstruct his masculinity. It demonstrates his wealth and ability to financially support the reconstruction or purchase of this artificial body, which fits into Kimmel's "cycle of 'conspicuous consumption'—the frenzied and competitive consumption of expensive items that demonstrate high status."[91] In consumer culture, consumption of products is always a status symbol. The continual reconstruction of the Iron Man suit is a consumption of technology that demonstrates Tony's high status and masculinity. He treats the suit the same way consumer culture discards highly advanced technological items the second a similar item with a few improvements is produced. Its artificial nature, in consumer culture, implies that it is a body for sale, and with enough money or technological prowess anyone could possess it. Superior masculinity is available to everyone and only needs to be cultivated. This implies that superior masculinity is innate and the inability to produce it is a flaw in someone's gender configuration. As with Captain America, the real man needs only a serum or a scientific method to bring out his true nature. Mike Featherstone writes that "With appearance being taken as a reflex of the self, penalties of bodily neglect are a lowering of one's acceptability as a person, as well as an indication of laziness, low self-esteem and even moral failure."[92] In a culture where dieting, bodybuilding, and cosmetic surgery can change one's appearance completely and are becoming increasingly available to a wider audience, not participating in appearance-based gender identity is suspicious. As this ideal body is a body that anyone can possess, not having it must be a lack of desire to possess it, implying a lack of innate masculinity. The Iron Man is simultaneously unique and generic: it is superior, but also for sale.

Conclusion

Superman, Captain America, and Iron Man demonstrate how superheroes perpetuate a pre-existing script for ideal masculinity. This construction is based on the elimination of the feminine, which includes anything defined as nonmasculine, anything that is soft, weak, connected to nature, biology, and the domestic sphere. Through the inverted triangle body shape, emphasized by the chest chevron and the Underwear of Power, the superhero constructs a powerful body reflecting an innate masculinity, representing the mastery over the (feminine, natural) body via masculine technology and science. The evolution of the American masculine ideal between the 1940s and contemporary times reflects the rise of consumer culture and its influence on all levels of society. Increasingly, masculinity is defined by how much can be earned, spent, and bought. Men are encouraged to buy their way into ideal masculinity by moving up the corporate ladder, providing for their family, and being able to purchase luxury items and status symbols. From the 1940s' working-class masculinity's connection to the military and technology, to the 1950s' rise of middle-class Cold War sentiments and Momism paranoia, the 1960s and 1970s' occupational consumer culture and second wave feminism, and the 1980s and 1990s' bodybuilding action hero, masculinity has evolved to continually produce bigger and "better" bodies. Underlying this evolution is the increasing faith in technology's capacity to improve the human body beyond its natural abilities, as if feminine nature can continually be upgraded or replaced by masculine technological powers. The superhero movies of the 2000s and 2010s have perpetuated this ideal masculinity. At the second annual superhero conference, in 2016, Daniel J. Connell and Drew Murphy each presented papers on hypermasculinity in superhero films. They discussed how, every time a new X-Men or Wolverine film is released, audiences marvel at Hugh Jackman's ability to be bigger and more muscular, especially now that he is in his early fifties.[93] Chris Pratt's transformation from chubby Andy Dwyer in *Parks and Recreation* (2009–2015) to superhero Peter Quill in *Guardians of the Galaxy* (2014) was widely covered by celebrity news outlets, and his chest close-up was a focal point for the film's trailer.[94] Robert Downey Jr., whose portrayal of Iron Man made the superhero more famous than ever before, has maintained a striking physique for the films even though Tony wears a robotic suit and does not need a superhero body.[95] No matter which media format is being accessed, the superbody is there, bigger and more powerful than ever before.

The promotion of these immense bodies can have serious consequences. *The Adonis Complex* documents how the promulgation of these bodies causes many young men to develop negative self-images and contributes to the rise of bodybuilding and steroid addiction. The psychological effects of steroids resemble paranoia and hypermasculine frames of thought, which include violence as the foundation of hypermasculinity, especially violence aimed at women, gay men, and men of color.[96] Simultaneously, the powerful masculine body exists side by side with masculinity's constant anxiety about its own strength. In the 1930s and 1940s, many men could not afford to feed their families or themselves, lost physical strength, and became malnourished even while mass media constantly produced images of the physically powerful working-class body. This was replaced by the image of the soldier, who was masculinized by his military service but whose Double—the conscientious objector and the shell-shocked sufferer—haunted American society. In the 1950s, men were becoming too soft and weak as a result of luxury and had to go camping, fishing, or hunting to become harder and stronger. Counterculture and the panic about Momism in the late 1950s and 1960s produced a crisis about long-haired and soft men who refused military service side by side with the rise of corporate masculinity. In the 1980s and 1990s, masculinity was under siege through the slow deconstruction of male privilege, and the bodybuilding action hero quickly appeared to reinforce the idea of the male as the protector of the female. In contemporary times, a brief glance at websites such as Roosh V and blogs such as *The Athefist* will prove that many men are convinced that feminism means the oppression of men instead of gender equality.[97] "If only we could go back to the good old days when men were men and women were women." But there were no good old days, and the toxic ideas and constraints of patriarchal hegemonic masculinity have always forced men into a state of panic and overcompensation.

Superheroes offer compensatory images of powerful masculinity as well as scripts on masculine behavior countering the narratives of masculinity in crisis. They are a power fantasy attempting to purge male anxiety. Superman would never be anxious about his status as a man. He might suffer from existential angst in relation to his humanity or alien nature, but Super*man* is always a man. Captain America and Iron Man continually construct their own masculinity and do not need to be told how. They possess the innate knowledge required to forge the ideal masculinity. They always come out on top, as real men do. In comic books and other forms of mass media, the superhero remains at the top of the social hierarchy, dominating all others in the universe. The ideal masculinity promoted in superhero comic books overlaps with some behavioral patterns and ideology associated with hypermasculinity, such as violence as inherently masculine, elimination of the feminine, and risk-taking behavior as heroic masculinity, but also includes an insistence on American nationality, whiteness, and wealth as a gateway to power in consumer culture. Furthermore, through the use of the chevron, this masculinity is also marketable, which allows it to be perpetuated and exported to a massive audience. This ideal masculinity fits into hegemonic and heteronormative gender roles, perpetuating the status quo.

CHAPTER 2

The White Female Body

This chapter examines the femininity represented by two female combatant superheroes, Supergirl and Wonder Woman. These female superheroes represent femininity and womanhood outside of the stereotypes previously identified in comics, such as Brokeback, fridge-ing, and the "strike a pose and point" powers. While female superheroes can perpetuate stereotypes about women and femininity, they are inherently disruptive to the heteropatriarchal status quo on which the genre of superheroes rests: the male soldier/warrior/protector and the female civilian. This chapter focuses on how this disruption is mitigated and reframed as compliance. It investigates Wonder Woman's representation of the American female soldier and, in later decades, the female warrior. Considering the traditional "pose and point" powers, this analysis will dig into how muscularity's intrinsic connection to masculinity impacts the female physical combatant. Female superheroes, like their counterparts, are increasingly subject to impossible bodily standards. Through the analysis of Supergirl, also a physical combatant, this chapter explores the link among the female superhero's body, plasticity, and combat. Mirroring the relationship with the male superhero and the action figure, the female superhero is linked to the Barbie doll and her dark Other, the porn star. Even the female soldier is not exempt from this comparison.

The Female Warrior: Wonder Woman as the American Female Soldier

Superhero comics have been dominated by male superheroes from the very beginning. In the 1940s and 1950s, few child care professionals were worried about this lack of female role models in mass media influencing girls. While most critics and professionals were concerned with comics' violent content, William Moulton Marston, a psychiatrist and teacher, was more concerned with the absence of female superheroes. A staunch supporter of the suffragette movement, Marston believed that women had a superior moral and loving character that could tame men's warlike nature through love bonds.[1] Marston believed that neither boys nor girls appreciated femininity or even recognized female power, which needed to be corrected through "a feminine character with all the strength of Superman plus all the allure of a good and beautiful woman."[2] Marston created the *Wonder Woman* comics to provide girls with a suitable role model and to promote his theories on female power. For example, Wonder Woman came from Paradise Island, populated solely by women, which reflected his belief that if women were empowered, they could create utopia. Women should use love to make men submit to women's superior nature, and Wonder Woman was equipped with a magic lasso that compelled everyone to tell the truth. All men really wanted was a strong and beautiful woman to submit to, and in 1941, Diana of Paradise Island became Wonder Woman and embodied that powerful feminine ideal. To that end, Wonder Woman's looks were carefully designed by Henry George Peter, whose work was inspired by the Gibson girl, a forerunner of many of the later pinup girls popular during World War II, and suffragette art, which often included strong women breaking the bonds or chains of the patriarchy. Marston wanted a woman "as powerful as Superman, as sexy as Miss Fury, as scantily clad as Sheena the Jungle Queen, and as patriotic as Captain America."[3] The design that Peter came up with was remarkably similar to the patriotic pinup girl.[4]

In the late 1930s and early 1940s, the pinup girl was an increasingly popular art form, used in advertisements, pulp magazines, and paperback novels, as a celebration of American femininity. As Charles G. Martignette and Louis K. Meisel state, "Artists chose to paint pin-ups because they wanted to capture and celebrate the femininity of American women."[5] The American girl in pinup art was bold and independent, and she enjoyed a freedom of movement unparalleled in more conservative European societies, at least from the American point of view. The American woman's independence resulted in a more beautiful and refined femininity, which was lacking in European women, as evidenced by the pinup girl's gaze often starting directly at the viewer.[6] Wonder Woman, as a reflection of Marston's ideas about powerful women, had to be drawn as a celebration of powerful femininity. Like the pinup girl, Wonder Woman's costume is form revealing and resembles a bathing suit. The strapless, backless top was designed to showcase that, despite her strength, her arms and shoulders remained slender and feminine. The belt hugs her figure, and the booty shorts completed the look with a patriotic motif while the kinky boots created an air of sexual allure. Additionally, because she is dressed in the colors of the American flag, Wonder Woman's identity as a non-American is effectively erased, as she clearly represents America in her fight against the Axis. The style of the pinup girl was combined with the conventions of suffragette art. Marston found the movement's art, with women blindfolded and breaking free of chains, appealing as a metaphor for his theory of love binding, and most comics found Wonder Woman breaking free of the chains of patriarchal oppression while using her lasso to bind men instead. Additionally, the suffragette can also be found in Wonder Woman's bracelets. According to the origin story of the 1940s, the Amazons were once bound by men; when they broke free, Aphrodite led them to an island they could rule in peace. To remind them that they should never again let men bind them, the Amazons wear the cuffs of the chains with which they were bound. Wonder Woman is "the suffragette as pin-up," a celebration of femininity and a symbol of female power.[7] Marston aimed to create an image of the feminine ideal that some of his readers would already be familiar with and that would be appealing to a mass audience, while incorporating his untraditional views.

The pinup girl celebrated the 1940s' American ideal of feminine beauty, independent and fierce, but she remained a traditional wife and mother underneath the glamour. While the question of women and work occupied the cultural landscape in the 1920s and 1930s, most popular authors urged women to remain in the home. Leila Rupp writes that "Motherhood and housekeeping, women were told, were professions one could practice with pride."[8] However, in the 1930s, the working class increased significantly due to the Depression. Many women who had been professional housewives had to take on the kind of work that working-class women had always done, such as waitressing, laundering, cleaning, and various kinds of factory work. In the 1940s, America entered World War II, and the surplus of male labor created by the 1930s' Depression quickly dried up as men either gained employment in the growing war industry or joined the military. The shortage of workers had to be filled by women. Because of the professional housewife ideal, the cultural narrative insisted most women were unemployed and had to be persuaded to join the workforce, something they had never done. The real cultural change was that, for the first time, middle-class and upper-middle-class women left the home in large numbers to pursue life in the public spheres, which created anxiety about the future state of femininity in America. Supposedly, femininity was best preserved in the home, and women participating in the rough public and professional spheres would become too masculine. Therefore, the government propaganda of the time presented the idea that war demanded extraordinary sacrifices of housewives, not only having to miss their husbands but also having to leave their homes and children. Government campaigns emphasized that if women took war jobs, the war would end and women could return to their homes and children, reuniting the family. Women joining the workforce changed the way women were presented in popular media, but the widespread dissemination of the pinup working girl "did not mean that the ideal American woman had changed beyond recognition. Beneath the begrimed exterior, she remained very much a traditional woman."[9] Underneath it all, she was still a housewife.

Wonder Woman may not have been a housewife, but her story followed the cultural narrative. Paradise Island, functioning as a metaphor for the domestic sphere populated exclusively by women, had been entirely cut off from the outside world, the public sphere, and only came out of seclusion because of the war, or because Steve Trevor crashed his plane on the shores of Paradise Island. Wonder Woman volunteers to leave her home and fight for America in "man's world," the phrase Amazons use to describe the outside world. Through this narrative,

Wonder Woman fits into the cultural idea of the woman who was comfortably and happily living at home but does her bit in the war effort to save the life of her sweetheart. Throughout the *Wonder Woman* comics, the narrative implies that, after the war, Trevor and Wonder Woman would settle down together. The comics presented the idea that Wonder Woman's participation in the public "man's world" was temporary, just like women's participation in war work. The image of working women became increasingly normalized even while the idea that women's true place was in the home persisted. Furthermore, the working woman was more acceptable when she was unmarried and childless, as she did not have responsibilities in the home, even though plenty of married women with children did work. Wonder Woman was also unmarried and without children and did not challenge the idea that wives and mothers should be in the home. Despite Marston's radical policies, Wonder Woman followed the cultural narrative surrounding the working girl as a temporary phenomenon.

During World War II, Wonder Woman participated in what was considered traditionally women's work in her secret identity as Diana, the air force secretary. In 1942, the Women's Army Auxiliary Corps was founded, which became the Women's Army Corps (WAC) in 1943.[10] These women existed in the new cultural concept of the female soldier, which was created to preserve the hegemonic masculinity of the military. Male soldiers were defined as heroic combatants, and female soldiers as noncombatants who did the increasingly feminized jobs of managing a professional army in an industrialized world. They were clerks, typists, telephone operators, technicians, secretaries, and sometimes translators. In this manner, the role of the protector and the heroic warrior ideal could be preserved as a masculine role. The female soldier was portrayed as honorable, self-sacrificing, and chaste while the work itself was promoted as essentially feminine, and thus naturally suited to women. This substantial effort to reconfigure women's place in the home to women's place in the war, on a temporary basis, was further aided by recruitment strategies promoting the idea that women's natural and essential skills would be further developed through military service, which would help women become better wives when their husbands returned from the war: "The flip side of this new recognition of women's place in the war was that the special skills that made Wacs so valuable were often precisely those nurturing and caring skills that were traditionally assigned to women. To accept Wacs as fellow soldiers now, to give them proper credit and support, would make them better wives when the war was over."[11] While this statement by Michaela Hampf specifically discusses women in the WAC, this can be extrapolated to women in all branches of military service during the 1940s. The American media insisted that military service was reinvigorating and masculinizing for men because of the warrior ideal, while the creation of the female soldier as a separate concept allowed the media to simultaneously claim that women were feminized by military service. In this way, the military fulfilled an important function in the cultural imagining by not only protecting the nation but also reinforcing the traditional gender roles on which the nation was built.

The narrative that framed the roles women performed in the army as inherently feminine was used to legitimize female soldiers, and Wonder Woman, as a celebration of femininity and a secretary in the air force, further perpetuated that discourse. Wonder Woman rarely fought enemy Nazi soldiers directly, as she was more likely to fight spies and infiltrators on the home front while working as a WAC. Even when fighting, she remained explicitly feminine and her official state-sanctioned profession was that of a military secretary. While this can be read as a reduction of Wonder Woman's radical potential, it is important to understand that Wonder Woman continually insisted that her femininity was the source of her strength and power, and that this was a radical message. Considering that femininity or behavior associated with femininity is still often dismissed as frivolous and unimportant, this was a transgressive message for young children. Moreover, Wonder Woman's participation in the military was promoted as positive and empowering. It contributed to the normalization of working women in the military and the war industry. Wonder Woman admonished women to resist cruel husbands and abusive marriages, to submit to military discipline, and to become strong and make men submit to them instead. The Wonder Woman created during the Golden Age (1930s–1950s) was a complicated figure who straddled the divide between conventional and transgressive ideas about women in the home and in the war. These contradictory significations would vanish from the *Wonder Woman* comics after the death of William Moulton Marston in 1947, when Robert Kanigher took over the series.

In the 1950s, with the Comics Code Authority (CCA) and the increasingly conservative cultural landscape, *Wonder Woman* comics became less effusive in their message of empowerment for women and took on a more traditional gender narrative. A large part of the conservative turn taken by the comics can also be attributed to Kanigher, who "hated the character he called 'the grotesque inhuman original Wonder Woman.'"[12] Increasingly, the *Wonder Woman* comics began to emphasize a more traditional depiction of gender roles compared with the 1940s' run. After the end of World War II, Wonder Woman no longer fought Nazi spies or Japanese agents. Instead, like many women in the 1950s, she returned home. In the American imagination, the home became the nexus of peace and relaxation, a hiding place from the outside world full of the burdens of corporate culture as well as foreign forces threatening to invade American society and the nuclear family. Mitra C. Emad discusses how, after World War II, "sparked by American postwar propaganda directed at women, Wonder Woman's identity moves further and further into the domestic, feminine realm and away from the masculine realm of politics and war."[13] Most of Wonder Woman's story lines now revolved around her family on Paradise Island. Through the Amazons' technological marvels, the adult Wonder Woman could interact and have adventures with her younger selves, Wonder Tot and Wonder Girl.[14] Along with her mother, Queen Hippolyta, they protected Paradise Island and the planet from outside forces together, as a family. Wonder Woman no longer protected humanity from its own dangerous impulses such as war, but from a hostile galaxy or the supernatural. These stories reflected the Cold War rhetoric of the domestic sphere as a bulwark against the threat of the world beyond America. Women, as the keepers of the domestic sphere, played a key role in the ideology of the domestic. They had to maintain the home as a pleasant and comfortable environment and raise good and able citizens. In these stories, Hippolyta functions as the mother who raised a good, feminine daughter, Wonder Woman. Together, they protected Paradise Island, their home, and, by extension, the world. By doing so, they promoted Marston's belief that strong women working together could save the world. The enemies they faced were often male or identified through masculine pronouns, implying that masculine greed and destructive tendencies needed to be contained by strong women in order to protect the paradise women could create together.[15] However, this powerful message was mitigated by the domestic frame in which Wonder Woman now appeared.

Throughout the 1950s and 1960s, Wonder Woman's transgressive message was consistently dismantled. Kanigher fired Harry Peter, who had drawn Wonder Woman in the powerful suffragette and pinup tradition, and, as Carolyn Cocca documents, "On the covers drawn by Irwin Hasen and panels by Ross Andru, Diana's boots were replaced with delicate laced sandals, her formerly flat bustier was drawn with more defined curves, her hair was longer and her eyes and mouth larger, and more dynamic posing followed for more focus on her curves."[16] With a more romance-focused story line, the art no longer drew Wonder Woman as a fierce and powerful warrior and made her more conventionally attractive instead. Other changes included cutting a traditional section in the comic called "Wonder Women of History," celebrating female scientists, artists, and athletes, and replacing it with the section "Marriage A La Mode," dedicated to discussing different marriage customs around the globe.[17] Romance, while regularly present in *Wonder Woman* comics, was now a far more central plot point. Wonder Girl often struggles with her feelings for Merboy and her duty to become Wonder Woman. Trevor and Mer-Man compete for Wonder Woman's affection. Trevor keeps asking Wonder Woman when she will finally marry him, while she struggles with the desire to be his perfect wife in light of her duties to the world. She continually reminds him that she cannot marry him as long as there is work for her to do, because she cannot possibly combine her duties as Wonder Woman with the duties of a wife and mother, reflecting the idea that wives and mothers should remain in the home. Wonder Woman also had to compete with herself for Trevor's love. In her secret identity, as Diana Prince, the air force secretary, she often laments that Trevor never notices her and cares only about Wonder Woman. However, when he does show interest in Prince, she is often jealous and wonders how much he really loves Wonder Woman if he can be attracted to other women. It perpetuates the idea that women cannot be friends, even with themselves, because they are always competing with each other for men's affections. While the comics seem to imply that Trevor and Wonder Woman's marriage is inevitable, that Wonder Woman will one day be unable to refuse Trevor because she loves him, the reader also knows that Wonder Woman's work would never be done, and according to her logic, she cannot be both Wonder Woman and a wife. The tension between these two truths could not be explored indefinitely, and the stories grew stale throughout the Silver Age (1950s–1970s). As a result, *Wonder Woman*'s sales began to drop.

It became clear that the *Wonder Woman* comics needed a new direction, and DC appointed a new editor, Mike Sekowsky. In 1968, Wonder Woman was summoned to Paradise Island and told that the Amazons had to retreat into an alternate dimension to recharge their fading powers and youth. Wonder Woman chooses to stay behind to save Trevor, who has been accused of murder. When the Amazons leave Earth, Wonder Woman becomes entirely human. She loses her Amazon strength and eternal youth. With the loss of her feminine power, she turns into Diana Prince permanently. She cuts her ties to her feminine support network and erases her connections to her female gods, Athena and Aphrodite. The consistent elimination of the female seems incongruous because these changes were, according to DC editorship, a move toward feminism, as Kelli E. Stanley documented: "The professed idea behind the transformation was to make the character more 'human,' and therefore more 'inspirational,' in keeping with the changing times; however, cover after cover reinforced not only her dramatically decreased physical strength and sense of helplessness, but even a 1950s' style concentration on romantic plot entanglements."[18] As Diana Prince, Wonder Woman would be more like everyday modern women. She owned a boutique, dressed in fashionable mod-style clothes, and pursued an active dating life. These elements do not constitute a sexist narrative on their own, but other elements in the comics demonstrate a complete lack of understanding of the contemporary feminist movement. Wonder Woman was unique because she had a whole network of supportive women; the Amazons of Paradise Island were her sisters, friends, teachers, and fellow soldiers. Prince, however, became the martial arts student of a male, Chinese teacher. With her Amazon strength depleted, she seemed to have forgotten her training on Paradise Island with her female instructors and needed to learn a new way of fighting from a male teacher. Instead of focusing on female friendships, Prince had few female connections and focused mostly on male attention. Lillian Robinson notes that "Significantly, the covers from this period show her battling more female foes than ever."[19] The Diana Prince era eliminated and destroyed the focus on female empowerment by placing Wonder Woman in male-controlled isolation. Instead of focusing on women's radical power, the stories now focused on proving that Diana was as good as any man. Instead of working with women to fight abusive and destructive men, and showing women how to make men submit to good and loving women, Wonder Woman was now competing with men. Infused with sexist stereotypes of what women really wanted—fashionable clothes, plenty of men to date, and not having to compete with other women for men's attention—the Diana Prince era, through the patriarchal destruction of female ties, eliminated Prince's feminine power.

In the early 1970s, Gloria Steinem began to lobby DC Comics to reinstate Diana Prince as Wonder Woman and, in 1972, even featured Wonder Woman in her traditional costume on the cover of *Ms.* magazine.[20] In 1973, Wonder Woman was reinstated, with costume, lasso, and kinky boots intact. The Bronze Age (1970s–1980s), with its cultural context of the feminist movement and its backlash, the antidraft movement in response to the Vietnam War, and its debate about female soldiers in combat, saw the emergence of several female superheroes whose powers were rooted in the physical.[21] For instance, Power Girl first appeared in *All Star Comics #58* in 1976, and She-Hulk first appeared in *Savage She-Hulk #1* in 1980. Wonder Woman returned in her costume and resumed her original role as a female warrior in the fight against the forces of evil, at a time when the cultural construct of the female soldier as a noncombatant was called into question. In 1971, *Rowland v. Tarr* challenged the draft, partially based on its gender discrimination against women. In 1979, the enlistment qualifications became the same for men and women, but women were barred from active combat zones, although this rule was not legalized until 1994. In 2005, this legislation was reversed, and the ban on women in combat was lifted. Women's place in combat, in the military, and in society has been an ongoing debate for decades.

Several key issues inform this debate, including the traditional view of women as mothers and homemakers in need of male protection as well as the cult of the body, which posits that women are physically unsuitable for combat. Helena Carreiras and Gerhard Kümmel challenge the cult of the body in their work, *Women in the Military and in Armed Conflict*: "The military traditionalists primarily stress what they see as the perennial and genuine physical and psychological qualities of men such as aggressiveness, physical strength, action orientation, boldness, stamina, willingness to endure exposure to extreme physical danger and readiness to taking lives and withstand the bloody requirements of war. These are mirrored in adherence to the myth of the genuinely peace-loving, passive, gentle and squeamish woman which denies these attributes to women and the female body and psyche."[22] The cult of the body, intersecting with patriarchal gender roles, perpetuates the argument that male and female bodies have different capabilities. Men can be muscled and physically powerful, but women are incapable of achieving such muscularity.[23] Men can be aggressive, but women, who give birth and rear offspring, are soft and persuasive. The female body is burdened by the uterus, menstruation, and pregnancy and does not have the necessary stamina for combat training. However, as Carreiras and Kümmel discuss, there are far larger differences between individual members of the same sex than there are categorical differences in fitness or strength between the sexes. Given similar amounts of training, men and women can attain similar levels of fitness. Female superheroes, despite their power and ability, have often supported the cult of the body through their "strike a pose and point" powers that keep them from the battlefield and their lack of muscularity, as documented by Mike Madrid.[24] Banning women from combat allows comics to present the female body as pristine and soft, perpetuating the cult of the body.

Despite her status as a physical combatant, Wonder Woman has often perpetuated this cult of the body in her comics. In the 1940s, Wonder Woman was never shown sweating, bleeding, or injured when fighting enemies, which fit into the image of women in the war industry as removed from combat, preserving their femininity. As a female soldier, she was a noncombatant and never fought as an American soldier at the front. Although Wonder Woman was physically very powerful, her unique Amazonian physique prevented her from bulking up. In the 1950s and 1960s, Wonder Woman remained slim and dainty, and the loss of her costume framed her as a civilian instead of a combatant. In the 1970s, when the debate on female soldiers gained media attention and second wave feminism made inroads on social attitudes, Wonder Woman returned in full battle regalia.

By the Dark Age (1980s–1990s), in 1987, the *Wonder Woman* comics were rebooted again by Greg Potter, Janice Race, and George Perez, who is often credited with the success of this run. Wonder Woman returned to her roots, closely tied to the Greek gods and Greek mythology and focused on Diana's own potential godhood as well as her physicality. Throughout many of these comics, Joan Ormrod notes, Diana marvels at her own strength, taking delight in her bodily powers.[25] The Wonder Woman of this era was more physically powerful, with more pronounced musculature.[26] Other female superheroes, such as She-Hulk, also increasingly had physiques following the bodybuilding tradition. The popularity of bodybuilding in the 1980s had a massive impact on the looks and designs of male action heroes and superheroes. Female action heroes and superheroes, while they did not bulk up in the same degree as their male colleagues, also gained noticeable muscle mass. Yvonne Tasker writes that "The soft curves presented as defining the ideal female form in the 1950s, has shifted to an emphasis on muscle tone in images of the 1980s and early 1990s."[27] Bodybuilding constructed a narrative of building a better body. The original 1940s *Wonder Woman* comic books had also focused on building strength, with (moderate) muscle tone taken as a sign of good health. This narrative returned in the 1987 *Wonder Woman* run, and muscular female action heroes became increasingly present in popular culture, as evidenced by the popularity of heroes such as Ripley in *Alien* (1979) and *Aliens* (1986) as well as Sarah Connor in *Terminator 2* (1991). The trend of drawing Wonder Woman as a more muscled superhero continued throughout the following two decades, as evidenced by figure 2.1.

This striking image of a muscled Wonder Woman from 2010 follows the tradition of the more muscular female heroes established in the 1980s and 1990s.[28] Wonder Woman is facing the reader, with an angry, determined expression, and her legs stand firmly apart. With her arms side by side, but lifted in action, and her fists clenched, she adopts a very active pose traditionally associated with male superheroes. Her abdominal muscles are defined with as much lavish detail as her male colleagues enjoy. Her shoulders are wide, and the tendons and muscles in her arms and legs are clearly visible. These are all depictions of power, typically associated with masculinity. Yet, she carries markers of femininity. Her long hair is loose and unbound. She is clearly wearing makeup and has large breasts. This depiction incorporates both feminine and masculine cultural signifiers to present a more complex and empowered image.[29] It is true, according to Jeffrey A. Brown, that

Figure 2.1. Simone's Wonder Woman. *Source*: Gail Simone et al., *Wonder Woman: Contagion* (TPB) (New York: DC Comics, 2010). © 2010 DC Comics.

tough, muscular female superheroes "run the risk of re-inscribing strict gender binaries and of being nothing more than sexist window-dressing for the predominantly male audience" because they can be read as "simply enacting masculinity rather than providing legitimate examples of female heroism."[30] When female superheroes enact masculinity and are read as empowered through that masculinity alone, the female superhero inadvertently dismisses and eliminates the feminine. This reading itself can be problematic. Are female superheroes read as tough and empowered because they enact masculinity? Or is the female superhero read as masculine because she is tough and empowered? Often, power is read as masculine because masculinity is predicated on the ability to overpower weakness, which is coded as femininity. The link among power, strength, and masculinity is an established part of masculine discourse, and it prohibits feminine discourse from being read as powerful because of the systematic denigration of femininity and nonmasculinity in the American cultural landscape. It demonstrates "our inability to imagine femininity as anything but a condition of vulnerability," as Carol A. Stabile writes.[31] Reading a tough, empowered female superhero as a woman merely inhabiting a male space can be a form of sexism. Considering the research done by Carreiras and Kümmel, automatically reading the possession of muscularity as masculine can be a form of sexism. Instead, the elements in this image that add to Wonder Woman's embodiment of power, while they can be and certainly are often read as signifiers of masculinity, also function as part of Wonder Woman's female warrior identity. In this iteration, Wonder Woman reconfigures the social mold of womanhood and challenges the culturally accepted gender binary by incorporating both feminine and masculine gender markers, which implicitly challenges existing relations among femininity, masculinity, and power. Figure 2.1 is a prime example of how Wonder Woman can function as a symbol of female empowerment through her status as a physical combatant.

While Wonder Woman has enjoyed an increase in muscularity and can present a very powerful image, this reading can be rendered harmless and nonthreatening through her costume. One facet that is immediately noticeable about Wonder Woman's costume is that it is basically a bathing suit. The practicality of such a costume, except as a tool to draw the male gaze, is questionable. Certainly, there is no way for her to prevent any nipple slippage during battle or any friction while flying at super speed, when, according to the laws of aerodynamics, the air should slip between her breasts and pull at the fabric.[32] It also provides the enemy combatant with an easy hold to pull Wonder Woman closer and leaves vulnerable parts of her body exposed. Wonder Woman, with her training in military combat, would, logically, choose heavy armor to wear in combat, especially in light of the plate armor stereotypically associated with ancient Greek culture, which is associated with the Amazon. It would be more practical to cover at least the most fragile parts of the body, even if the (heavy) protection of plate armor is discarded in favor of speed and maneuverability. While this kind of criticism may seem harsh for a fantasy genre, superhero comics consistently attempt to design realistic and supposedly functional armor for male superheroes. For example, Batman's utility belt helps him carry gadgets into battle, or the padding used in the Batman costumes for most of the Batman films protects him because he does not have any superpowers. Superman's current costume is explicitly labeled as a battle uniform and has an armored look, because Kryptonians would have needed protective gear in combat on their home planet.

Criticism aimed at Wonder Woman's bathing suit among fans has been consistent. Female fans tend to point out that the bathing suit helps objectify Wonder Woman and exposes her in ways that male superhero costumes do not expose male bodies.[33] A common counterargument is that a revealing costume is sexually empowering and that if a woman chooses to dress in such clothing, she has a right to do so. It is important to remember that the empowerment argument is always flawed in regard to fictional characters, because even though the narrative provides the illusion that female characters have agency, they remain under the control of the author. It is never Wonder Woman choosing to dress in the bathing suit, but always the artist choosing to portray her in the bathing suit. Additionally, there is something suspect about a society where women are surrounded by images of naked women and encouraged to dress provocatively to please men while claiming that they feel empowered by being (almost) naked. However, the argument is not entirely without merit. While it dismisses objections against Wonder Woman's costume as old-fashioned concerns with propriety and as sexist and oppressive to women, it does combat criticism based in the slut-shaming of female superheroes for wearing revealing clothing. Yet, the general argument against tropes for female superheroes' revealing costumes concerns the double standard for men and women, specifically how ubiquitous such revealing costumes are in regard to female characters. The artist of figure 2.1 has managed to evade the objectification of female characters through revealing costumes by giving Wonder Woman a powerful physique and stance. But superheroes are often drawn by different artists who produce completely different images of the same superhero, such as figure 2.2.

This image is a variant cover for *Wonder Woman #36* (2011), published only a year after the 2010 image, when Gail Simone handed over creative control to Meredith and David Finch.[34] In this image, Wonder Woman looks much younger, reduced to an uncertain-looking girl despite being Wonder *Woman*. She is posed in a way that simultaneously highlights her buttocks and breasts. While not a concrete example of the Brokeback Pose, it is very reminiscent of the trope. She does not seem to possess any kind of muscle mass. Despite Wonder Woman's being streaked with blood and holding a sword and shield, the image does not really convey the aftermath of an arduous battle. The bloodstains are minimal and are placed to draw attention to the slim stretch of her arm and the wide curve of her thigh, which tapers off into an unlikely small knee and, by implication, thin calves. Her breasts are central to the image, framed by the shield and the sword. The curve of her ass is framed by the lasso. Her waist and ribcage are strikingly thin, as evidenced by the concave lines underneath her breasts, emphasized by her pose and the painful arch of her spine. Her facial expression is unsure, vulnerable, and her mouth is drawn in a luscious pout. The sexualization of her body leaves her open to both objectification and ridicule, undermining her power and authority as a superhero. She does not look threatening or powerful. To the presupposed male reader, she is harmless, providing him with the pleasure of watching her in voyeuristic close-up panels.

The pleasure experienced by the assumed male reader is scopophilia, which Norman K. Denzin defines as experiencing pleasure in taking "other people as objects of a controlling and curious gaze."[35] As Denzin discusses, this controlling

Figure 2.2. Finch's Wonder Woman. *Source*: Meredith Finch et al., *Wonder Woman #36* (New York: DC Comics, 2011). © 2011 DC Comics.

gaze in mass media is masculine, exercising control and objectifying female characters. Denzin goes on to say that "every gaze is regulated, structured by underlying systems of power and gender."[36] The gaze is constructed by the viewer and their place in society: where social categories (such as race, sex, sexuality, class) intersect. For instance, in *Practices of Looking*, Marita Sturken and Lisa Cartwright argue that when men are depicted and subjected to the gaze of the audience, they are also empowered with "particular codes of resisting the power of the gaze upon them."[37] Men depicted in action or with powerful physiques "negates attempts to objectify them because they are shown as powerfully within

Figure 2.3. Wonder Woman in full armor. *Source*: Meredith Finch et al., *Wonder Woman #41* (New York: DC Comics, 2015). © 2015 DC Comics.

the frame."[38] As in the 2010 image of Wonder Woman, this also works for women. It is the pose of the 2011 version—the uncertainty and vulnerability, Wonder Woman's youth, and the emphasis on the exposed parts of her body—that makes her vulnerable to the gaze. As a female physical combatant, this image of Wonder Woman fits into the cultural impulse that ensures "Women in media [are] frequently portrayed as in need of rescue, as sexual objects, or a seductress."[39] To disarm Wonder Woman's physical capabilities and strength, she is framed as a sexual object reduced to her breasts and her ass. Yet, even the very same artist can produce different images. Consider the cover of *Wonder Woman #41* (2015), also drawn by David Finch, as shown in figure 2.3. While this image does have thigh-high boots fetishized in porn and her concave ribs are still in evidence, she is also heavily armored and has an active, powerful stance. The image of the powerful female combatant is arresting and transgressive, because it uses codes traditionally used by male characters to resist the gaze. Thus, she can symbolize rebellion and freedom, utilizing the potential of the powerful female body to the fullest.[40]

Wonder Woman's body can signify a multitude of things. It can indicate independence, strength, and power, and it can be objectified and sexualized. Figure 2.2 leaves Wonder Woman sexualized. She becomes an object on display instead of a subject in action and perpetuates the idea that female superheroes, and women everywhere, are nothing but window dressing. Yet, the other two images challenge that. These three images being produced so close together in time, in 2010, 2011, and 2015, respectively, indicates how the dominant hegemonic narrative increasingly exists in conflict with narratives that challenge the status quo. These narratives exist separately, in different comics and individual issues, but as they exist within the same title, which is expected to maintain some level of continuity, produce an ongoing struggle to consolidate two conflicting narratives of female gender roles. On the one hand, feminist movements and activists have encouraged artists and authors to move away from stereotypical images of women as helpless victims and to think of ways in which warrior womanhood can exist in the world. On the other hand, the increasingly powerful conservative forces present in the American cultural landscape since the events of 9/11 have made traditional gender roles once again appealing, because they are familiar and safe in a changing, dangerous world. These discussions also reveal the ways in which sexism and conservative gender roles evolve to incorporate and appropriate feminist dialogue, or at least to pander to it on the surface while perpetuating toxic messages concerning femininity, vulnerability, and the objectification of women's sexuality.

Barbie Dolls and Porn Stars: Supergirl and the Plasticization of the Female Body

In the late 1940s and early 1950s, America was transforming into a new consumer society, which promoted the idea of the teenager as a good consumer to combat a perceived rise in juvenile crime. Michael Barson and Steven Heller document how "a kinder, gentler, *nicer* sort of American teenager—who we will dub the KleenTeen—was being imagined, refined and promoted by the popular arts."[41] This new teenager served as the direct opposite of the juvenile delinquent dominating the cultural landscape in the late 1940s and early 1950s. The juvenile delinquent, as a cultural construct, reflected rising fears about America's moral fiber and whether future American citizens would be able to safeguard the American way of life.[42] The charges aimed at young girls, specifically, were mostly about sex and prostitution, revealing a preoccupation with women's chastity and procreative abilities. Women were expected to function as a moral compass, and their "corruption" seemed especially sinister and demoralizing. If young girls, as the media reported, did not value their virtue, spread venereal disease, and had increasing numbers of illegitimate children, how could they raise virtuous citizens or construct the ideal American nuclear family in order to withstand the threat of communism and the breakdown of civilization? Early 1950s mass media promoted the KleenTeen as a virtuous alternative that young children could look up to and emulate.

The KleenTeen functioned as a new consumer, and advertisements increasingly targeted teenagers instead of their parents. Most of the advertisements aimed at female KleenTeens concerned the growing commercialization of romance. The teenager became a dedicated romantic for whom dating was an important financial endeavor and part of his or her civic duty.[43] Girl KleenTeens had to financially invest in femininity by buying products like cosmetics and fashionable clothes. In return, the boy KleenTeen would spend money on the date, equating her monetary value with his own status display. During the date, he would press for romantic or sexual contact and she would establish the boundaries of that contact, guarding her chastity. This financial exchange bolstered heteropatriarchal norms surrounding men and women's sexual behavior and supported the assumed inevitable construction of the nuclear family. For girls, it was a demonstration of maintaining beauty with a budget, which American culture considered to be her moral obligation to her country, community, and the men in her life. The quintessential KleenTeen magazine, *Seventeen*, "as it ventured further and further into the post-war era, increasingly promoted male approval and marriage, cornerstones of traditional models of gender relations."[44] Fashion, virtue, and femininity were qualities young women had to cultivate to gain male approval and to resist any possible communist influences penetrating American society.

In this context, Supergirl first appeared in the Superman-focused *Action Comics #252* in 1959. *Action Comics* served as a monthly comic book where writers experimented with new characters and plotlines outside of the "official" story lines, which would eventually be identified as canonical. By introducing Supergirl in *Action Comics*, it would be easy to drop her if she failed to satisfy readers. The introduction of a superpowered girl in the comic was the last attempt in a long line of new strategies to cash in on the steady popularity of Superman-inspired comics. After World War II, Western, horror, and jungle comics had become extremely popular, but sales waned after the introduction of the CCA in 1954 and superheroes became popular again. With declining sales in other genres, precipitating a need for renewed profits, DC attempted to expand the Superman universe by adding related titles. This meant new stories focusing on Kryptonian culture, Superman's adventures as a young boy (Superboy), and his pets (Krypto the Superdog and a superpowered monkey). The expansion of the Superman universe created a family centered around Superman, which fit into the Cold War popular media's focus on the family. Adding a female character, especially a harmless "little sister" archetype, would further cement the expanding Superman cast as a family unit resisting threatening outside forces. *Action Comics* had several story lines focusing on a Supergirl. For example, in one story Lois Lane briefly became Supergirl, and in another, Supergirl was created through magic. The character who would eventually take on the Supergirl title in a more permanent capacity was Kara Zor-El, also known as Linda Lee Danvers. Introduced as a new family member, Supergirl had kid-sister appeal that rendered her safe. As Aldo J. Regalado writes, "The fact that she was a junior member of the growing super family allowed her to escape the criticisms levied against Wonder Woman, Sheena and other powerful female characters who operated as loners in the world of men. Supergirl's deference to her older, more experienced male cousin helped contain any threat posed by her displays of powerful femininity."[45] By crafting a female character who was powerful but also deferential, sweet, and subordinate, like a KleenTeen, Supergirl could fly under the CCA's radar.

The addition of a female character had to be handled carefully, as the CCA heavily policed female characters, far more so than male characters. The 1954 version of the code had a "Costume" section, which stated, "Females shall be drawn realistically without exaggeration of any physical qualities."[46] While the same section also stated that, in general, "Nudity in any form is prohibited, as is indecent or undue exposure," there were no rules specifically aimed at containing male bodies.[47] At no point did the code include a rule that male bodies should not be exaggerated, allowing the rise of extremely exaggerated musculature and unrealistic portrayals of male bodies. The first administrator, Judge Charles F. Murphy, took his position very seriously, and a large number of the changes the code wrought in its first few months concerned the drawing of female characters. In 1954, "Murphy told reporters that more than a quarter of the changes involved 'reducing feminine curves to more natural dimensions' and having clothing cover a 'respectable amount of the female body.'"[48] Considering how strictly Judge Murphy interpreted the code and the time-consuming nature of the approval process, which could become extremely costly, Supergirl's creators had to make sure she fit the standards of the CCA. Therefore, she had to fit into the wholesome KleenTeen model. The KleenTeen would never take her clothes off in front of boys or participate in indecent or morally suspicious behavior. Like many superheroes in the code-created Silver Age, Supergirl had imaginary, impossible, and wholesome adventures with no lasting impact on the narrative. Tailored for a supposed female audience, those adventures were filled with romance even while Supergirl remained chaste. She was pretty, conventionally feminine, and subservient to the (male) authority figures in her life. To the guardians of teenage culture and the CCA, she seemed harmless. However, her debut on the cover of *Action Comics* #252 creates some sense of ambiguity about her place in the Superman mythos.[49]

To reinforce the idea that Supergirl is just like Superman and is part of his family, she essentially functions as his female counterpart. The chevron on her chest indicates her connection to him and marks her as affiliated with his franchise. On her introductory cover, she is even mimicking his typical flying pose.

Underneath the title, Supergirl is centered on the page and ascending from a crashed rocket, while Superman descends from the left. Judging from the angle of the rocket and the direction of the smoke, Supergirl has just hurled onto the scene from the right, directly opposite Superman. He is angled away from her and is pushed to the side with his left elbow off-page, as if she has forced him out. Supergirl's arrival negates Superman's status as the solitary survivor of Krypton. The phrase "and I have all your powers" could be interpreted as "I have taken your powers from you" rather than "I have the same powers as you." The question "Is She Friend or Foe?" printed on the cover frames her arrival as a possible challenge to the existing order, implying that her very existence has shifted the balance of power away from Superman.[50] However, Superman claims that she must be an illusion and that she could not really have the same powers as him, making the reader doubt the accuracy of her claims. The hierarchical structure is also reaffirmed by her name: Supergirl. Superman is a man—a powerful, autonomous adult. Supergirl, however, is a *girl*, which relegates her to the position of the infant.

Supergirl is consistently coded as a child. While she is meant to have Superman's strength, she does not have the physicality to match and is portrayed as slimmer and shorter. Not only does this play into gender stereotypes about women's bodies being smaller and weaker than men's, but it also frames her as a young girl-child. Her cape is much shorter than his, and younger superheroes typically have shorter capes or no capes at all. Her flowing knee-high skirt, with bare legs underneath, further codes her as a child. Short skirts were, traditionally, worn only by children. But with the rise of the teenager as a consumer, many fashion companies created teen clothing lines specifically geared toward girls younger than college-age women, who wore longer, more respectable skirts. According to Thomas Hine, this specific kind of "clothing indicated young people's acceptance, and even celebration, of less-than-adult status in society."[51] At an age where only a few decades earlier they would have been expected to contribute to the household and take on adult responsibilities, teenagers had become in-between creatures and their clothing reflected that. The KleenTeen especially was considered more innocent, wholesome, and naive. Consequently, Supergirl's slightly parted legs also seem innocent and girlish as she appears completely unconcerned with suggestions of impropriety or sexual innuendo. She maintained this attitude throughout the 1950s and 1960s. For at least two decades, Supergirl seemed content to float around in the whimsically romantic story lines of the KleenTeen. By 1972, a decade after the first stirrings of second wave feminism, Supergirl finally attempted to grow up. Now in her early twenties, she moved to San Francisco to lead a more independent life away from Superman and her adoptive parents' influence. However, the various story lines imply that there was some uncertainty about the direction her character should take. Constantly changing careers, boyfriends, and superhero costumes, Supergirl never seems to alight on a fixed, solid, and mature identity. Supergirl donned a new costume for almost every issue, and fans were encouraged to send in their own costume designs, hinting at a greater concern for her looks than her superpowers or feats of heroism.[52]

Compared with the stability of Superman's long-standing and successful career as a newspaper journalist, his love interest Lois Lane, and his iconic costume, Supergirl's instability is telling in that the comics failed to consolidate the new and changing gender roles arising in the wake of second wave feminism into a strong and confident female superhero. With the greater sexual freedom for women, Supergirl gained a variety of boyfriends, although this was, in essence, perhaps not very different from her 1950s romantic adventures. Supergirl attended college and had entry-level jobs in various industries, indicating an awareness of the increasing educational and professional opportunities for women. However, the comic was also filled with negative stereotypes. Her numerous boyfriends and jobs indicated a flaky nature, and she was more concerned with the look of her costume than her duties as a superhero during the entirety of the Bronze Age (1970s–1980s). Eventually, in the crossover event called *Crisis on Infinite Earths* (1985–1986), Supergirl sacrifices herself in an attempt to save the multiverse. Unfortunately, all the alternate universes melt into one main universe, which the heroes manage to save, but nobody remembers Supergirl or her sacrifice. Arguably, this version of Supergirl fits the fridge-ing stereotype where women are killed only to further the plot, rendering their deaths meaningless. She is killed to resolve the universe reshuffle, but remains unremembered and has no lasting impact on other characters' emotional lives.

Crisis on Infinite Earths was a reboot of the DC universe designed to streamline different continuities and make it easier for new audiences to start reading comics. Supergirl did not become part of this new continuity and remained out of print during most of the Dark Age (1980s–1990s), although she had a (failed) film in 1984 and appeared in *Superman: The Animated Series* (1996–2000). In 2004, during the Modern Age (1990s–ongoing), Supergirl returned as Superman's older niece, who was younger than him because she was trapped in suspended animation for two or three decades. This Supergirl physically resembled her original 1950s look, although she now had a bare midriff. A second series based on this story line was launched in 2005, and the New 52 reboot (2011) established a *Supergirl* series with its first issue published in 2011. This new series maintained elements from the 2004 run, such as the fact that Supergirl was a teenager on Krypton when Superman was a baby, but, because of suspended animation, she is still a teenager when she lands on Earth. This reversal of the age dynamic only reinforces the idea that Supergirl will never grow up, because even her baby cousin became an adult before she did. Aside from her connection to her male cousin and their shared heritage, her eternal physical attractiveness and youth are the only aspects that remain unchanged. She remains the little blonde Barbie doll who never really grows up. Mike Madrid writes that Supergirl "is not a woman, and therein is the secret of her appeal. Supergirl isn't a threatening Superwoman, who might develop ideas of her own. She is the sweet kid sister."[53] No matter how much time passes, Supergirl remains a young superpowered *girl*. Cartoons and comics typically freeze time or exist in a nonspecific "neverwhen," which lacks historical awareness and is simultaneously occurring right now, at the time of reading, and in whatever chronological order the events unfold in the comic universe, as discussed by Orion Ussner Kidder.[54] This means that superheroes often age very slowly or not at all, and yet long-established sidekicks do grow up. The most famous of these is Nightwing, who fought crime as Robin, Batman's sidekick, during his childhood. Supergirl, however, never really goes on to establish an adult identity separate from her adult male counterpart.

Supergirl never grows up and, in fact, cannot grow up, as her youth is a vital part of her identity as a female superhero. According to Hine, "The concept of the teenager rests in turn on the idea of the adolescent as a not quite competent person, beset by stress and hormones."[55] Supergirl, as a female teenager, is often portrayed as silly, incompetent, and volatile. This made Superman's parental relationship with her inevitable because she could not be expected to control herself and her powers. It demonstrates Hine's point that cultural notions about teenagers "emerged as useful ways of explaining and controlling youthful behaviour."[56] Because Supergirl is a silly teenager, she needs the adult Superman to parent her, not only to make sure she does not accidentally hurt herself or others but also to make sure she does not rebel. Being a teenager is considered an inevitable period of transition, marked by "surliness, self-absorption [and] rebelliousness."[57] In American media, teenagers signify the fear that the young will strike out against the established order and displace the adults as the authority, which they will inevitably do when they grow up. Therefore, framing youth as a lack of maturity and decision-making capabilities provides a legitimate reason for the social and legal control of teenagers by adults. Supergirl, who ages but never grows up, is a perpetual teenager and thus stuck in the cyclical nature of rebellion and control inherent in young characters, full of youth's potential and anxieties. Her age implies that she is good and obedient, for now.[58] Supergirl's youth provides a reasonable rationale for other characters to assume parental control over her even while her youth is used to signify her femininity. Youth is culturally connected to femininity as both are "conceived as passive, immature and vulnerable," while adulthood is a male space associated with rationality, control, and stability.[59] Like femininity, youth is a state of constant change that needs to be controlled. Unlike the culturally accepted tom*boy*ish girl, an adult woman transgresses gender roles by inhabiting a male space. Adult women are often erased from public spaces because they lack the young and fit body associated with femininity.

In consumer culture, women are encouraged to use antiaging creams and to undergo cosmetic surgery as a way to stay young and attain an ideal of beauty conflated with specific notions of femininity epitomized by the Barbie doll. In *Barbie Culture*, Mary F. Rogers theorizes that "Barbie is a body centered selfhood, increasingly shaped by technologies extending way beyond the plastic surgeon's office. She represents the plastic selfhood celebrated in mass advertising."[60] Barbie represents the selfhood that is dependent on the construction of the body as malleable, an unruly biology that needs to be controlled by technological advancement, which is coded as a masculine force controlling feminine nature. The image of Barbie re-creates the biological body as plastic and does away with its imperfections and excesses. Helen M. Malson writes that the body's excess is most obviously identified in menstruation and body fat, which "comes to stand for all that is negative about the body" because "body fat is also culturally and physiologically related to the reproductive female body."[61] While women in general are often made to embody excess, the large woman in particular is seen as wanting and being too much. Above all, she is too sexual and represents the fear of being consumed or drained of masculine virility. Women's procreative power is framed as something that saps men's virility and is a form of feminine excess, as Jane M. Ussher discusses in *Managing the Monstrous Feminine*: "The apparently uncontained fecund body, with its creases and curves, secretions and seepages, as well as its changing boundaries at times of pregnancy and menopause, signifies association with the animal world, which reminds us of our mortality and fragility, and stands as the antithesis of the clean, contained, proper body."[62] The female body, with its capacity for change and excretions, has come to signify debilitating decay and excess. The uncontrolled female body signifies contamination. The pregnant form "is infused with sexuality—swollen belly and breasts sign of her fecundity and embodied being," and threatens to bring forth something outside of male influence.[63] As Sandra M. Gilbert and Susan Gubar discuss, a man "cannot verify his fatherhood by either sense or reason, after all; that his child is *his* is in a sense a tale he tells himself to explain the infant's existence."[64] Considering Karen Horney's concept of womb envy as male jealousy of women's procreative power and the cause of motherhood's increased denigration, the female body's symbolization of excess explains the need for elimination of the female in procreative and body-enhancing technology. The (Barbie) doll, in its plasticity, is a representation of the need for women to control their bodies via masculine technology or for men to control female bodies. The doll is seen as a body controlled and shaped by technology. It is made plastic: firm, beautiful, and perpetually young. The inability to sustain such a body is considered a loss of femininity, a gender transgression. Early KleenTeen culture already hinted at the current obsession with body maintenance as it stressed grooming the body to attain the romantic ideal. The evolution of American culture into consumer culture further encouraged the perception that spending money will guarantee a beautiful, plastic body. Supergirl is like Barbie, the physically impossible girl; and like Barbie, Supergirl is a doll for play, sex, and decoration. Rogers points out that Barbie "plies her influence on a cultural terrain where people . . . inhabiting contemporary post-industrial societies—know that to be female is to be seen significantly as a decorative object, an aesthetic contribution, or a sexy presence."[65] Barbie might be an astronaut or a doctor, but she is known for her beauty and accessories.

The Barbie doll—or any female doll that wears makeup and caters to traditional modes of femininity, such as Bratz or Disney's princess collection—is increasingly younger, and there is something pedophiliac in the way contemporary American culture has conflated hairlessness as a signification of childhood with a desirable sexual trait, which contributes to the ongoing sexualization of women and girls at increasingly younger ages. Children are hairless and require adult supervision, and so do women. In many ways, they are considered incapable of making their own choices. This reappears in the image of the doll, which is also hairless and can be moved and played with at the owner's convenience. The doll becomes the porn star in the increasing pornification of Western culture, which normalizes hairless women to the extent that women in commercials for razors are shaving their already hairless legs. The presence of body hair implies a lack of proper maintenance and femininity. As Mike Featherstone notes, "The tendency within consumer culture is for ascribed bodily qualities to become regarded as plastic—with effort and 'body work' individuals are persuaded that they can achieve a certain desired appearance," as long as they spend the money required.[66] Any lack of maintenance "becomes interpreted as signs of moral latitude."[67] Everyone must maintain their body and make it plastic, permanently young, tight, and beautiful. This plasticity must be maintained in the same way that a car or computer or any advanced technological item requires maintenance, which safeguards the consumption of cosmetics, cosmetic surgery, dieting, and exercise. For example, Barbie has multiple successful careers but is still most famous for being beautiful, young, and fashionable. It is not the accoutrements of her professions or her success that has made her famous, because Barbie is equally recognizable, or more so, when she is naked. It is her plastic body that signifies her identity. The porn star is the persona hidden behind the plastic facade of the doll. Supergirl is both the doll and the porn star because they have become extensions of each other. Over the years, Supergirl has remained identifiable through her youthful looks and the big *S* on her chest, but like Barbie, she has had numerous different costumes, careers, and identities.

The new *Supergirl* comics published in 2011 is the first new run that stabilizes the character. Although the 2004 version also had a costume that remains mostly the same in every issue, unlike her previous Bronze Age counterpart, she once again lacked a stable identity. She jumped from living in the twenty-first century to the thirty-first and back, briefly assumed the identity of Flamebird (a superhero from Kryptonian mythology), and eventually returned to Kryptonian society with the founding of New Krypton. The 2011 version offers a more stable identity and a new permanent costume. Similar to Superman's costume update, hers is a blue bodysuit with thin black lines to suggest the edges of interlocking panels and give a more armored, military look. Her red cape is lined with gold and is tied around her neck, while her boots have been updated with a wedge heel to create the illusion of practicality. Now that Supergirl has evolved from a childish KleenTeen to a modern teenager, she has been given a staple of the accoutrements of femininity: a pair of high heels. However, wedge heels are not "proper" high heels and are increasingly common in the footwear of preteens. The boots come up to her kneecaps but do not cover them, although the knee is one of the most fragile areas of the leg. The pointed ends of the boots point toward her crotch. The boots' edge comes up high enough to qualify the boots as the type fetishized in pornography, but the wedge heel disarms the pornographic connotations and reconfigures Supergirl's position as a girl. Once again, Supergirl straddles the divide between sexually available and sexless child.

Being both explicitly underage and sexualized, the modern Supergirl contributes to the sexualization of young girls in contemporary American media. In *Supergirl, Volume 2: Girl in the World*, a flashback shows the audience how Kara received her costume from her father and wears it for the first time. The graphic novel includes a story line about Supergirl's preparations for the final trials, an exam that grants adult status to any Kryptonian that passes it. The costume should denote that Kara has passed those trials and is seen as both an adult and a representative of her house. At this time, Kara has not yet attempted her trials and is sent away from Krypton before she can do so. In other words, Kara will never be an adult according to her own cultural standards, and her pose in figure 2.4, taken from this story line, reinforces that idea. Her body language is hesitant, and her hands are clenched in the fabric of the cape, scrunching it up and holding it away from her body. She is displaying herself for her father's approval. The pose invites scrutiny. Her thighs are clenched together in uncertainty, her knees touching while her calves twist away from each other with one ankle turned out so her toes are touching. This is a very cliché image of innocence and naïveté, which is oddly flirtatious. The girlishness of the pose is undermined by her naked thighs, which signify sexuality. Instead of the knee-high skirt the KleenTeen and 2004 Supergirl wore, the modern Supergirl wears a bodysuit that closely resembles a bathing suit. The red panels at the front and the back draw attention to her crotch and bottom. The suit's panty lines are so high that some pubic hair should be showing, except that her vulva is seemingly completely bald (or clean shaven), like that of a doll, a porn star, or a child. This panel uses imagery associated with children, where the main female character is sexualized and posed to invite the reader's scrutinizing gaze.[68]

In this iteration, Supergirl is still a *girl* even as she tries to inhabit adult spaces. At first, Supergirl is clearly uncomfortable and uncertain in the clothing of adulthood, complaining that the boots are too tight. The narrative insists that Supergirl is not guaranteed to pass the final trials because she is not studying enough, implying she lacks the responsibility necessary to become an adult. Supergirl approaches, but is ultimately rejected from, adulthood. Her youthful irresponsibility reappears when she refuses to let Superman guide her when she arrives on Earth. She has no memory of how she got there and is completely incapable of assimilating because she does not speak any Earth language. Supergirl has never been more helpless and infantilized, and yet she has never been more independent and rebellious. She continues to wear the dress of Kryptonian adults, a subversive act by Kryptonian standards. She refuses Superman's help, finds housing and friends, and builds the foundations of her own support network outside of Superman's influence. She also works to discover how she arrived on Earth, beginning her own coming-of-age story. This narrative carries the anxieties that American society harbors toward young people, especially young girls: the

Figure 2.4. Modern Supergirl *Source*: Mike Johnson et al., *Supergirl*, vol. 2, *Girl in the World* (TPB) (New York: DC Comics, 2013). © 2013 DC Comics.

potential for destruction, subverting the established order, resisting adult control, challenging male control, and birthing something monstrous.

The modern Supergirl represents changes in American culture concerning young women—the ongoing sexualization of young female bodies and the increased resistance fostered by online communities—and its anxieties about women and immigration. Post-9/11 American society has much in common with Cold War ideology and rhetoric, with a return to conservative gender roles and the persistent fear of America being invaded by sinister outside forces. While 9/11 was a direct hit to corporate America and most victims were men, Susan Faludi writes that the press framed the event in conservative gender terms, using a traditional cultural narrative: "The articles seemed to gravitate toward the argument: 'maleness' was making a comeback because New York City's fire*men* were heroes on 9/11, and they were heroes because they had saved untold numbers of civilians—especially *female* civilians. One would never think from studying the photos the press chose to publish that the survivors (the victims) of the twin towers attack were predominantly male."[69] In light of an attack on American soil, no matter the realities of that attack, protection and security were framed as masculine and femininity as weak and helpless in order to reaffirm traditional American values. This led to "the denigration of capable women, the magnification of manly men, the heightened call for domesticity, the search for and sanctification of girls," and the depiction of women in mass media as helpless.[70] It heralded a return to traditional values in the interest of preserving American society as a whole. Supergirl's helplessness in America mirrors these traditional gender values, further reflected in her tenuous control over her powers and her refusal to accept help when she obviously needs it, suggesting that competent and rebellious women who refuse masculine aid and protection are delusional and a danger to themselves and others. However, her helplessness and stubborn resistance to male supervision further intersect with her status as an immigrant who is either incapable of integrating into American culture or unwilling to do so. In the past, Superman and Supergirl were the embodiment of the American Dream: white immigrants who assimilated completely without any visible effort and who were extremely loyal to their adopted country. Now, Supergirl is both unable and unwilling to assimilate. When she arrives on Earth, she is confused and unaware of her abilities, inadvertently causing extensive property damage and killing or heavily maiming at least two people. As a helpless young woman, she needs to be controlled by a male authority figure. As a foreigner on Earth/American soil, she is a threat. As a blonde-haired, blue-eyed girl, cast in the image of the ideal American girl, Supergirl embodies the fear that the threat to American civilization has infiltrated American society and will eventually arise from within.

The fears surrounding immigration and infiltration are fully revealed in the *H'el on Earth* story line (2012–2013), where Supergirl is persuaded to sacrifice Earth in an attempt to bring Krypton back by a third survivor of Krypton.[71] At the start of this story line, Supergirl is a refugee actively mourning the loss of her homeland. Instead of celebrating her adoptive country and giving it her undivided loyalty, Supergirl is willing to destroy it to bring back her old world. Unable to emotionally connect to Superman because of his distance from Kryptonian culture and his allegiance to America, Supergirl is eager to trust and believe in H'el, a fellow Kryptonian survivor. He presents himself as the only one who can understand her because they are the only two people who remember Krypton, which represents the existence of immigrant communities as dangerous and threatening. The seduction of Supergirl by H'el also raises the ghost of sex and reproduction, the fear that the immigrant community will grow too numerous and out of control. While Supergirl passes as white American, H'el's physical appearance is more monstrous and less human. He represents the dangerous (non-white) immigrant seducing the (white) refugee into betraying and destroying her adopted country. The *H'el on Earth* story line carries traditional fears about immigrant communities rising up and destroying the status quo. Supergirl is an ambiguous figure, both perpetuating and challenging dominant and conservative gender roles that frame women as subservient and decorative. She is young and pretty, conforming to the cult of the doll, but youth itself can be a site of anxiety and rebellion. She is the embodiment of both the cultural fears and the desires that surround young women, who are continually cast as plastic bodies. Supergirl represents the cult of the doll, even while she exhibits rebellion and power. Inside her slim and plastic body, she contains all the elements that American culture fears it cannot control.

The Supergirl of today, with her immigrant identity highlighted and her rebellion against Superman's efforts to control her, is very different from the sweet kid sister who first arrived on Earth in the 1950s. Supergirl's narrative seems to incorporate elements of the classic coming-of-age story as she is continually seeking to discover her own identity, rebelling against the space of teenage-hood she is confined to. While she is infantilized and sexualized through the depictions of her body, the physical power of that body continually undermines those depictions. Supergirl is a superhero in flux: perpetuating and rejecting the formation of the body as a doll. The dominant gender script perpetuated by most mass media is that of women as plastic, controlling their biological, changing, and unpredictable bodies through masculine technology. Biological procreation, with its excesses and swollen bodies signifying fecundity, must be banished through plasticity, maintained through masculine technology, and eventually replaced by masculine procreation. Women who conceive children with technological aids often face a narrative where the (masculine) technology is praised as miraculous and their female biological bodies are shamed as nature's volatile and unreliable failures. Women and young girls are encouraged to transform their bodies, to chase plasticity, but they must do so in secret, to preserve the illusion of femininity as inherently young and beautiful.

Conclusion

Through the social upheaval of World War II and the growing female workforce, the 1940s allowed for a progressive and powerful female superhero, such as Wonder Woman. The 1950s, however, and its cultural push for a return to the home, required a return to more conservative gender roles. This prompted the creation of the KleenTeen Supergirl and turned Wonder Woman, as well as her younger selves, into romance-obsessed girls. The 1960s created confusing story lines, where narratives supposedly influenced by second wave feminism created unstable female superheroes who rejected femininity. The 1970s and 1980s saw the rise of the muscled female superhero, which continued into the 1990s. The 2000s and 2010s, while catering to more progressive ideas about gender, still tap into conservative gender ideas that infantilize and denigrate capable women. It is clear that, throughout the years of publication, both Wonder Woman and Supergirl emerged as complex figures in terms of gender signification.

Female superheroes inevitably challenge the status quo because they complicate the idea that women need to be protected, which is a fundamental rationalization for American culture's "natural" gender roles. Much as the way forces in 1940s American media worked to de-radicalize the female soldier to protect the status of the male soldier, female superheroes are de-radicalized to protect the male superheroes' status. Through the cult of the body, the Barbie doll, and the porn star, female superheroes' power is undermined. Both Wonder Woman and Supergirl are subject to the increasing plasticization of the body in the pornification of American culture, which supports cultural narratives positing the need for masculine technology to control the unruly, excessive female body. Similar to the ways that male superheroes are pushed to control their bodies and substitute weak, soft flesh for hardness, women are pushed to control all their natural "excess" and flabbiness by transforming into a plastic doll. The key difference is that this transformation is a source of power for men, and they are often lauded for the achievement. After all, as discussed in chapter 1, what men do takes determination and skill and is evidence of their ability to conquer feminine nature. For women, this transformation into plasticity is required, and a failure to adhere to bodily standards often results in a social death.

While female superheroes often articulate powerful messages about womanhood and resisting the female-denigrating status, these messages often occur in conservative narratives through exploitative images. However, it is clear that female superheroes, when possessing a muscular body, are often read as mimicking a masculine power and inhabiting a male space. And yet, appearing traditionally feminine with powers that are not centered on the body reduces female superheroes to having "point and pose" powers. No matter what the female superhero does, she "fails" to live up to her male counterparts. To reiterate Carol A. Stabile's point, this only serves as further evidence that both those reading and writing comics fail to imagine the heroic condition as rooted in womanhood or femininity due to American culture's obsession with masculinity as a state of action and femininity as a state of plastic passivity.

CHAPTER 3

Gay Characters and Social Progress

This chapter discusses Billy, Teddy, and Batwoman as some of the first gay and lesbian characters to be published by Marvel and DC. All three were written as gay from the beginning of their series, although Billy and Teddy were initially more "subtle" with no direct references to homosexuality within the *Young Avengers* series. Together, Billy and Teddy enact homonormativity as a route to social acceptance through Teddy's performance of the masculine partner and Billy as the feminized counterpart. The perpetuation of heteronormative gender roles in gay relationships in popular media is often used to legitimize gay characters and provide them with the protection of social acceptability. Yet, even heteronormative gay characters are still Othered when taken out of the domestic setting of their relationship. This is especially true for Batwoman, whose struggles between homonormativity and the Other result in a monstrous transformation and death. The tension between heteronormative characterization and the Othering of gay characters illustrates Suzanna Danuta Walter's point that visibility does not automatically indicate genuine social acceptance or the liberalization of public sentiment as "media saturation of a previously invisible group can perpetuate a new set of pernicious fiction, subduing dissent by touting visibility as the equivalent of knowledge."[1] Visibly queer characters can perpetuate stereotypes or embody traditional fears even while presenting humanizing and heroic portrayals. Furthermore, increased visibility can lead to a sudden spike of resistance, a violent backlash against people who were once ignored but are now in the public eye.

The Rise of Homonormativity: Wiccan and Hulkling

Billy and Teddy are two members of the Young Avengers team, whose titular series first began publication in 2005. Originally, the team had seven members: Wiccan (originally Asgardian, William "Billy" Kaplan), Hulkling (Theodore "Teddy" Altman), Patriot (Elijah "Eli" Bradley), Stature (Cassandra "Cassie" Lang), Hawkeye (Kate Bishop), Iron Lad (Nathaniel Richards), and Speed (Thomas "Tommy" Shepherd).[2] The initial series remained in print until 2007, after which the Young Avengers team appeared in several miniseries that tied into major crossover events such as *Civil War: Young Avengers* (2008), *Young Avengers Presents* (2008), *Secret Invasion: Young Avengers/Runaways* (2008), *Young Avengers Dark Reign* (2009), and *Young Avengers: Siege* (2010). The next series that focused on the characters outside of a crossover event was *Avengers: The Children's Crusade* (2010), followed by a limited run of fifteen issues published in 2013 and 2014, known as *Young Avengers* (volume 2). In *New Avengers* (2015–2017), Billy and Teddy joined the Avengers Idea Mechanics, who disbanded in 2017. They next appeared in *The War of the Realms* (2019).

The Young Avengers' first publication in 2005 occurred in the wake of several legislative changes in the United States regarding the lesbian, gay, bisexual, transgender, queer, intersex, asexual, and other nonstraight identities (LGBTQIA+) community. The first would be *Lawrence-Garner v. Texas* in 2003, which decriminalized sodomy in Texas, setting an important legal precedent for LGBTQIA+ rights.[3] In New York, where *Young Avengers* takes place, "anal sexual conduct" and "oral sexual conduct" were no longer legally classified as "deviant sexual intercourse" and do not result in "sodomy in the third degree charges" as of 2003.[4] In the same year, the Massachusetts Supreme Court upheld same-sex marriage and was the first state to legalize it. These changes in legislature seem out of character considering how, post 9/11, mainstream American society became more conservative, as discussed in chapters 1 and 2. This can be partly explained through the increased perception of the gay community as a white, middle-class community capable of sustaining American heteronormativity by maintaining a public/private split. Lisa Duggan discusses how the concept of the public/private split first gained traction in the 1980s as a result of "antigay forces" redefining "privacy as a kind of confinement, a cordon sanitaire protecting 'public' sensibilities."[5] In other words, it inscribed the private sphere as a separate entity, containing the personal from the public, which was defined as the political. Duggan writes how "conservative forces worked to define the private sphere as an isolated, domestic site completely out of range of any public venue."[6] Instead of a political issue influencing public rights, access to citizenship, and modes of exclusion and discrimination, sexuality became a personal issue that should not have an impact on the public sphere, which is controlled by heteronormativity. It is culturally framed as masculine and heterosexual, which is the invisible "norm" people are required to uphold. The public/private split sustains the public sphere as the political sphere, which should not be impacted by private matters such as sexuality or gender or race, which are private whenever they differ from the public norm: straight, white male. Everything else is someone's "private" business, which means that it is required to remain out of the public eye. Essentially, the public/private split forces gay people into the closet even while it professes to provide a safe space for gay people to exist.

This public/private split became entrenched in the American cultural landscape of the 1990s with the rise of neoliberalism and was institutionalized through legislation, such as *Lawrence*. In 2003, it decriminalized sodomy on the basis of a right to privatized liberty, barring government intrusion into the private affairs of two consenting adults. As Katherine M. Franke points out, "*Lawrence* puts an end to the interpellation of gay male and lesbian couples as criminals based on their private sexual conduct."[7] However, the decriminalization of sodomy "merely signals tolerance of the behaviour, so long as it takes place in private and between two consenting adults in a relationship."[8] In effect, *Lawrence* creates a premise that heteronormalizes homosexual couples and conduct. The private sphere is equated to the domestic sphere of the heterosexual nuclear family, of the couple, and domesticizes homosexuality as it confines homosexuality to the home. *Lawrence* implicitly "renders different legal treatment to those who express their sexuality in domesticated ways and those who don't."[9] It creates a framework where the acceptable homosexual is in a committed relationship, which contains their homosexuality to the private sphere, implicitly creating the unacceptable homosexual who is single and whose sexual conduct is outside the private setting, which should/could still be considered criminal.

While *Lawrence* furthered the decriminalization of homosexuality and created new political avenues for gay rights advocates, it foreclosed political action that resisted heteronormativity or domestinormativity (as used by Franke). It allowed activists to define LGBTQIA+ rights as gaining access to rights defining the domestic experience (marriage, adoption, etc.) and framing those rights as being inherently private matters that the government should not interfere with instead of the public rights and conditions of citizenship that they actually are. Combined with dominant social strata such as whiteness and the middle class, a community emerged that is privileged or legitimized above other gay communities: white, affluent, gay, and heteronormative. The drive to legitimize a specific homosexual identity—not only through *Lawrence* but also through the legislation of gay marriage and gay adoption, which directly connects gay rights to the heteronormative hegemony—occurred after the World Trade Center attack on 9/11. The attack was followed by the rapid vilification of Islam in the Western press and the rise of Islamophobia at a time when the American government needed the middle class to stand united on issues such as the wars in Afghanistan and Iraq. Providing additional civil rights to the gay, white, middle-class community would ensure their support of American hegemony by creating a sense of homosexual nationalism, or as Jasbir K. Puar has dubbed it, homonationalism.[10] The concept of homonationalism describes how homonormative communities can access forms of belonging in the hegemony by punching down on people from Muslim and other non-white communities, similar to other historical racial bribes. This performative belonging was reserved for the white, American, middle-class community, made visible through TV series such as *Queer as Folk* (2000–2005), *Queer Eye for the Straight Guy* (2003–2007), *The L Word* (2004–2009), and, more recently, *Modern Family* (2009–2020). All of these series had a predominantly white, middle-class, and American cast. Black, Asian, rural, working-class, bisexual, transgender, asexual, or other minority LGBTQIA+ communities were absent

Figure 3.1. Billy and Teddy close-up. *Source*: Allan Heinberg et al., *Young Avengers #1* (New York: Marvel Comics, 2005). © 2005 Marvel Comics.

from this wave of gay acceptance in popular culture, and it is in this context that Billy and Teddy's relationship was first published.

While Billy and Teddy were a gay couple from the beginning of the *Young Avengers* series (2005–2007), it is not clear that Billy and Teddy are in a romantic relationship. The first issues only subtly referenced their relationship and caused audiences to speculate in online message boards and fan fiction. This subtext was neither substantial nor overt. In one of their very first close-ups, such as in figure 3.1, a panel taken from *Young Avengers #1* (2005), their interaction can be read as flirting.[11] The phrase "thanks for watching my back" can be interpreted as an innocent thank-you from one teammate to another, or it can be read as an invitation to flirt, especially when paired with the response "it's a pleasure," implying that Billy is literally deriving pleasure from watching Teddy's behind.[12] With the close-up of their faces, which are in proximity, the panel exudes an intimate moment in the middle of a fight. Other clues consist of Billy and Teddy pairing off together when the team disbands and both of them responding in a distressed manner when the other is hurt. *Young Avengers #2* (2005) depicts Teddy with his arm casually draped around Billy's shoulder, but there is no further physical contact.[13]

However, it is only in the sixth issue that there is any explicit reference to Teddy and Billy's relationship. When they are discussing their superhero code names, Hawkeye says that Billy will "need a name that won't become a national *joke* when the press finds out about you and Teddy."[14] At this time, Billy is still going by the name Asgardian, and Hawkeye is referring to the possibility of pronouncing Asgardian as "Ass Guardian"—referencing anal sex in relation to Teddy, conflating anal sex with gay sex. Their relationship is only made vaguely explicit six months after their first appearance without using the words "gay," "relationship," "couple," or "dating," and they only touch platonically. Considering that the

Young Avengers are teenagers, Marvel may have wanted to avoid explicit romantic, and implied sexual, contact between young and possibly underage characters. Gareth Schott also writes that in mainstream comics "sexual intimacy is merely hinted at, occurring off-panel. . . . When this occurs for gay characters, this is more readily understood as a political act, rather than a genre or medium driven shortcoming."[15] Kara Kvaran also points out that the author of the *Young Avengers*, Allan Heinberg, who is gay, had complete control over the characters and that the decision to keep Billy and Teddy's relationship mostly off-page was not an editorial decision but an attempt to keep the story moving forward because, as Heinberg said, "When you're fighting Kang the Conqueror, it's tough to find the time to make out."[16] But this does not explain why Stature and Iron Lad are shown kissing in close-up three times within hours of meeting each other. They even get a tearful goodbye scene when Iron Lad has to return to the past, even though their romantic attachment is hours old at best. While emotional intimacy and the development of long-term relationships, past the "will they/won't they?" stage, often occur off-page, casual physical demonstrations of love or sexual interest between heterosexual partners does happen regularly, and it definitely occurs in the *Young Avengers* comics. The double standard here is clear: homosexual couples do not have time to make out, but romantic contact between heterosexual characters who are virtual strangers is normalized to such an extent it becomes invisible and is omitted from the rationalization barring homosexual contact.

There are numerous other instances in which the *Young Avengers* comics refuse to directly engage with Billy and Teddy's sexuality. For instance, in *Young Avengers #7* (2005), Billy and Teddy attempt to tell Billy's parents that they have assumed superhero identities, which Billy's parents instead interpret as Billy and Teddy coming out, although the word "gay" is never used. Billy's mother says that "we're just so happy you boys *found* each other," and Billy's father says, "Welcome to the family, Ted."[17] This frames Billy and Teddy's coming out as part of a domestic narrative of family even while the lack of explicit language, such as "gay" or "homosexual," ties into the public/private split. They do not publicly acknowledge something that needs to remain private (i.e., silent). It depoliticizes the moment as Billy and Teddy are primarily identified as being in a relationship instead of being gay. Combined with the lack of physical intimacy, such as hugs or hand-holding or kissing, the comic clearly follows the public/private split where sexual/romantic conduct between two consenting homosexuals in a committed relationship is acceptable as long as it cannot be seen. The public/private split is primarily normalized in white, middle-class, urban communities, to which both Billy and Teddy belong as they live in New York and have parents with decidedly middle-class professions. And the white, middle-class, urban gay culture we find in popular media performs heteronormativity through its framing of gay men or lesbian women not only as ordinary, white middle-class American people but also as domestic and monogamous. Billy and Teddy's gay experience is only just visible enough to signal it to the reader, but it remains largely in the private, off-page sphere and maintains the public/private split as set out by Duggan because the audience can ignore most of it if they want.

Their relationship remains framed in this manner until 2010, when it becomes a significant part of the *Avengers: The Children's Crusade* story line. In this series, Billy and Teddy are more physically demonstrative. They are depicted embracing, holding hands, and sharing a bed (while sleeping). At the start of the series, the Avengers attempt to detain the Young Avengers at Avengers Mansion.[18] They are provided with a room, and Billy uses his magical powers to transform the two single beds into one double bed. Giving the boys two beds instead of one to share can be read as the Avengers being responsible adults when housing a young teenage couple, although separate rooms would have been more efficient. However, considering Captain America's previous reference to Billy as Teddy's "friend" instead of "boyfriend," this can be read as the Avengers refusing to acknowledge Billy and Teddy's relationship. Billy's transformation of the two beds into one is an act of defiance that physically manifests their relationship. Combined with their intimate embrace taking up more than half of the page, this image demonstrates that Billy and Teddy are comfortable with physical intimacy. The specter of homosexual sex threatens the public/private barrier and emphasizes Billy and Teddy's homosexual desire. The threat of possible physical intimacy is dissolved when Speed interrupts them. A later panel depicts Billy and Teddy sharing a bed in another hideout, but they are fully clothed and only sleeping. In the last issue, *Avengers: The Children's Crusade #9* (2012), Teddy asks Billy to marry him, and when Billy accepts, the couple kiss. The issue where they kiss was published in 2012. In other words, Billy and Teddy had been a confirmed, out gay couple since their first publication in 2005, but it took seven years for them to kiss on-page. The context of the marriage proposal is crucial here as it frames the kiss as an affirmation of their commitment to emulating heteronormativity and maintaining the public/private split. It is only in the service of homonormativity that Billy and Teddy can display their homosexual desire, safely contained in their monogamous relationship and inside their apartment, behind closed doors. While the gay community is still underrepresented in all media and the mere depiction of a gay couple can be read as progressive, Billy and Teddy typify the representation of homosexuality that equates gay culture with the white middle class and normalizes them at the cost of other gay communities. This reaffirms Walter's point that visibility is not enough to create adequate representation.

When Billy and Teddy are presented as a unit, they perpetuate homonormativity and its conservative, heteronormative gender roles. Billy is framed as the performer of the feminine role and Teddy as the masculine one. For instance, it is clear in the panel where Billy and Teddy are kissing that Billy is smaller and less broadly built. In comics, smaller bodies can be read as feminized because they lack the exaggerated musculature associated with masculinity. Teddy—tall, buff, blond, and all-American in his civilian identity—is framed as the masculine partner in the Billy/Teddy relationship, but appears to lack masculinity when isolated. In his superhero identity, he uses his shape-shifting abilities to assume a hypermasculine body. Green and large, he assumes a form that resembles the Hulk, to which his name also refers. The Hulk, who is green and hugely muscular and is known for his nearly uncontrollable rage

Figure 3.2. Hulkling in motion. *Source*: Allan Heinberg et al., *Young Avengers Presents* (TPB) (New York: Marvel Comics, 2008). © 2008 Marvel Comics.

and violence, is a form that symbolizes the hypermasculine, considering that "To a large extent, not only is aggressiveness and aggression expected to be a significant part of a man's make-up, but also it is increasingly viewed as normal."[19] Teddy's body, when transformed, is extremely powerful, with the kind of padded shoulders and musculature typically associated with masculinity in comics, as seen in figure 3.2. The Hulk projects a hypermasculinity Teddy consciously and explicitly performs. However, the name Hulkling seems to undercut this image of powerful masculinity. The diminutive "ling" implies that Hulkling's hypermasculinity is only a derivative of the Hulk's.[20] As a gay character, Teddy can approximate masculinity, and even hypermasculinity, especially when compared with Billy, but his masculinity is questioned when isolated from a feminized counterpart.

Teddy's diminutive masculinity is further underlined through his origin story. Teddy is a Kree/Skrull hybrid, two alien races with a long and complex history in the Marvel universe. Due to his alien parentage, Teddy is a shape-shifter. It cannot be said that Teddy's body is singularly male, because it can produce multitudes of gender. The Hulk can only transform into the Hulk or back into Bruce Banner, while Teddy can transform into many forms, which renders him suspect. The gender binary, as the invisible norm within American culture, creates only two modes of gendered bodily identity and erases multiplicity, which Teddy's body, through its abilities, automatically generates. While Teddy grew up and identifies as a white male, his shape-shifting abilities mean that he could transform into a woman if he so chooses. Such a confusing, changing, or unstable identification is often culturally understood to signify femininity.[21] Jane M. Ussher writes about how the female body is viewed as constantly caught up in its own biological cycles of production and is considered unstable and perpetually changing.[22] While Teddy controls the shift, the fact that his body *can* change signifies a bodily instability that is threatening because it is feminizing. Compared with the male body, which is always hard and stable, controlled by masculine technology, the potential for softness and change inherent to female nature frames Teddy's body as nonmasculine. His body becomes a site of unease, as his changing body mimics women's procreative power, as he re-creates his own body into a weaker, diminutive derivative of a hypermasculine monster.

When viewed in isolation from each other, Teddy represents the cultural stereotype of the homosexual who lacks masculinity but aspires to it, while Billy is almost completely feminized and cast as the Other through his relationship with the Scarlet Witch (Wanda Maximoff) and his twin, Speed (Tommy Shepherd). In the *The Children's Crusade* story line, it is confirmed that Billy and Speed are the reincarnation of Wanda's children. When Wanda was married to the synthezoid Vision in the 1980s, she used her magic powers to find two lost souls and give them physical bodies, creating twin boys named William and Thomas. Later events revealed that those souls were part of the demon Mephisto, whose soul had split into five parts during a previous story line. Mephisto reabsorbed the two souls, but the power used by Wanda to bind them to physical bodies destroyed him. This resulted in the deaths of William and Thomas. The Avengers erased Wanda's memories of the events. Years later, Wanda regained her memories, lost control over her powers, killed several Avengers, and subsequently vanished. *The Children's Crusade* reveals that Billy and Speed are William and Thomas reincarnated and that Billy is far more powerful than he initially assumed. Instead of a magic caster, his powers actually resemble Wanda's reality-warping abilities. Through these similar abilities the dominant theme of the series is revealed, which is that history repeats itself, and thus, Billy will end up driven mad by his powers as Wanda was.

The cyclical nature of time is indicated by the repetition of two sets of mutant twins in different generations. Ivor Morrish discusses how twins are often written as opposites of each other, representing binary forces: male and female, good and evil, light and dark, with the dark twin as the Other embodying all the evil impulses of the light twin.[23] Billy's mother, Wanda, is the twin sister of Quicksilver (Pietro Maximoff) and had twins herself, William (Billy—Wiccan) and Thomas (Tommy—Speed). The original mutant twins are analogous with the second-generation mutant twins. Both Billy and Wanda have magical abilities, and Tommy and Pietro are speedsters with inexplicable white/silver hair. Tommy and Pietro function as the good/light twin compared with the black-haired Billy and Wanda, who embody the evil/dark twin, the Other. Wanda and Pietro both have Romani heritage, but Wanda is the one who resembles their Romani mother, while Pietro resembles their German father, Max Eisenhardt (Magneto). Billy is reincarnated into a Jewish family, while Tommy's new family is never mentioned and he is phenotypically white. Although Jewish identities have been folded into the concept of whiteness in the 1940s, as discussed in the introduction, anti-Semitism continually seeks to frame the Jewish identity as non-white. Furthermore, Ritchie Robertson discusses how, in the late nineteenth and twentieth centuries, there was a consistent trend in ethnography where anti-Semitism was expressed through pseudoscientific terms framing Jewish men as feminized figures. For example, Robertson writes, Jacques Le Rider was one of the first to express how "the male Jew could be imagined as unmanly, as located between the masculine and the feminine."[24] While Billy's Jewish heritage can be read as another stereotypical signification of his intellectual and wealthy background, it can also be read as his non-white heritage signifying a feminine nature that plays into the widespread paradigm that "gay sexuality negates masculinity."[25] Historically, gay men have often been associated with a lack of masculinity and an affinity for the feminine, much like Jewish men. In the few instances where gay sexuality has been associated with an overabundance of masculinity, this has often incorporated the idea that men have sexual needs that a (proper) woman does not. This creates the specter of the predatory gay man who sexualizes and seduces straight men and can somehow spread his homosexuality like a contagion because he bears sexual signification: "Men want sex, but don't allow themselves to be the object of sexual desire. Women, and not men, should be the bearers of the sexual. They should be the ones to be desired. They should contain within their 'being', their social relations, their sense of fashion, all the promises of sex. Gay men blow that careful distinction."[26] To ward off the specter of the predatory gay man, gay men are often desexualized in mass media and placed within safe, nonsexual domestic settings.

But even the domestic sphere can be Othered. Both Wanda's and Billy's romantic partners can be read as indicative of perverted sexual appetites as neither the Vision, a robot, nor Teddy, an alien, is a human man. Wanda is heterosexual and the Vision clearly presents and identifies as male, but he is still a cyborg. Wanda's attraction to the Vision signifies her status as the Other. This sexual perversion is hinted at through her superhero name. Barbara Ehrenreich and Deirdre English discuss how "witches are accused of every conceivable sex crime against men. Quite simply, they are 'accused' of female sexuality."[27] Witches are women

Figure 3.3. Billy and Wanda. *Source*: Allan Heinberg et al., *Avengers: The Children's Crusade* (TPB) (New York: Marvel Comics, 2012). © 2010 Marvel Comics.

who are in control of their sexuality, and therefore, women who are too powerful threaten the established order and must be destroyed. Wanda's relationship with the Vision is a crossing of boundaries of gender, sex, and humanity, and so is Billy's relationship with Teddy. By making Billy and Tommy analogous with Wanda and Pietro, the narrative, as well as the artwork in *Avengers: The Children's Crusade #3* (2010), as depicted in figure 3.3, implies that they are extensions of each other.[28]

Figure 3.3 frames Billy as an extension of Wanda. Her cape flows into his, and their bodies seem to melt into one another. Both display expressions of fear and uncertainty. It almost looks as if Wanda's cape is strangling Billy, implying that Wanda's destiny will destroy him. For Billy, as a feminized character, the story line and imagery imply an affinity or overlap between the homosexual and the female body, which needs to be destroyed when it becomes too powerful. The danger of femininity, especially excessive femininity, becomes evident when considering how many comics have narratives where female characters are killed to maintain the status quo.[29] *The Children's Crusade* implies that Billy and Speed are destined to replay the lives of Wanda and Quicksilver with Billy (as Wanda) losing control and killing his friends. In *Avengers: The Children's Crusade* #3, fellow superhero Wolverine says: "The Scarlet Witch murdered our friends—she stole their lives—and then she took out about a million mutants. And not *one* of you can tell me she won't do something like that—or worse—again. So the only permanent solution is to *kill* her. And if we were smart, we'd get rid of *Wiccan* too."[30] Billy and Wanda are considered too dangerous to be left alive because of their feminine powers and their bodily existence.

The power that Billy and Wanda, as the dark, feminine, and Other twin, possess is excessive and originates in their mutant bodies. In the Marvel universe, mutants are the next evolution of mankind, and mutant-ness is passed on from parent to child through DNA. Mutant powers are thus framed as deeply rooted in the body, and the female body in particular "is constructed as bodily uncontrollable and excessive."[31] Therefore, when female mutant superheroes lose control and need to be destroyed, it implies that female bodily excess, when it cannot be contained, must be eliminated. Placing Billy in the ranks of women who are too powerful frames him as a feminized character, implying that women and gay men cannot handle responsibility and power. Additionally, magic has often been linked to women and fits into what Mike Madrid calls the "strike a pose and point" powers associated mostly with female superheroes as it allows them to be powerful without needing to be in the physical battle.[32] Like Wanda, Billy has "pose and point" powers. These powers can warp or "pervert" reality, and through this perversion, he takes on her role in the cyclical nature of history.

Not only is Billy Wanda's Double, but he is also her demonized offspring. Barbara Creed discusses how, in horror films, the fear of female procreative powers is represented through mothers who "create monstrosities through the power of their imagination."[33] Women create life without any physical evidence of the involvement of a biological father. Every pregnant woman contains the anxiety that whatever she is bringing forth is foreign, is alien, and cannot be controlled by men. The Scarlet Witch harvested Billy's soul and gave him a flesh body by imagining it without any input from the father figure, the Vision. Billy may be reincarnated as the son of a heterosexual couple, but his origin as the son of the Scarlet Witch frames him as a child produced solely by a woman.[34] Such an origin story plays into stereotypical views of homosexuality caused by the domineering mother, who overtly feminizes her son and does not allow for any masculine influence. The stereotype of the effeminate and flamboyant gay man has a long history in American culture through its obsession with Momism, as discussed in chapter 1. Supposedly, Momistic mothers created overly dependent male children who identified with women and became attracted to men, which became a popular "explanation" for homosexuality.[35] Billy's fatherless conception plays into those fears of the all-powerful woman whose procreative powers cannot be controlled or subverted by men. Billy's powers, rooted in the body, are also essentially reproductive. Billy can create almost anything with his powers, and other characters fear this ability. They fear that Billy's creation will be destructive and monstrous, mirroring the fear of women's reproductive power. Billy's inheritance of Wanda's powers, the ability to re-create reality itself and taking her place in the cycle of history, implies that he will also produce an excessive, monstrous offspring. Billy's status as a feminized character manifests in his relationships with Teddy, Wanda, Tommy, and his powerset. Billy's signification of femininity remains complex as, like that of most male superheroes, his costume (consisting of a full bodysuit and a cape) covers him completely.[36] In the ten years since Billy's creation, his costume has gone through three changes. The first one, from 2005, when he still went by the name Asgardian, had a few round chest panels, and his headband had wings, as a tribute to Thor's costume. At this time, Billy was unsure what his powers actually were, and he seemed to mostly produce something similar to Thor's lightning. While Billy's initial code name Asgardian has a connection to the traditionally masculine Thor, who comes from Asgard, his subsequent name, Wiccan, is affiliated with witches and women.

Billy's second costume, updated in 2010, was similar to the first, only without the round panels and wings, as shown in figure 3.4.[37] The third and most recent change, from the 2013 run, also remained very similar to the original two.[38] It consists of a black bodysuit with a galaxy pattern on the sides and the sleeves, a red cape, and a belt, as demonstrated in figure 3.5. The galaxy pattern is a reference to Billy's destiny as the Demiurg: a godlike being with cosmic powers who will rewrite the rules of magic and create a paradise dimension.[39] The full bodysuit completely covers Billy's body and erases all trace of it. In figure 3.4, a panel drawn by Jim Cheung, Billy demonstrably has some musculature with lightly toned abs and forearms. In figure 3.5, drawn by Kate Brown and Jamie McKelvie, none of that musculature is visible through the suit. This is partly due to the different art styles used by Brown and McKelvie compared with Cheung. The Brown/McKelvie team shy away from the exaggerated body shapes traditionally used in comics. While they adhere to the inverted triangle body type, it exists in a much smaller degree than in most other comics. Billy lacks the inverted triangle shape and yet is not sexualized in the manner of many female superheroes.[40] While the degree to which the inverted triangle shape is exaggerated changes from artist to artist, Billy's lack is noticeable. He does not exist as either a fantasy subject or an object.

In the *Young Avengers* (volume 2) miniseries, the plot is haunted by both the specter of the predatory gay and the uncontrollable creations of monstrous femininity. In the first issue, Billy accidentally pulls an interdimensional mind-controlling parasite into his own dimension. This parasite is called "Mother," once again referring to the monstrous feminine and the fear of female reproduction. To fight Mother, the Young Avengers team up with four new characters—Noh-Varr,

Figure 3.4. Original Wiccan. *Source*: Allan Heinberg et al., *Avengers: The Children's Crusade* (TPB) (New York: Marvel Comics, 2012). © 2010 Marvel Comics.

Loki, America Chavez, and Prodigy (David Alleyne)—and begin traveling through dimensions to find a way to destroy her.[41] During their time hopping from one dimension to the other, Loki addresses the possible consequences of Billy's power by claiming that Billy imagined Teddy into reality:

> LOKI: A long-lost heir to the Skrull empire at the same school in the same city. *And* gay. *And* falls impossibly in love. . . . You are an *improbably* dashing prince.
>
> TEDDY: Billy wouldn't d—
>
> LOKI: No. I agree. He's lovely. But *choosing* to do it is kind of beside the point. Whims and daydreams are all that it takes.[42]

Figure 3.5. Modern Wiccan. *Source*: Kieron Gillen et al., *Young Avengers, Volume 2: Alternative Cultures* (TPB) (New York: Marvel Comics, 2014). © 2014 Marvel Comics.

Loki claims that the odds of Teddy existing and being in love with Billy are improbable and that, while Billy may not have consciously chosen to bring Teddy into existence, "whims and daydreams" are all it takes.[43] He implies that Billy cannot control his powers and that the strength of his (homosexual) desire changes reality itself. Of course, neither the audience nor Teddy can ever know for sure if this is true. Loki is an untrustworthy character and is known to lie or twist the truth. Teddy does become concerned that everything he is feeling or thinking might be created by Billy, which implies that Billy made Teddy gay, raising the specter of the predatory gay man. Furthermore, if Teddy was created by Billy, there would be an additional incestuous dimension to their relationship, further raising the specter of Billy as the monstrous mother. In light of this, it is significant that Billy is the one who brought Mother into their dimension. At the end of the miniseries, Billy and Teddy decide that all that matters is that they love each other, and the Young Avengers defeat Mother. Billy comes into his powers fully for the first time and transforms into the all-powerful Demiurg, but decides to walk away as he is not ready to wield its power. None of this resolves whether Teddy's feelings are genuine or artificially created and how monstrous Billy will become. The question of whether Billy will be able to control the destructive potential of his procreative powers remains unanswered and lies constantly in wait.

Externalizing the Queer: Batwoman and Her Monstrous Doubles

In the 1950s, comic books were recovering from a considerable decrease in sales after World War II, the implementation of the Comics Code, and the competition with other forms of mass media, such as television. Comics featuring superheroes became popular again with their use of whimsical fantasy or sci-fi story lines, and companies sought to capitalize on this popularity by expanding the superhero's cast of characters. Superman, for example, gained several pets and a cousin, as discussed in chapters 1 and 2. The success of expanding the Superman family precipitated a boom in distaff characters, and in 1956, DC introduced Batwoman. While Batman and Robin were, supposedly, written as partners with a father/son dynamic, allegations that they were in a homosexual relationship and promoted a homosexual lifestyle to young children had been cropping up since the early 1950s and had been expounded on by Fredric Wertham in his book *Seduction of the Innocent* (1954).[44] Due to the panic surrounding comic books and their influence on children, these accusations had to be refuted and Batman was provided with a new love interest. Additionally, Batwoman would hopefully increase the sales of *Batman* (1940–2011) and *Detective Comics* (1937–2011) by bringing in a female audience.

Batwoman's civilian identity was Katherine Kane, a wealthy socialite from Gotham who was inspired by Batman to use her wealth for good. She had a utility purse, to conceal weapons disguised as stereotypically feminine items such as lipsticks, hairnets, and compact mirrors. Batwoman appeared regularly in the comics in the 1950s and 1960s and was relatively well received by fans. But by 1964, Batwoman and other characters created in the 1950s were cut in the series' overhaul to create a "darker" tone.[45] Nonetheless, characters continued to refer to Katherine Kane, and she appeared briefly in a few issues in 1979, coming out of retirement to assist Batgirl (Barbara Gordon). Later that year, Batwoman was killed by the League of Assassins. The new Batwoman first appeared in *Countdown to Final Crisis* (2006–2008) and *Final Crisis* (2008–2009), after which she briefly took over as the lead character in *Detective Comics*. In 2009, DC began publication of the *Batwoman: Elegy* miniseries (2009–2010), which launched her regular titular series, *Batwoman* (2010–2014). Batwoman continued to make regular appearances in *Detective Comics* until DC relaunched the *Batwoman* comic with a new first issue in March 2017, which is still in circulation at the time of writing. This new Batwoman is Kate Kane, a wealthy Jewish heiress and, in an ironic twist, a lesbian. She is the cousin of the original Katherine Kane, who is Batman's aunt through marriage in DC's current continuity, making Bruce Wayne (Batman) and Kate Kane (Batwoman) related. This section will focus primarily on the Kate Kane Batwoman, specifically the *Batwoman: Elegy* and the *Batwoman* series (2010–2015), both of which engage almost exclusively with the more fantastical and gothic elements of the DC universe.

In comic scholarship, *Batwoman: Elegy* has received positive criticism, and while it is true that *Elegy* is the first Batwoman story that fully engages with Kate's sexuality in a transgressive and progressive manner, to consider it as containing only positive representations of heroic lesbianism is a simplification of the series' complexity. Paul Petrovic states that "through its intricate layout and thematic design," *Elegy*'s artwork visualizes how Kate's lesbianism is used to "challenge the heteronormativity of comics."[46] Instead of using traditional linear panel layouts, the series is structured by panels in spider-web formation or like shards cracking the page. It disregards traditional use of borders and the gutter space in comics, symbolizing how Kate, as the Batwoman, transgresses the limitations of society and its interpretation of her identity. This style is also used in the *Batwoman* comics (2011), especially in the first story line, *Hydrology*, where panels are drawn in fluid streams flowing into one another, jumping backward and forward in time, forcing the reader to investigate and construct the narrative. While Petrovic's argument that the art informs the narrative, underlining its themes of familial fragmentation and the multiplicity of Kate's identity, is eloquent and significant, the interpretation of *Elegy* as fully transgressive or consistently invested in the politicization of Kate's lesbian identity lacks some nuance. Both *Elegy* and the subsequent *Batwoman* comics are complex narratives that attempt to challenge the status quo and promote diversity but fail to interrogate heteronormativity.

The *Elegy* series contains damaging stereotypes about lesbians and gender performance through Kate's relationship with her sister and her father, as well as the codification of the domestic and public spheres. In *Elegy*, flashbacks reveal how Kate was kidnapped at twelve years old, along with her twin sister, Elizabeth "Beth" Kane, and her mother, Gabrielle "Gabi" Kane. Both her mother and sister die, and Kate is rescued by her father, Jacob "Jake" Kane. While this origin story fits a traditional narrative where the hero gains motivation from the death of a parental figure, Kate losing her twin sister is unusual. Most superheroes do not have brothers or sisters, much less a twin sibling, or even extended family, which allows for a team of superheroes to function as a surrogate family without displacing the traditional biological family. Of course, for those that do, biological siblings are often a source of conflict and tension within the narrative. Morrish considers how twins exist in opposition to each other and are used to symbolize humanity's double nature:

> Twins, however, have always been regarded as something special and, if not related directly to divinity, yet as possessing some unusual power or *mana* which works in opposition, rather like the positive and negative forces of electricity or the north and south poles of a magnet. There is, thus, in the concept of the twin a certain balance or equilibrium implied, a closeness and similarity without a complete identity; and ultimately, at least in mythology, a certain opposition which may lead through increasing hostility to an attempt by one twin to destroy the other.[47]

As discussed previously, twins represent opposing dichotomies: light and dark, male and female, good and evil. Throughout *Elegy* and *Batwoman*, Kate is framed as the masculine twin and Beth as the feminine twin. In the flashbacks to Kate's childhood, she is often shown as having more affinity with her father while Beth is closer to her mother. During their childhood, Kate was Beth's protector and engaged in tomboyish behavior. The alignment of Beth as feminine and Kate as masculine is also hinted at by the color motif used in the flashbacks to Kate's childhood. When they are not drawn wearing the same thing, Beth is often depicted wearing white and pink colors, which are considered soft and feminine. Kate is drawn in black and red, often read as masculine colors, while foreshadowing her identity as Batwoman and allowing the reader to identify her.[48]

The twins' signification of gender is reinforced through their relationship with their parents and the family's relationship to the military. In *Batwoman #7* (2012), Kate's father explicitly states that Kate more closely resembles him, while Beth was more like her mother, reaffirming Kate's symbolic position as the masculine twin. When both Beth and Gabi die, the feminine is completely annihilated in the Kane nuclear family. Only the masculine survives in the form of both Kate and her father, reaffirming her parallelization with him in the family unit. While both of Kate's parents were in the military, scenes with her mother are obviously parental, set in the domestic sphere. The family is seen moving from base to base to accommodate Jacob's career, framing him as the career military man in the family unit, while Beth's mother is the one making the girls' dinner, helping them with homework, or driving them to and from school. Although Gabi is also a military woman, we only see her performing traditionally motherly duties. As discussed in chapter 2, the masculine soldier identity depends on the construction of the female soldier as a fundamentally feminine role, which Gabi maintains. We never see her exercising, following orders, or working as a soldier. As discussed in chapter 1, the warrior masculinity of the male soldier often depends on his ability to destroy the feminine within himself and his unit. Following the destruction of the feminine in the family unit, the Kane family takes on the structure of the military unit, with Kate assuming the role of the male soldier following her superior/father's orders. Jacob uses the tenets of the military as the moral code with which to raise his daughter, which culminates in Kate joining the military academy at

West Point, where she attempts to consolidate her identity as a soldier, but the masculine warrior-protector role instead of the feminine role.

Kate joining the military is an attempt to cement her citizenship and access to its rights in American society. Aaron Belkin and Jason Dittmer discuss how the military is considered quintessentially American, a place where citizens can affirm their American nationality.[49] Joining the military is not only an attempt by Kate to find a masculine role as protector but also a way to solidify her place in heteronormative society by affirming her American nationality through her status as a white (Jewish) woman. As discussed in the introduction, superhero comic books assisted with breaking open the category of whiteness to include all phenotypically white persons, instead of Anglo-Saxon or Germanic whites only. Kate's whiteness as well as her closeted homosexuality, which automatically frames her as heterosexual within public spaces, allows her to temporarily gain access to the privileged military space. It is her performance of masculinity that endangers that access. Kate's desire to be a soldier and protect people explicitly originates from a desire to prevent what happened to her mother and sister from happening again. Kate wants to assume the male protector role to protect signifiers of the feminine. Her identity as a soldier is framed in masculine terms, instead of the feminine soldier role that women like her mother performed.

At West Point, Kate excels not only in her academic classes but also in the physical requirements. While this can, and should, be read as challenging stereotypes surrounding the cult of the body, which frames the female body as inherently weaker than the male body, her lesbian identity can complicate this straightforward reading. Depicting the lesbian as too masculine or depicting masculinity as the source of lesbianism is a familiar, damaging stereotype. If Kate's desire to protect is read as a desire to inhabit a role that is explicitly masculine because of her childhood trauma, compounded by the fact that her father raised her without any feminine influence, Batwoman could be read as perpetuating the idea that lesbianism stems from an overabundance of masculine influence, an inability to process childhood trauma, or the result of such trauma interfering with the "correct" construction of gender identity, which are homophobic and Freudian constructions of female homosexuality.[50]

The *Elegy* series also undermines Kate's transgressive political potential through its portrayal of the military and the Don't Ask, Don't Tell policy (DADT). During her time at West Point, Kate begins a romantic relationship with her roommate, Sophie Moore, and is reported for homosexual conduct to her superior officer, Colonel Reyes. While it is impossible to ignore the accusation, Reyes will look the other way if Kate publicly denounces her sexuality. Kate refuses. This scene demonstrates Kate's refusal to compromise her individual identity for the sake of discriminatory military policies, but it also cements Kate's loyalty to the military and its code of ethics. Kate states that "a cadet shall not lie, cheat or steal, nor suffer others to do so" and admits that she is gay.[51] Kate's refusal to reject her lesbianism is not only a personal loyalty to her own identity but also a performance of the values elevated by the military industrial complex, which renders her complicit with its discrimination. She never voices a critique of the discriminatory policy. When she tells her father, he says that he cannot fault her because she maintained her honor. This perpetuates neoliberalism's public/private split, incorporating how *Lawrence* forecloses political action that challenges institutionalized heteronormativity. The series clearly presents gay women's capacity to serve in the military without compromising its code of honor or the effectiveness of its fighting force through Kate's exemplary behavior and record, but never discusses how the policy is discriminatory. Her expulsion is framed as a personal loss, not an institutionalized injustice. This reaffirms that homosexuality should be kept private and separate from privileged or public spaces to safeguard the institution as Kate's silence safeguards the military within the comic book pages. Kate's sexuality is thus divorced from its political power.

While the series never digs into the institutional and community-wide repercussions of policies such as the DADT, it does demonstrate how such discriminatory policies are destructive on a personal level. When Kate is discharged from West Point Military Academy, she descends into a self-destructive spiral. Left without a purpose, she drinks too much, drops out of college, and lives on her stepmother's wealth. Similar to the *Iron Man* comics and films, this slide into frivolous consumption is presented as part of the corrupting gluttony of the upper class, which is framed as feminine, as discussed in chapter 1. Rejected from the ultimate masculine sphere, the military, Kate sinks into a completely feminine space of wealth and luxury characterized as excessive, toxic, and destructive. After an encounter with Batman, Kate is inspired to become a vigilante and stops partying. Batman, as a signification of the masculine, guides her out of toxic femininity. After fighting as an unnamed vigilante for a time, Kate is caught by her father, who threatens to use his position in the military to prevent her from fighting crime unless he can provide her with sufficient training. With a masculine authority figure to give her structure, guidance, and validation, Kate can escape the feminine space of excessive consumption. It is her father who suggests she use Batman's chevron as her own, to identify her as "one of the good guys," and Kate agrees, assuming the Batwoman moniker and chevron.[52] Traditionally, Batman is the male warrior protector of the city of Gotham, which is often identified through female pronouns within the DC universe. Aligning herself explicitly with Batman means that Kate assumes a male warrior identity, protecting the female domestic sphere (Gotham), through male mentorship (her father) and male signification (the bat chevron).

In her Batwoman identity, Kate combines signifiers of masculinity and femininity and performs a monstrous gender transgression through her uniform and character design. The trade paperback edition of *Elegy* has three design sheets in the back, one for Batwoman and two for Kate Kane. The design sheet for Batwoman reveals a preoccupation with practicality typically reserved for male superhero costumes. As the top lines say, the look used in *Countdown to Final Crisis* and *Final Crisis* is preserved, but altered with "more sensibility and functionality."[53] Batwoman's originally long hair is cut and hidden underneath a wig

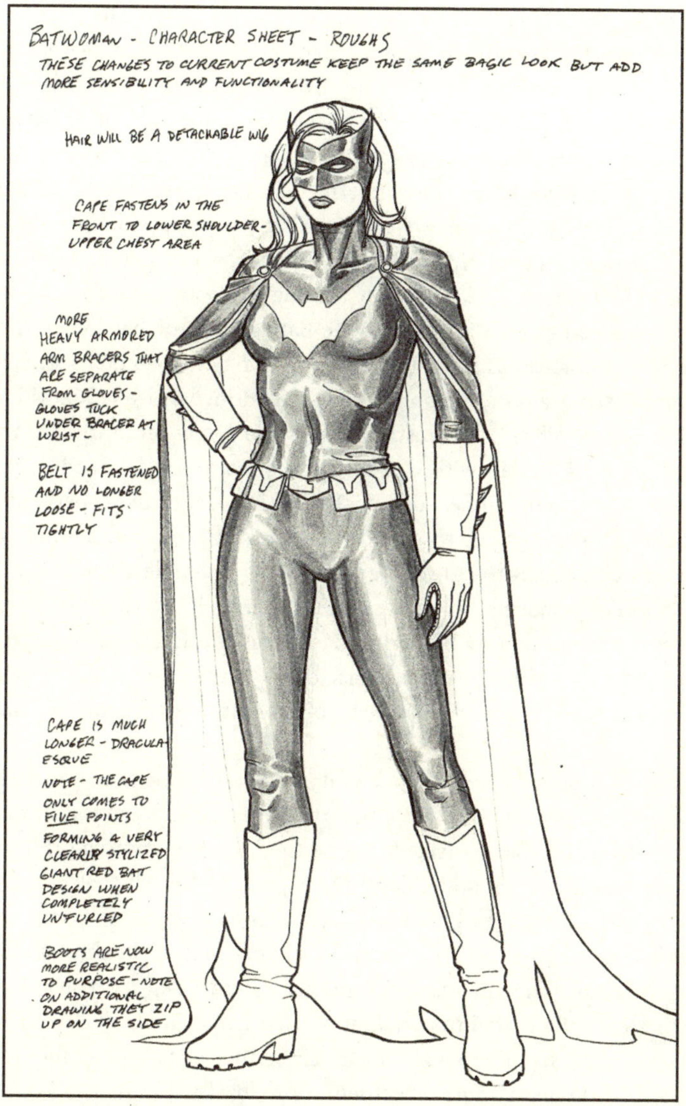

Figure 3.6. Batwoman design. *Source*: Greg Rucka et al., *Batwoman: Elegy* (TPB) (New York: DC Comics, 2010). © 2010 DC Comics.

that detaches when gripped. The cape is fastened in the front to preserve mobility and has been refitted to function as a paraglider. Her costume has added armored panels in the gauntlet and gloves, and the boots, instead of fashionable high heels, are sturdy and resemble combat boots. While formfitting, this look is the complete opposite of that of most female superhero costumes, which resemble bathing suits or bikinis or are so skintight they might as well be naked. It is more reminiscent of male superhero costumes: formfitting enough to display musculature without sexualizing the character, as demonstrated in figure 3.6.

Batwoman's look is reminiscent of the way comics typically represent masculinity. Her suit has both the belt, as a replacement for the Underwear of Power, and the chest chevron, but without the inverted triangle body shape. Yet, it is not *her* chevron, but Batman's. Despite these masculine signifiers, Batwoman is still recognizably a woman and her body conforms to some tropes associated with femininity in comic books. For instance, the tight-fitting suit does not cling to a set of powerful abs but to the concave curve of her rib cage, which makes her look underweight instead of powerfully muscled, and her breasts sit high on her chest. In most panels throughout the series, they are slightly pointy, as if she is wearing a push-up bra instead of a sports bra. As the Batwoman, she has long red hair and wears blood-red lipstick. Through the role of the physical combatant, *Elegy* steps away from the "strike a pose and point" powers identified by Mike Madrid. Petrovic argues that "*Elegy* offers a deconstruction of the hyper-feminine," not only by "showing Kate working out with weights, with sweat rolling down her grimacing face and grimy workout clothes, desexualizing the aura of the superheroine," but also by adding typically male tropes to her costume.[54] It is a mingling of gender signifiers that challenges the idea of femininity as a complete contrast to masculinity. Batwoman performs a blurring of gender roles by inhabiting the male soldier role as a woman and by blending masculine and feminine signifiers as the Batwoman. In *Elegy* and *Batwoman*, masculinity and femininity are each other's Double, and Doubles inevitably seek to break boundaries and seep into each other.

Superheroes exist in a constant state of doubling: the superhero and their secret, civilian identity. Especially in the Batman universe, the superhero is a consciously crafted monstrous Double to strike fear into the hearts of criminals. Batwoman is Kate's monstrous other: embodying all those parts of herself that belong outside hetero/homonormativity. As a civilian, Kate seeks to exist in the homonormative, but her dark Other (Batwoman) contaminates Kate's civilian life through the superhero's other Double. The villains that superheroes must defeat are also Doubles of the superhero, often created to match and mirror the superhero. If, as Friedrich Weltzien claims, the superhero is automatically connected to masculinity, the superhero's Double, the villain, must reflect femininity back on him, as is the case with Batwoman.[55] Her villains are all Doubles of herself, monstrous and sexually destructive, invoking images of blood, monstrosity, and femininity. One of these Doubles is the main villain of *Elegy*, the High Madame of the Religion of Crime, named Alice, who plans to release a toxic nerve agent over Gotham. According to the acolytes of the religion, "The apostle of the First would come to Gotham and there he would murder 'the twice-named daughter of Cain,'" which would either bring about the apocalypse or make the Religion of Crime the rulers of Gotham.[56] The organization assumes that "twice-named daughter of Cain" refers to Batwoman, also named Kate Kane (pronounced as Cain). The cult sends its high madame, Alice, to murder Batwoman and destroy Gotham. Alice is obsessed with *Alice in Wonderland* and speaks only in quotes from Lewis Carroll's work. For example, when she meets Batwoman for the first time, she says, "I can't explain myself, I'm afraid, because

Figure 3.7. Batwoman/Alice 1. *Source*: Greg Rucka et al., *Batwoman: Elegy* (TPB) (New York: DC Comics, 2010). © 2010 DC Comics.

I'm *not* myself, you see."[57] In both *Alice in Wonderland* and *Through the Looking Glass*, Alice exists as a Double, either as a dream or as a mirror image, which exists as a distorted copy of Alice in the "real world." In *Elegy*, Alice is the distorted Double of Batwoman, who is her direct opposite, the hero to her villain, and they are often depicted as two parts of the same whole, as demonstrated by figures 3.7 and 3.8.[58]

In these panels, Batwoman and Alice form a single body and a single face, representing the Double—the Self and the Other—while foreshadowing the plot twist near the end of *Elegy*, which is that Alice is actually Beth Kane.[59] Some members of

Figure 3.8. Batwoman/Alice 2. *Source*: Greg Rucka et al., *Batwoman: Elegy* (TPB) (New York: DC Comics, 2010). © 2010 DC Comics.

the Religion of Crime believed that "twice-named daughter of Cain" referred to a set of identical twins and that one needed to kill the other to fulfill the prophecy. They kidnapped Beth and brainwashed her into becoming Alice, to become her Double's Double and a Double of herself: Alice is Beth's Double, who is Kate's Double, who is Doubled by Batwoman, whose Double is Alice—like a fractured mirror reflecting its distorted mirror image back at itself again and again. This brings the thematic use of twins full circle as the dark twin, the villain Beth-as-Alice, attempts to destroy the light twin, the superhero Kate-as-Batwoman. Yet, the use of color complicates this initial reading. Alice's costume consists of white and pastel colors, pointing to Beth as the light, heterosexual twin, while Kate's black-and-red costume frames her as the dark, homosexual twin. Both Beth and Kate are complicated versions of each other and exhibit the blurring of boundaries, where unstable identities seep into each other and become each other.

Other villains, or Doubles, in the *Batwoman* series are the Mother of Monsters, Nocturna, and Morgan La Fey. During Batwoman's investigation into the disappearance of several children in Gotham, she discovers that they are being used as sacrifices to bring monsters from urban legends to life. For example, the legend of the Weeping Woman, a woman who drowned her own children, and Bloody Mary are brought to life. These villains link maternity and monstrosity as well as blood and femininity.[60] These monsters are summoned and sacrificed to summon the Mother of Monsters, who gave birth to Medusa, the snake-haired woman from Greek mythology. By teaming up with Wonder Woman, Batwoman finds out that in the ancient past of the DC universe, the Mother populated the Earth with monsters. Eventually Zeus, the patriarchal god, decreed that the earth belonged to mortal men and he ordered the Mother locked away, her children hunted down and destroyed. This villain's origin story reflects historical and contemporary anxieties surrounding motherhood and women's creative power, as discussed previously. Not only does Mother give birth to monsters that exist outside of man's control (the only way to safeguard the world is through control by a powerful patriarch), but she also devours her children to gain the strength to enter the world, symbolizing the fear of the devouring or Momistic mother who corrupts and destroys her husband's offspring. The Mother's return to Gotham can be read as a crossing of gender boundaries: a refusal to accept heteropatriarchal limitations on motherhood and femininity, which need to be stopped at all costs to save the world, or preserve the heteronormative status quo.[61]

When the villains finally succeed in summoning the Mother, they do so by opening a portal over the shoreline. The being that spills out is made entirely of eyes and tentacles and, possibly, brain matter. Three different versions of the Mother—one drawn in black, another in green, and the last in red—are improperly overlaid, creating an effect of distortion, like an eldritch horror crawling out of the void. It seems as if the edges of her form are unstable and she is about to burst out of her lines. This lack of bodily integrity reinforces the theme of seeping boundaries and the blurring of categories as another dimension opens up into our own and she spills out. Mere mortals cannot recognize her form; she can only be identified as a horrific, monstrous Mother. Of course, in the end, she is vanquished. The Mother's defeat at the hands of Batwoman is the defeat of a woman made monstrous by escaping the bounds of the homo/heteronormative and transgressing traditionally subservient feminine gender roles. As Batwoman's Double, the Mother also represents the struggle in Kate herself to prevent the dark and twisted Other from spilling into her homonormative civilian life.

Kate, in her civilian life, is invested in constructing homonormativity, which frames white, middle-class homosexual couples in long-term relationships as acceptable versions of homosexuality at the cost of other LGBTQIA+ communities, as discussed previously. Kate attempted to perform heteronormativity by joining the military, which traditionally provides spaces of belonging and legitimization to minorities. Rejected by these spaces, Kate looks for belonging through a homonormative relationship. She has several female partners, most notably Renee Montoya, Maggie Sawyer, and Natalia Mitternacht. When Kate leaves the military, she breaks up with her girlfriend and roommate, Sophie Moore, who maintained the public/private split and denied her sexuality to retain her position in the military. While in her self-destructive phase after leaving West Point, Kate meets Renee Montoya when Renee, a beat cop in the Gotham City Police Department (GCPD), pulls her over for speeding. While Renee and Kate enter into a monogamous relationship, they are not able to fulfill the tenets of the homonormative. Renee is Hispanic and, at the time of meeting Kate, in the closet. Neither her parents nor the people she works with are aware that she is gay. While this maintains a public/private split, it also prevents her from fully committing to the construction of a family with Kate, a requirement of homonormativity. The public/private split requires gay people to either be in the closet entirely, without engaging in homosexual behavior at all, or be in committed relationships, which function as a cordon sanitaire keeping homosexuality from entering the public space. Essentially, gay people can only be gay when they are in a relationship to ward of the specter of the single, predatory lesbian by embodying the acceptable lesbian, who is in a relationship. While Renee is concerned about the repercussions to her career if she were to come out, her remaining in the closet is framed as preventing her from committing to Kate and the performance of homonormativity. Remaining in the closet also clashes with Kate's own morals, which prohibit lying, even by omission, at all costs. Furthermore, homonormativity is often accessible only to white, middle-class couples who can perform normative gender roles within their relationship. Renee is Hispanic and working class per her low-income beat-cop job. Neither Kate nor Renee can be framed as the masculine or feminine partner in relation to each other, causing the relationship to transgress the heteronormative gender roles required in homonormativity.

The closest Kate comes to inhabiting the homonormative is through her relationship with Maggie Sawyer. They meet at a fundraiser event for the GCPD, where Maggie approaches Kate because they are both wearing tuxedos, breaking conventional dress codes and signaling queerness to the outside world. In doing so, it breaks the public/private split as it makes both Kate's and Maggie's lesbianism readily apparent, as evidenced by Kate's stepmother expressing discomfort with Kate's chosen attire. Maggie claims that wearing a tuxedo is always lucky because "you don't feel bad when other people show up wearing the same thing," implying that a woman in a tuxedo or a suit instead of an elaborate dress at a formal event automatically signals lesbianism.[62] While this is certainly true in the higher echelons of Gotham society, outside of the comic book pages, the image of a woman in a stylish suit is no longer as radical as it once was and cannot automatically be taken as an expression of lesbianism or lesbian desire.[63] Women in suits and tuxedos are increasingly normalized and co-opted by the fashion industry, an example of how heteronormative culture appropriates and de-radicalizes lesbian signification. While Kate's signaling of her lesbian identity is transgressive within the comic book pages, the audiences outside those pages are presented with a nonradical and increasingly heteronormalized identity statement.[64]

During this initial meeting, Maggie reveals that she broke up with a lesbian partner in Metropolis when she moved to Gotham and is currently single. Kate and Maggie start dating and quickly progress to a committed relationship, settling into the homonormative. Maggie is the ideal partner for Kate. She is openly gay in the GCPD, citing Commissioner Gordon's strict antidiscriminatory policy as part of her success, which frames Renee's insistence that being out would jeopardize her career as paranoia in the face of a progressive, liberal society. Maggie's career as a detective frames her as middle class, compared with the beat cop, with its higher social status and wage. Furthermore, Maggie is a mother. Before she came out as gay, she was married to a man and had a child. Her daughter resides in Metropolis and occasionally visits Maggie in Gotham. The link to motherhood frames Maggie as the feminine partner in their relationship. Although Maggie is a detective and often works the same cases as Batwoman, during the Mother of Monsters story line, Batwoman consistently expresses concerns and fear for Maggie's position as a defender of Gotham's citizens. Even when Maggie is a physical combatant herself, Kate assumes that, as the Batwoman, she has more resources and training to withstand the rigors of combat. She effectively casts Maggie as the (female) civilian who needs to be protected and herself as the (male) soldier who will protect her. At the end of the Mother of Monsters story line, Kate asks Maggie to marry her, reaffirming her position as the "active" male partner in traditional gender roles. Throughout the next few issues, Kate and Maggie move in together, and Maggie even encourages Kate to see a psychiatrist so Kate can resolve her childhood trauma and the posttraumatic stress disorder she is suffering from as a result of her vigilantism.

At this point in the story line, Batwoman's original creative team, W. Haden Blackman, J. H. Williams III, and Amy Reader, planned for Kate and Maggie to marry and completely settle into the homonormative, but DC editors intervened.[65] They rationalized that superheroes could not have happy personal lives and Kate and Maggie could not get married. While editorial interference is normally not so widely publicized, DC had no choice but to openly justify its position as Blackman, Williams, and Reader publicly threatened to quit if DC interfered with their artistic vision. Considering that they had won a GLAAD Media Award for their work on Batwoman, having them quit over an editorial dispute concerning the marriage of gay characters would have been a public embarrassment. Instead, DC removed them from the title before they could leave in protest and released a statement that the editorial differences over the wedding were not because of Batwoman's sexuality.[66] Considering that many of DC superheroes have been or are currently married, the excuse that superheroes cannot be married falls flat and lends credence to the theory that Kate and Maggie's wedding was canceled out of fear of a public backlash against a happily married lesbian couple. While Marvel's

Northstar wedding in 2012 received plenty of positive publicity, DC's fear of a backlash against two gay female characters marrying hints at the way lesbian homonormativity prevents lesbianism's fetishization by straight men and is therefore less acceptable.

Instead, in *Batwoman #34* (2014), Maggie and Kate break up. Maggie's ex-husband sues for full custody of their child, citing Kate as a bad influence on their daughter. Kate contacts Maggie's ex-husband and promises to leave Maggie if he drops the lawsuit. Kate never informs Maggie of this deal, but stresses in her goodbye letter that "a daughter needs her mother."[67] Kate is clearly referring to her own motherless childhood, playing into the stereotype that only male/female couples are suited to raise children. Additionally, the comic never depicts Kate and Maggie parenting together successfully, and Kate does not have a relationship with Maggie's daughter. The only time they interact is when Kate inadvertently scares her. While the comic portrays the breakup with Maggie as a personal sacrifice on Kate's part and implies that using someone's sexuality as leverage is wrong, the clash over Maggie's daughter also seems inevitable. In the same issue, a villain named Nocturna or Natalia Mitternacht, who has discovered that Batwoman and Kate are the same person, breaks into Kate's apartment and seduces her while biting her on the neck like a vampire.

From this point on, the narrative descends into stereotypical portrayals of the predatory, vampiric lesbian. Once bitten by Mitternacht, Kate is plagued by nightmares and regularly transforms into a vampire. The transformation is marked by Batwoman having sharp canines, speaking in a strange purple speech bubble with a gothic font, and displaying an increased aggressive attitude. While these transformations occur regularly, Kate never remembers her episodes as a vampire. Mitternacht also becomes romantically involved with Kate, whose emotional turmoil over her breakup with Maggie evaporates. As a lesbian vampire, Mitternacht represents the fallen/evil woman who refuses to perform the traditionally female role of wife/mother, threatening the survival of the heteronormative nuclear family. According to Barbara Almond, in her discussion of Dracula as a monstrous mother, the vampire has often been a stand-in for deeply rooted psychological fears about "perverse maternity."[68] The vampire represents monstrous procreation as it can reproduce on its own, using its blood, linking images of procreation, menstrual blood, femininity, and monstrosity, as well as sexual taboos. Mitternacht perpetuates this signification through her relationship with her stepson, Anton. She seduced him into killing his father, her husband, so she could inherit the family fortune. This invokes the taboo of incest as well as the image of the controlling, vengeful mother who dominates her son, destroys his masculinity, steals his inheritance, and turns him into a weapon against other men. Through the controlling mother, Mitternacht, as the female vampire, represents the fear of women's sexual appetites as disproportionate and capable of sapping men's strength and virility. With her sharp canines and heavily applied lipstick, she raises the specter of the vagina dentata that will literally, not just symbolically, devour the man and consume his power. This overwhelming sexual desire is a gender transgression as "normal" women are portrayed as not having sexual desire, which is the prerogative of men. Mitternacht embodies the fear of female sexual hunger as she serially seduces, marries, and then murders rich men. Her greed and gluttony continually destroy men who are too weak to resist her, themselves already corrupted by an excess of money and luxury.

Through its signification of monstrous procreation, the vampire also presents as a figure of contagion. The lesbian vampire becomes a figure who spreads her homosexuality like a virus, seducing women away from socially acceptable partners. Mitternacht seduces Kate and erases her desire to perform heteronormativity, literally making Kate monstrous. By transforming her into a vampire, Mitternacht becomes a mother figure to Kate but is also her lover. By infecting both Kate's and Batwoman's lives, Mitternacht further blurs the boundaries between Batwoman and Kate, pulling Kate away from the homonormative and allowing the dark Other to invade her civilian life. At this time, Beth, redeemed, returns to Gotham and reveals that Kate has been under hypnosis the whole time. Mitternacht only made Kate believe she was a vampire, but Mitternacht insists that hypnosis cannot force people to do things they do not really want to do, implying she only set Kate's hidden desires free. While Kate seemingly consented to their sexual contact, Mitternacht's hypnotic abilities make it clear that Mitternacht raped Kate, because Kate was not capable of informed consent while under the influence of mind-altering powers. The insistence that, deep down, Kate must have wanted it parrots the kind of accusations women are confronted with when they (attempt to) report their (sexual) assaults. However, the comic does not explicitly engage with any of this, skimming over Kate's potential sexual trauma and her response to it. Instead, the comic immediately skips ahead to the conflict with Morgan Le Fey.

Morgan Le Fey is the last villain and Double in the *Batwoman* series and, as a witch, symbolizes the sexually powerful woman. Morgan Le Fey's quest for world domination through the use of magic represents the woman who uses her sexual power to control men. Morgan is the destroyer of Camelot, the ancient city of King Arthur. She seduced one of his knights to betray his king, once again highlighting women's sexual power as destructive. In other DC canons, this becomes even clearer. For example, in the DC Animated Universe, containing the animated cartoon series *Justice League* (2001–2004) and *Justice League Unlimited* (2004–2006), Morgan also represents the monstrous, controlling mother who subverts masculine power. She casts a spell over her son, Mordred, keeping him young throughout the centuries they spend trying to take over the world. He is a perpetual ten-year-old, playing into the Momistic idea that mothers baby their sons in order to control them. In *Batwoman*, she is once again attempting to take over the world by mixing feminine magic and masculine technology, a gender transgression. Batwoman's entire gallery of villains is women and monstrous mothers who represent the struggle between the queer and the homonormative in Kate herself. In the end, Kate loses this struggle. After the *Batwoman* series ends in 2014, the single *Batwoman: Future's End* issue (2014) reveals that Kate has become a vampire (for real this time) and Beth, as the new superhero Red Alice, has to kill her.

This issue demonstrates that Kate, as the Batwoman, the lesbian, the dark twin, cannot resist being swallowed up by the horrors the lesbian invokes through her gender transgression.[69] She must be destroyed by her opposite, her Double, her twin. Her gender transgression first made her Nocturna's target, seduced by what appeared to be an evil vampire, and eventually turned her into one. The *Batwoman* comics narrate the struggle between Batwoman's quest for order and justice, on the one hand, and Kate's attempts to construct a homonormative life in the heteropatriarchy, on the other, while the Batwoman's existence in the realm of terror and monsters keeps invading Kate's life. Being Batwoman, Kate becomes literally haunted and controlled by her enemies, possessed by the dark Other. While *Elegy* and the *Batwoman* comics attempt to engage with Kate's sexuality in a transgressive manner, before DC editorship interfered, Kate signified the homonormative. When DC editorship intervened, she was turned into a toxic lesbian stereotype. It seems that the gay superhero either performs homonormativity or is destroyed, perpetuating the cultural narrative where the homonormative, white, middle-class gay community is the only acceptable gay community. While Batwoman is clearly an attempt at positive representation, the comics fail to question and challenge patriarchal hegemony.

Conclusion

It is clear that gay and lesbian characters' representation of homosexuality is often complex. For instance, while Billy and Teddy can (and should) be read as a positive step forward to include more homosexual characters performing feats of heroism successfully, it is important to understand that they represent a specific kind of gay community, which is white, middle-class, and homonormative. Billy and Teddy perpetuate the homonormative, and when they are represented in isolation from each other, they signify troubling and problematic stereotypes. The comics consistently conflate femininity with homosexual signification and perpetuate fears of the gay man as destructive, predatory, and contaminating. The early comics imply that homonormativity is the only acceptable way to be gay. The new 2013–2014 run seems the most progressive so far, despite the implication of Billy making Teddy gay. It has better representation of the full spectrum of human sexuality, including gay, bisexual, and gender-fluid characters, and Billy and Teddy are often shown kissing and embracing, casually referring to each other as "boyfriends." Recent comics present gay characters more directly, suggesting a more liberal attitude to gender and sexuality present in American culture. However, the manner in which they are represented, with somewhat persistent stereotyping, contradicts this, revealing the persistence of conservative attitudes to gender and sexuality.

Batwoman's performance of gender is transgressive, but the narrative problematizes it. The destruction of the monstrous, the search for the homonormative, and the eventual death of Batwoman all represent the destruction of the queer as punishment for her gender role transgression. In this way, the narrative plays into the popular "bury your gays" trope. In this trope, usually one partner, or sometimes both, in a gay couple is killed. The trope mostly affects women, revealing how female lesbian relationships are less acceptable when lesbianism is not fetishized for male consumption. It has historically been present in American mass media—for example, the death of lesbian character Tara McClay in *Buffy the Vampire Slayer* (1997–2003) in 2002. More recently, in the spring finales of several shows in 2016, several lesbian and bisexual characters were killed. Autostraddle "tracks all the lesbian and bisexual women who have died in the history of television. When its list began in March 2016, it had 65 women on it. It now [in 2017] has 182."[70] As of September 2019, this list has climbed to 208.[71] While comics do not match these numbers, it is important to realize how dominant this trend is in the American cultural landscape and how comics tie into this through both their lack of female gay characters and the deaths or torture of those characters.

Billy's, Teddy's, and Batwoman's representations of the homonormative ideal and the construction of the gay character as the Other make clear that comics still have a long way to go in terms of positive representation of gay characters. It is telling that some of the most famous gay characters are part of a twin: Billy (and Tommy), Batwoman or Kate Kane (and Beth Kane), and Northstar (and his twin sister Aurora). The gay character is canceled out by their twin, a straight version of them. Additionally, both Billy and Teddy, and Batwoman face horrifying monsters called Mother who raise fears of miscegenation and monstrous femininity, hinting at the dangers of destructive sexuality.

The comics maintain the public/private split on which homonormativity rests. This is not necessarily through the characters themselves but through their surrounding cast and the society these characters live in. The reader knows that these characters are gay, but the general public in the DC or Marvel universe does not. While their colleagues, family, and friends might know that they are gay, do the citizens of Gotham and New York know their heroes are gay? Doubtful. Kate Kane is an out lesbian, but is Batwoman in the closet? Billy and Teddy are openly committed to each other, but their allies, the adult Avengers, refer to them as friends. By divorcing the superheroes from the LGBTQIA+ community and having them remain in the closet, the comics isolate their superheroes. They present the gay superhero as an anomaly who needs to keep their sexuality in the closet when superhero-ing. While the incorporation of gay superheroes into the narrative promotes a more diverse and progressive attitude, it fails to construct a narrative that challenges heteronormativity as the foundation of hegemonic homophobia.

CHAPTER 4

Legacy, Community, and the Superhero of Color

This chapter grapples with Black or non-white superheroes and their relationship with whiteness through white communities, white partners, or the inheritance of a white legacy title. With whiteness being an essential and fundamental aspect of American culture, all non-white superheroes exist within a white hegemony. This chapter seeks to understand how the non-white superhero is positioned in relation to that white hegemony within the comic book. Two of the most notable Black male superheroes are the Falcon, who was the first African American superhero, and Luke Cage, the first Black superhero who did not have "Black" in his name *and* starred in a titular comic. This chapter discusses the Falcon's construction of the hero through his powers/abilities following the retconning of his origin story from a social worker to a brainwashed criminal in the context of blaxploitation and historical stereotypes of Black men. This first section also explores Luke Cage's blaxploitation roots in order to consider the evolution of Luke's relationship with his Black community. Kenneth Ghee considers the only "real" Black superhero to be a Black superhero that is culture bound and subverts whiteness' status quo by advocating for his culture, requiring him to unhook from whiteness.[1] Considering the need to unhook from whiteness, this chapter also analyzes Storm and Kamala Khan as Ms. Marvel. Examining the communities that Storm belongs to and is rejected from, as well as how Storm is positioned within them, this chapter will discuss Storm's relationship to whiteness and her community. The chapter then analyzes Ms. Marvel's representation of a young, female Pakistani American, her position within her community, and the question of how non-white femininity is positioned within the white heteropatriarchy.

Seeking the Black Male Superhero in the Falcon, the Black Captain America, and Luke Cage

First introduced in 1969, the Falcon entered a cultural landscape mired in antiwar protests following the Vietnam War and the civil rights movement. Throughout the early 1960s, there were no mainstream Black superheroes in self-titled comics, and the few Black characters that did exist appeared in comics dedicated to other, white characters. These comics often engaged with race, promoting racial unity based on color blindness. Whether someone had blue, green, purple, or Black skin had no impact on their abilities as a hero, comics proclaimed, and so they easily sidestepped engagement with real-life racism that white characters might benefit from. As Aldo J. Regalado writes, "In most cases, . . . African American characters were objectified and employed to express white concerns."[2] Comics championed against civil unrest and framed racism as a problem that could be defeated only if everyone involved, including Black people, could be reasonable. Comics rarely, if ever, engaged with the civil rights struggle from the point of view of a Black person. After all, Stan "Lee's primary objective was to entertain his audiences" and appeal to a broad consumer base. Therefore, "he made certain that Marvel's comics remained dramatic, exciting, and fun, with enough countercultural sentiment to keep them relevant but not enough to alienate more conservative fans."[3] Comics included references to poverty and "the man," and for the Falcon, a struggle to gain full parity with his white peers due to what he perceived as weaker abilities, but never explicitly articulated an antiracist agenda. While Sam does not explicitly link his "lower" status to his race, the terms he uses and the solution he presents hint at a racial element.

Sam first appeared in *Captain America #117* (1969) when Captain America and the Red Skull swapped bodies and Cap-as-Red-Skull was transported to Exile Island by Red-Skull-as-Cap with the power of the Cosmic Cube. When the Exiles, who are ruling the island and subjugating its native peoples, meet Cap-as-Red-Skull, they attempt to kill him. They are stopped by a falcon named Redwing, Sam Wilson's pet. Initially, Sam was a Harlem-born Black man and a former social worker, who had an affinity for birds and a well-trained falcon, Redwing. Answering a newspaper advertisement for workers, he'd traveled to Exile Island. Seeing what the Exiles were doing to the local population, he attempted to organize a rebellion. Captain America persuades him to put on a costume and adopt the moniker "the Falcon" to inspire and lead the locals. He also trains Sam, and together they defeat the Exiles. Once they go back to America, and Captain America's body has been restored, Sam and Captain America, or Steve Rogers, team up regularly. From 1971 until 1978, the series was billed as *Captain America and the Falcon*. This origin story was retconned in 1975, when Sam was revealed to be Snap, a mafia-connected criminal whose memories had been altered by the reality-warping Cosmic Cube, which also established a telepathic link between Sam and Redwing, courtesy of the Red Skull. Sam was then planted on Exile Island, poised to become Steve's perfect partner, and set to betray him at the most opportune moment.

The introduction of a criminal past achieves two things: it establishes Sam as a *victim* of the Red Skull and frames Sam's heroism as unnatural. Unlike Steve Rogers, whose heroic masculinity is innate, as discussed throughout chapter 1, Sam is a criminal who needs to be brainwashed into becoming a hero. While a criminal past is not a damaging character trait in and of itself, as many superheroes are former criminals atoning for past sins, it is telling that the first African American superhero was given such a past retroactively, during a time when blaxploitation was particularly popular. According to Novotny Lawrence, blaxploitation is a genre in which "the conflict operates as a metaphor in which whites represent the oppressive establishment."[4] Blaxploitation films traditionally included a Black protagonist, "who is both socially and politically conscious" and consistently challenges a white villain with a range of Black supporting characters in an urban setting.[5] These films included extreme violence committed by the protagonist in order to triumph over the oppressive establishment in all its forms. Additionally, "blaxploitation films frequently depict overt displays of black sexuality."[6] While these films engaged frankly with Black experiences in America, the term "blaxploitation" is now often used in a derogatory capacity, referring to the exploitation of the Black experience to generate financial profit that did not benefit Black communities. Furthermore, the increasingly excessive violence and nudity of the films eventually caused a backlash from Black audiences, who felt that blaxploitation reduced Black characters to violent stereotypes living in a violent community.[7] Like many art forms that were initially created by Black people for a Black audience, blaxploitation was co-opted by white institutional and cultural forces (Hollywood, white TV networks, comic publishing industries controlled by white people) and scrubbed of its most radical, political elements to become palatable to white audiences. Eventually, blaxploitation devolved into depicting crime and violence in an urban setting with Black characters as a form of trauma porn for white audiences.

Comics sought to capitalize on blaxploitation's popularity by introducing character elements that blaxploitation had made popular: violent and criminal Black male characters. While the comic did strip the more volatile elements to maintain the moral righteousness associated with traditional *Captain America* comics, as well as ignored blaxploitation's challenge of the white establishment, it completely reframed Sam's status as a hero. The introduction of a criminal past ties into the stereotype of all Black men as criminals and gangsters who require the injection of whiteness to become heroes. After all, it is the Nazi Red Skull who brainwashes Sam into becoming Steve's perfect partner and compels Sam to do good. Without the Red Skull, Sam might have remained a petty criminal. Instead, Sam becomes the protégé and partner of the white Steve Rogers, achieving superhero status. Throughout history, the subjugation of Black men has been justified through the claim that Black men are inherently violent and need white paternal intervention to become civilized. For Sam, this is made true.

After the cancellation of *Captain America and the Falcon* in 1978, Sam appeared as a member of various teams (e.g., the Defenders and the Avengers) in team-titled comics and remained a regular supporting character in various Captain America titles. He had a self-titled miniseries in 1983, but the continuity in that comic was erased in 2001. In 2014, Marvel announced that Sam would take over the mantle of Captain America, and in 2015 the series *Captain America: Sam*

Wilson (2015–2017) was launched. He went back to being the Falcon in 2017, with his own titular comic, which lasted only eight issues and was canceled in 2018. The most consistent context in which Sam appears is through his partnership with Captain America, who is the source of his heroism, which remains the defining element of his character.

In the first *Captain America and the Falcon* series (1971–1978), Sam and Steve live together while teaming up to protect the innocent people of their neighborhood. While the comic focuses on both characters equally, Sam consistently struggles with feelings of inadequacy. Compared with a (white) supersoldier, Sam Wilson is an ordinary human being, and all the training in the world cannot give him Captain America's enhanced strength or speed. For example, in *Captain America and the Falcon #169*, Sam is attacked by a group of men who run away when Steve shows up to help him. Sam asserts that the reason the men ran away is because Steve is Captain America, while Steve insists they ran because there were suddenly two of them.

> STEVE: Well . . . that was because there were *two* of us then.
>
> SAM: Bull! I'm sorry, man, but—*BULL!* We *both* know they were plain scared of your *power* and I didn't faze 'em one *bit!* We can't play hide-an'-seek with it any longer, Cap—If I'm gonna stay your *partner,* I have to be something more than a "costumed athlete!" Otherwise, I am to you what Redwing is to me: a *PET!!*[8]

Because of their unequal abilities, Sam does not consider himself an equal in their professional partnership. At this time, Sam is not the only non-superpowered individual serving on the Avengers (others include Iron Man and Hawkeye), but he seems to be the only one who keenly feels this inadequacy. The solution that Sam puts forward ties heavily into racial discourse. First, he insists that using technological compensation would level the playing field. Considering that Captain America's body is a technological or scientific product, as discussed in chapter 1, Sam and Steve would then both rely on scientific means to construct their superhero masculinity. Sam insists that the only person he could ask for help is T'Challa, the Black Panther. Like Sam, T'Challa is Black, and Sam explicitly does not want to rely on white assistance. This acknowledges that a racial dynamic exists between Steve and Sam, and between Sam and the other white superheroes. It hints at a white hegemony that Sam understands and seeks to undermine. This seemingly aligns Sam with Ghee's culture-bound superhero while simultaneously drawing on Black commonality. Sam claims that he and T'Challa have more in common than do Sam and the American Avengers because they are both Black, disregarding the fact that as the ruler of an African nation, T'Challa has a different cultural background and would have different racial experiences. The comic implies that the bonds of race supersede the bonds of nationality or cultural commonality and that Blackness is experienced the same way by all Black peoples everywhere.

Black Panther agrees to help Sam and they travel to Wakanda, where Black Panther designs "super-strong, *glider-wings*—Jet-powered from their *tips* by those wafer-thin *integrated circuits* feeding off a *sunlight-charged* power-pack—and all controlled by a direct link to my *brain*."[9] The wings fit into Sam's superhero theme, allowing him to fully inhabit his superhero persona. As they are wired directly into his brain, they are a bodily modification presented as if they were naturally occurring. In this sense Sam fulfills the requirements of superhero masculinity as established in chapter 1: a naturally appearing, scientifically enhanced superpowered phallic body. The addition of wings is especially significant because, as Adilifu Nama says, "Of all the superhero powers, the ability to fly literally and symbolically established the Falcon's agency and independence, in contrast to the landbound Captain America."[10] Not only do the wings serve as a signification of technologically infused masculinity provided by a Black man to another Black man, but they also elevate his status in the superhero hierarchy. While Sam's wings indicate a positive representation of Sam as a Black superhero through the special status they afford him, there are elements of his powers that are rooted in racist stereotypes. Aside from his physical abilities, developed by Captain America, Sam's other superpower is his telepathic link to Redwing, his pet falcon, and his telepathic command of all birds. This ability was implanted by the Red Skull, a Nazi supervillain from Steve's past. This is reminiscent of historical events where Black people were colonized and experimented on while furthering cultural narratives that normalize the brutalization of Black people. After all, Red Skull's modification of Sam's body is the cause of Sam's desire and ability to become a superhero. The narrative uses the violation of Black people as a vehicle for empowerment, which remains divorced from the context of white hegemony as the violator and beneficiary of this violence. In essence, the trauma enacted by whiteness is *required* for a Black man to be a superhero. Sam is powerful and a force for good *because* his Black body was violated and changed to fit standards set by a white man.

Because of this white construction of his superhero abilities, Sam is closer than many of his Black contemporaries to the masculine ideal that comics are infused with. His abilities are provided through technological innovation, and his close connection to Captain America, as well as his work for S.H.I.E.L.D. (Strategic Homeland Intervention, Enforcement and Logistics Division), connects him to the American military machine. The Marvel Cinematic Universe (MCU) further expanded this connection by making Sam a former U.S. paratrooper. Moreover, his body follows the inverted triangle shape necessary for the construction of the hypermasculine body, as demonstrated by figure 4.1.[11]

While the exact color pattern of the suit has changed across artists and comics, the red and white have been a staple of Sam's costume since very early in his publication history.[12] In the iteration depicted in figure 4.1, the white band around his hips functions as an Underwear of Power equivalent; and while it is not always present, most forms of the costume have some kind of detailing in the crotch area that functions in much the same way. The spreading of the wings adds bulk to the shoulders, accentuating the inverted triangle shape of his torso. Sam becomes a Black superhero who embodies the specific attributes of hegemonic masculinity that white male superheroes promote. However, Sam does not possess a chevron,

Figure 4.1. The Falcon. *Source*: Christopher Priest, Joe Bennet, and Jack Jadson, *Captain America and the Falcon #007* (New York: Marvel Comics, 2014). © 2014 Marvel Comics.

which denies him access to merchandising opportunities and their associated cultural capital in the world outside of comics. Black superheroes, even when they have nearly all of the same requirements of superhero masculinity as white superheroes, do not have access to the phallic body or mainstream popularity and recognition.[13] Both the Underwear of Power and the chevron work together to emphasize the inverted triangle body shape necessary for the construction of the hypermasculine. Sam's close adherence to the ideal, although he marginally falls short, provided him with the opportunity to embody one of the most popular and iconic superheroes ever: Captain America.

In 2014, the effects of the supersoldier serum were neutralized and Steve started aging rapidly. Subsequently, he picked Sam to become the next Captain America. Sam dresses in a modified version of the costume and takes up Steve's shield, which has long been used to symbolize Captain America. However, he keeps his wings and is still recognized as the Falcon by the other characters. The inheritance of the Captain America title by a Black man is significant, not only due to the high-tier status of the Captain America title but also due to the events of *Captain America: Truth* (2003), which explains how the supersoldier serum was initially tested on African American soldiers and brought about the Black Captain America, Isaiah Bradley, before Steve Rogers became Captain America. Because the military institution did not value the lives and bodies of Black people, their bodies were used to test the serum until it was deemed safe for white consumption. As a result, Isaiah Bradley was the only surviving member of his company. Steve essentially inherited a perfected means of masculinization from the suffering of Black people.[14] When Steve passes on the shield and the identity of Captain America, this narrative comes full circle: from the African American Isaiah Bradley to the white American Steve Rogers to the African American Sam Wilson. But, the origin stories of both Black Captain Americas involve the use of white science and power, the torture of the Black body, and nonconsensual experimentation. The Black body becomes heroic as it is infused with whiteness. Provided with the exterior trappings of whiteness, the Captain America title, costume, and shield, Sam can be read in two contrasting ways.[15]

The first would be that Black superheroes are fully equal to white superheroes and they can take on the mantle of established and high-tier white superheroes, which symbolizes the increasing parity between white and Black people in America, not only in social and economic terms but also in the performance of American masculinity. However, it can also be read as a Black man gaining legitimacy by performing whiteness. Has Sam, trained by a white man and inheriting his mantle, performed whiteness to such a successful degree that he has been given access to the highest status of American superheroes? Or is Sam a culture-bound superhero, a true Black superhero, and has that allowed him to achieve parity with white superheroes? The answer lies in what Sam does as Captain America.

As Captain America, Sam wears a costume similar to Steve's old one. It contains both the star as the chest chevron and the red-and-white paneling on the waist, highlighting the inverted triangle body shape, as seen in figure 4.2.[16] However, the first story line involving Sam as Captain America used the tagline "not my Captain America," which casts doubt on Sam's status, implying an inability to appeal to all Americans. The tagline echoes the phrase "not my president," which has been used to voice dissent by those who disagree with the election of a new American president. It expresses the sentiment that the speaker does not acknowledge the legitimacy of the sitting president owing to what that president represents, and was used during the presidencies of both Barack Obama and Donald Trump.[17] It is a phrase that speaks to the rejection of kinship with an authority figure or symbol. Through the tagline "not my Captain America," the reader is reminded that Sam is *a* Captain

Figure 4.2. Sam Wilson as Captain America. *Source*: Nick Spencer et al., *Captain America: Sam Wilson*, vol. 1, *Not My Captain America* (TPB) (New York: Marvel Comics, 2015). © 2015 Marvel Comics.

America, like Isaiah Bradley, William Burnside, and other copies, while Steve Rogers is *the* Captain America, the *real* one. It highlights how Sam's ascension to the role is cause for controversy as some people (both in the comic and in the real world) objected to a Black man embodying the national superhero.

During Sam's tenure as Captain America, Steve Rogers works as a consultant for S.H.I.E.L.D., and while he refuses to publicly condemn some of Sam's actions, the reader is privy to Steve and Sam's private disagreements, which reveal the racial tensions between the two. Sam insists that it is necessary for American society that he, as Captain America, speak out in favor of immigration and social reform, while Steve has faith that America will "do the right thing." He opines that superheroes taking public stances on political issues will diminish superheroes' abilities to serve all of the American people. This view is heavily influenced by whiteness, which frames the needs of oppressed minorities as "special interests" or inherently political in a way that the security of the rights of white citizens never is, as they are framed to be apolitical and universal. Essentially, whiteness promotes the idea that *not* acting on behalf of minorities is an apolitical stance that serves all of America. As a privileged white man, Steve can believe that, in the end, America will always represent truth and justice, democracy, and freedom. As a Black man, Sam is aware of America's historical and contemporary racial injustices and the difficulties of effecting legislative and social change. He understands that silence is compliance and that it is necessary for powerful cultural figures to speak out in support of minorities. Because Sam takes on a pro-immigrant political stance, publicly and as Captain America, it is clear that he adheres to Kenneth Ghee's concept of the culture-bound Black superhero. Ghee writes that "before we can determine if an *individual* Black fictional hero (created by Whites) is truly a Black hero at all," it must be determined if this hero is culture bound.[18] By culture bound, Ghee describes a hero who puts the needs of their own culture first, before the greater good. Essentially, the hero must not only defeat the villain but also challenge the status quo, which maintains the oppression of the hero's community and culture.[19] As Sam takes up one of the highest-tier superhero identities, he uses the political and social capital attached to that identity to speak out in solidarity with communities of color against the interests of the white status quo. However, the comic uses this to undermine Sam's ownership of the Captain America role through Steve's judgment of Sam's decision. When Steve, who is *the* Captain America and the white ideal that Sam is measured by, disagrees with Sam, it weakens support for him. Not only does Steve reaffirm that superheroes stay "above" politics, but he also reiterates the notion that the white man functions as the rational and objective norm while the Black man is emotional and selfishly divisive at a time when America needs to stand united against its enemies. This reiterates the often-used rhetoric that the enfranchisement of minority groups must wait until the national crisis of the time, in this case immigration, has passed.

Sam's internal monologue heavily implies that Captain America's attitude is old-fashioned and limited due to his own relative privilege. As Sam is the main character, the reader is encouraged to sympathize with his position by observing events from his point of view. However, while this is Sam's book, Steve's power as the original Captain America and its associated influence over the audience should not be underestimated. Of course, the way a comic speaks to the audience depends not only on the cultural forces that surround its production and reception but also on the social strata of the audience and their own particular context. It is worth noting that not all readers would receive the message positively or at all. A conservative audience might agree with Steve and read this as a fundamental failure on Sam's part to live up to the title. A progressive audience might see that Steve's perspective is limited and his inaction actively prevents the liberation of oppressed minorities. Regardless, by 2017, Steve's youth was restored and he took back the title while Sam returned to being the Falcon. In the face of a white challenger, the Black superhero can no longer claim ownership of the white legacy or role. While Sam did enact a culture-bound point of view, this was not enough to secure his ownership of Captain America. Perhaps this is for the best, as the role of the Falcon is Sam's alone, which may say more than a borrowed suit.

While Sam was the first African American superhero, Luke Cage was the first African American superhero to have a titular comic without the tag "Black" in his superhero name in *Luke Cage, Hero for Hire* (1972–1974). The series was rebranded as *Luke Cage, Power Man* in 1974 and ran until 1978, when Marvel changed the series to *Power Man and Iron Fist* when Luke Cage and Danny Rand decided to work together. This title remained in publication until 1986, when the series was canceled. *Luke Cage, Hero for Hire* was born in an era of municipal disinvestment as well as the emergence of benign neglect, a policy pushed by Sen. Daniel Patrick Moynihan (D-NY). Designed to "release" some of the tension in white communities caused by white jealousy of the gains of the civil rights movement, municipal and benign neglect allowed municipalities and local governments to divert funds away from poor communities. During the 1960s and the 1970s, when Black people moved into a (white) neighborhood, white people tended to abandon it as they considered their neighborhood "lost" and ensured that any federal or state contributions to municipal funds were rerouted, causing the decay of the neighborhood's municipal services and facilities.[20] The defunding of Black communities locked Black people into generational poverty, while the cultural debate framed poverty as caused by Black men's biological inferiority and welfare programs fostering dependence on government handouts. In response, the Nixon administration furthered a policy of benign neglect, which rested heavily on neoliberalism's insistence that economic prosperity required noninterference from the government.

Lisa Duggan discusses how neoliberalism has increasingly defined the federalist state as a mode of noninterference, safeguarding the freedom of the market. It limits the way the state can directly influence public life as it prioritizes economic prosperity through the mechanism of the free market.[21] Moynihan considered economic parity to be the true gateway to solving the "African American problem," which had been discussed too frequently in terms of political and legislative progress. Instead, it was time to allow the progress achieved in the 1960s to take effect while dismantling welfare programs, which created dependency on government handouts and prevented Black communities from managing their own local initiatives to alleviate poverty. Therefore, the best way for communities to achieve economic parity was to simply allow them to engage with the free market without government interference.[22] In reality, this allowed the government to disavow any responsibility for the conditions of Black communities. In effect, this trapped African Americans in cycles of poverty as schools were underfunded while a lack of investment in infrastructure dried up local businesses and employment opportunities, and a lack of public transport physically prevented people from finding work outside the neighborhood. By trapping and funneling Black people into these communities, whites could maintain segregation even when it became illegal and keep Black people out of suburbs and affluent urban communities. This context gave birth to the prison industrial complex, the popularity of blaxploitation films, and Luke Cage.

The first two series, *Luke Cage, Hero for Hire* and *Luke Cage, Power Man*, initially focused on Luke's past as a convicted criminal and his struggle to become part of the community in Harlem, pay his bills, and build a romantic relationship with Claire Temple, while his past continued to haunt him. Most of the surrounding cast and members of the community were Black, and while white characters did exist, they were rarely the sole focus of the plotline. Additionally, story lines frequently dealt with racism. For instance, *Luke Cage, Hero for Hire #1* (1972) covers the abuse Luke faces in prison from the white guards, who consider his "hard" and calm demeanor, as well as his refusal to work for them, as "uppity," obviously referencing the racist rhetoric that Black people need to "know their place."[23] At the same time, Luke's fellow Black inmates consider Luke to be too Tom-ish, referencing Harriet Beecher Stowe's novel *Uncle Tom's Cabin* (1852), which gave rise to the use of "Uncle Tom" as a derogatory phrase to describe a Black person whose behavior highlighted their acceptance of their inferior status while worshipping or catering to whites as their betters. These markers of racial awareness continue to pop up in the series' subsequent story lines. For instance, in *Luke Cage, Power Man #28* (1975), a large corporation owned by white people hires Black people to harass the Black community as a cover for its assassination of whistleblowers, trusting that no one will find a crime wave in a Black neighborhood suspicious.[24] In *Luke Cage, Power Man #32* (1976), Alex Simmons, a Black man who moves into a white neighborhood, is a victim of arson; and rather than helping, his white neighbors watch and are relieved that the Black man will have to leave their neighborhood. As a result of the arson, one of Alex's children dies before Luke arrives to assist. The villain, Wildfire, is eventually caught and screams: "You think because you're Black, you're the only ones that got any rights! Well, we got 'em too, understand."[25] This clearly references the violent methods used by white suburbs throughout the 1960s and 1970s to keep their neighborhoods white, a movement justified by rhetoric that focused on a white father's *right* to protect his family and choose/control his neighborhood.[26] It also speaks to the white backlash against the advances of the civil rights movement and how the dismantling of privilege is often experienced as an encroachment on civil rights. In this series, enemies were often rich white men or Black gangsters who had grown up in poverty, trapped in a vicious circle of arrest-prison-release. The narratives touched on racism-motivated crimes, the inhuman attitudes toward Black lives by institutions, and the distrust between Black community members and the police, who were not always portrayed positively (despite Luke's tentative working relationship with the white detective Rafael Scarfe). However, the narrative struggled to articulate the structural aspects of these issues and focused on the individual actions of a single person, often influencing scared, gullible, or desperately poor people. It did not identify whiteness itself as a structural part of American culture that systematically worked to destabilize and impoverish communities of color.

Time and again, the reader finds Luke on the side of the community and the victims of large corporations, even at the cost of his own paycheck. As discussed previously, Ghee requires the "real" Black superhero to prioritize his own culture and community of color over the maintenance of the white status quo. In this series, Luke helps and fights for his community, but only those individuals who have been victimized and who reach out for help. Luke is not a proactive superhero who seeks to actively better his community. The resolution of Luke's cases is always a return to the status quo, which relies on the ongoing oppression of Black people to maintain whiteness, instead of an attempt to change the status quo. Most superheroes function in this capacity. They are the protectors of the community against supervillains who seek to control or destroy the community as it is. Villains seek to change the status quo, and superheroes fight to maintain it.[27] The culture-bound superhero stands in contrast to this static and conservative superhero. However, Luke does not. While he comes close to functioning as a true Black superhero, fighting for a minority community against rich and more powerful enemies, he does little to advance the conditions or interests of his community as a whole in the face of its structural oppression.

It is through this contradictory history that Adilifu Nama considers Luke Cage to be "the superhero that has epitomized Blaxploitation" and yet simultaneously also the "most inherently political and socially profound black superhero to ever emerge."[28] As discussed previously, blaxploitation is a genre that often featured a politically conscious hero, whose sexual and violent prowess was unmatched, within an urban setting. Luke Cage's series had all of these elements, and, although the comics often failed to articulate a direct critique of institutionalized whiteness and the damage that benign neglect and white supremacy did to the community, it did have story lines that actively investigated the pain and suffering of Black people at the hands of racist whites. When blaxploitation's popularity dwindled, Luke Cage's sales also dwindled, and the series was rebranded as *Power Man and Iron Fist* in 1978.

James Owsley, also known as Christopher Priest, took over the series in the early 1980s, when the series de-emphasized the blaxploitation elements, increased Luke's vocabulary, and introduced the "Sweet Christmas!" catch phrase. In these comics, Luke is increasingly removed from his Black community. The comics split their attention between Luke's Harlem base and Danny Rand's apartment in a swanky white neighborhood uptown. The villains they face include Russian spies infiltrating the New York City Ballet, European crime bosses attempting to set up operations in New York, and mystical villains from the city of K'un-Lun, where Danny gained his powers. One of the most consistent narrative elements is the presence of soldiers and the military—specifically soldiers who find it impossible to return to civilian life and go on a rampage or join a private army as mercenaries, obviously tapping into mainstream audiences' increased dissatisfaction with the Vietnam War. The stories still take place in New York, but the surrounding cast is less racially diverse. While people comment on Luke and Danny's odd partnership and Luke is, at times, targeted by strangers because he is Black, racist hate crimes are far less present in this 1978–1986 series.

In the move away from blaxploitation elements, the comics lose the Black community and Luke's social and political consciousness. While Luke is consistently framed as "cooler" and more "with it" compared with his white partner, this mostly serves to play up Danny's lack of coolness to humorous effect, instead of an indication of Luke's political understanding. It also serves to underline Danny's cluelessness concerning American culture, as someone who grew up in K'un-Lun, and high-class status. Danny is white and rich, and he enjoys classical music. He says that he would be embarrassed by the attentions of fangirls, which Luke says he would enjoy in *Power Man and Iron Fist #86* (1982). Danny is often swayed by people's sob stories. Luke is Black and working-class, and he listens to hip-hop. He enjoys female attention. He is a harsher judge of character, and, while he seemingly understands societal factors for crime, he also considers people's inability to resist the pressures of modern, urban life as a moral and personal failure. The presentation of the white partner, raised in a foreign city and a stranger to many American customs, as the more civilized and forgiving one, compared with the Black character as angrier and having an easily provoked temper, plays into stereotypes of the angry and violent Black man being guided and controlled by the civilized white man. While, superficially, the comic shows us a Black, American born and raised superhero guiding an estranged American and helping him assimilate back into American life, we also have a deeper narrative about the white American teaching the Black man restraint and wisdom. Combined with the loss of his culture and community-bound narrative elements, the partnership takes Luke further away from politically impactful representation.

After the series' cancellation in 1986, Luke Cage did not return until 1992, when he appeared in a limited *Cage* series (1992–1993). In 1996, Luke appeared in a new *Heroes for Hire* series, which was only nineteen issues. Iron Fist also appeared on this team, as well as She-Hulk, Human Torch, Hercules, Black Knight, and others. Power Man and Iron Fist remained in charge of the team, but with the increased cast size, there were fewer stories focused on them. Cage continued to appear in group titles such as *New Avengers* (2005–2016) and *Thunderbolts* (1997–2003, 2005–2012, 2012–2014), or as a supporting character in comics such as *Alias* (2001–2004), *The Pulse* (2004–2006), and *Daredevil* (1964–ongoing). In 2010, a new *Power Man and Iron Fist* came out as a limited series with nineteen issues, ending in 2011. However, a new character called Victor Alvarez was using the Power Man name, and Luke Cage made only a brief appearance. It was not until 2016 that *Power Man and Iron Fist* returned with both Luke Cage and Danny Rand. However, this ran for only fifteen issues and was canceled in 2018. The miniseries was a mixed success, and while it did have characters reference the school-to-prison pipeline and the disproportionately high number of African Americans trapped in the prison industrial complex, it did not thoroughly or consistently engage with race.

Unlike the superheroes that precede him, Luke Cage has not experienced an increase in body size throughout the decades of his publication. His torso and body size have remained mostly consistent, except for the artwork of the limited 1990s Luke Cage series, where his body was displayed as thicker and broader overall. While we can witness an increase in detailed musculature, as with most comics, and the presence of the inverted triangle shape, Luke has always been drawn as incredibly big, even before the bodybuilding craze. This body fits into the image of the Big Black Brute that has been part of the American landscape since slavery and its associated anxieties of Black uprisings and violent reprisal.[29] It ties into the racist idea that Black bodies possess an animal physicality that white bodies do not. In contrast, the white body is cerebral, civilized, and controlled, especially when these white bodies are powerful, as they are the result of hard work and determination, as discussed in chapter 1. The Black body, however, is violent and animalistic through its muscularity and physical power. According to Ronald L. Jackson II, "The brute was almost always a tall, dark-skinned, muscular, athletically built character and often either bald or with a short haircut."[30] Luke certainly fits this description, with his original Afro shrinking until he becomes completely bald in the early 2000s. Furthermore, the costume that Luke used in the first series is slowly dismantled throughout the years of publication until Luke's standard getup in any *Avengers* comic is a T-shirt and a pair of jeans. Blair Davis writes how the very first issue of Luke Cage, *Hero for Hire* (1972), invites the reader to look at Luke's body and its Blackness as well as his costume through the cover and an introductory scene where Luke purchases his costume. This includes a yellow shirt open to his belly button, black pants, wide-brimmed boots, a silver headband, wrist chains, and a large chain wrapped around his middle like a belt. Initially, the comic admits that this is a hokey costume, but it acknowledges that such hokeyness is required to identify Luke as a superhero. Davis writes that "Cage therefore intends his costume to serve as a sort of uniform, one that identifies him as a protector, rather than an offender, and as a member of a higher rank that typically carries with it a certain amount of social status, respect and/or fear—much as the uniform of a police officer does."[31] The *Power Man and Iron Fist* comics certainly keep up with this theme as several scenes pause to allow Luke and Danny to change into their costumes before the action starts, highlighting how the costumes allow Luke and Danny to become Power Man and Iron Fist.

Following the discussion of Luke's original costume, Davis goes on to catalog how, in every subsequent iteration, the elements that were part of Luke's superhero identity, the Power Man, are stripped away. Increasingly, Luke stands out as the only character in the New Avengers not to have a costume. On the one hand, the removal of the costume or uniform is understood as a rejection of blaxploitation. The first issue's introductory scene of Luke selecting the costume highlights its inherently political nature and its removal as a depoliticizing of the Black hero and the Black body. It forces the reader to deal with Blackness directly, and yet, in the current political climate and the Black body's existence within white hegemony, the Black body is continually politicized and policed. The original costume was chosen to function as a quick explanation, a shortcut that immediately explained Luke's mission and presence in privileged spaces. Within the white hegemony, the Black person is continually asked to justify their existence and presence, and, without the costume, Luke's immediate justification against this racist demand is removed. Does this free him or put even greater pressure on him as a Black man on a team of superheroes? If we consider Luke sans costume to be depoliticized, does that make him less radical, less effective as a Black superhero? Or does it liberate him from the pressure of existing as a political body, a figurehead of representation, burdened with "saying something about the Black experience" in ways that his white peers do not have to speak to a racial experience? Effectively, the trend to consistently dress Luke down contributes to Luke's lack of cultural capital or recognizability.

The costume that Luke used in the first series, while hokey, is also not the standard spandex and mask configuration, marking him as an unusual superhero (especially compared with Iron Fist's more traditional getup). He is also lacking both the Underwear of Power and the chest chevron. While Marvel has more experimental heroes who lack the Underwear of Power and the chevron, its most prominent superheroes have some form of both. The current Luke Cage does not have a costume at all. Lacking an identifiable chevron locks Luke out of the merchandising possibilities that a chevron provides. Essentially, without a chevron, Luke is locked out of cultural capital that creates an instantly recognizable and marketable superhero outside of comic book fan communities. Lack of recognizability leads to a lack of popularity, which leads to cancellation or a lack of future publication—a cycle that is hard to break.

It is not surprising that two of the most important Black superheroes are known predominantly through their relationship with a white character. Both Sam Wilson and Luke Cage establish long-lasting partnerships with white superheroes, through whom the radical nature of the Black superhero can be undermined. The presence of the white character ensures that the spotlight is not solely on the Black character while simultaneously providing a "good white" character that softens the blow of any racism perpetrated by other white characters, preventing any white panic among a (white) audience. Through the white character, the Black character becomes more acceptable and can be kept in line.

Womanhood and Community: Storm and Ms. Marvel's Intersectionality

As discussed in the introduction, the X-Men have often been credited as an analogy for discrimination and oppression based on sex, gender, and race, even when most of the X-Men were straight, white men. In 1975, ten years after the first

X-Men were published in 1965, the X-Men gained their first Black member, Storm, also known as Ororo Munroe. Storm appeared in many X-Men–focused comics, such as *Uncanny X-Men* (1963–ongoing), *X-treme X-Men* (2001–2004, 2012–2013), and *Astonishing X-Men* (2004–2013). There have also been a few miniseries focusing primarily on Storm, such as *Ororo: Before the Storm* (2015) and *Storm* (2014–2015). While Storm is not the first Black woman to ever appear in comic books, or the first Black woman to wear a superhero costume, she did gain "recognition for being the first Black woman to be relevant in a comic book from a renowned publishing house," as Lucas do Carmo Dalbeto and Ana Paula Oliveira note.[32] Carolyn Cocca also points out that Storm was the first Black superhero to lead a superhero team and the first woman to be a superhero leader. It is important to note that Storm was added, along with a few other characters, to diversify the comic (even as the team remained mostly white and male). The 1975 relaunch of the *Uncanny X-Men* attracted a steady readership with medium-level sales. As the bulk of the characters presented a normative model (straight, white male), the comic provided the necessary conservative context to support Black and female superheroes while avoiding a conservative fan backlash and simultaneously attracting audiences looking for more progressive story lines. Storm thus benefited from being a member of a white, male-dominated team as it cemented her position as a mainstream and culturally relevant superhero through the increasing popularity of the *Uncanny X-Men* comics. Additionally, as Cocca states, Storm's status as a Black woman was also mitigated through her European facial features and hair as well as her isolation from a Black community.[33] Cocca points out that in the white-and-black reprints of the 1975 series, it is almost impossible to identify Storm as a Black character.[34] Like many Black superheroes, Storm is what Ghee calls a "white [hero] in blackface," which depoliticizes Storm's identity through the lack of "a sustaining black family, a viable black community, and continuity within black history or black culture." Essentially, Storm and other heroes in white face are "represented as black in color only while operating in all-white cultural context or world view."[35] There are a few attempts within the comic to engage with Storm's Blackness, but these are often only stereotypical and superficial.

Storm's very first appearance immediately uses African stereotypes lifted almost directly from Tarzan films and jungle comics. Responding to a plea for help to "Ororo, Great Goddess of the Storm," she appears dressed in a white loincloth using only her long, white hair to cover her breasts.[36] Her jewelry and headpiece are sufficiently exotic, along with her naked skin, to frame her as the tribal Other. Using her powers, she lifts into the sky, and with her hair and loincloth flapping around in the breeze, only a few strands of hair cover her nipples while most of her legs, belly, chest, and arms are exposed. After this sexualized display, Xavier arrives and explains to Ororo that she is not a goddess but a mutant. He says, "You have a *land*, Ororo—and people who *adore* you. I offer you a *world*—and people who may *fear* you, *hate* you—but people who *need* you nonetheless. The world I offer is not *beautiful*, but it is *real*. Far more real than the *fantasy* you are living *now*."[37]

In just a few lines, Xavier reframes Storm's actions, which save the lives of her fellow countrymen, and her status, as a powerful leader, as nothing more than a fantasy. Offering her civilization, he persuades Storm to leave behind people who love her, the only community she has known to support her, and let them fend for themselves so that she may work for a predominantly white community, which is feared and loathed by the white hegemony. She, too, will be feared and loathed because she is a mutant, but not, supposedly, because she is a Black woman. Storm leaves behind a position of power in order to serve a greater good, determined by a dominant, white hegemony. In a sense, this is demanded of all the X-Men, but Storm's intersectional identity complicates this because, unlike her white, male teammates, her relationship with the mutant community is also complex as she is Othered by them through her Blackness.

Like other Black superheroes, such as Black Panther, Storm fits into the ideal of the "noble savage," an idealized representative of the racial Other, through her heritage as a Kenyan princess. The term "noble savage" was first made popular in the late 1800s and denotes a racial Other who symbolizes the inherent goodness of mankind in its simplest and most natural state, freed from civilization and its corruption. Noble savage characters often appeared in both pro-slavery and anti-slavery narratives, perpetuating racist stereotypes about Black people's natural inferiority. These narratives implied that Black people needed a white patriarch to domesticate them so that they would not be corrupted by modern civilization, which was either prevented or caused by slavery. The noble savage often appeared as royalty or African nobility, representing the pinnacle of the Black man's possible racial development. He existed in a racist racial hierarchy, placed above the regular Black man, whose natural state was closer to that of animals, but lower than the lowest class of white men. Royal status was used to promote the idea of the exceptional Black who, unlike other Black people, has enough inherited nobility to be capable of education by the white patriarchy. Storm, as the daughter of a Kenyan princess, fits into this stereotype, which reframes her mutant powers as part of a specific African, racial heritage instead of the next stage of human evolution, like white mutants.

According to the comics, Storm is the last in a long line of Kenyan priestesses who all had white hair and blue eyes and were capable of weather magic. By reframing Storm's powers as an inherited ability shared among her Black ancestors, the narrative engages with stereotypes about Black people being closer to nature, animals, and spirituality compared with evolved, white mutants. As Jeffrey A. Brown points out, Storm's powers fit into a trend of Black female superheroes whose "powers 'explicitly associated with exoticized notions of Africa, nature, noble savagery and a variety of dark content themes.'"[38] Her powers are also closely tied to her emotional state, and there are several moments where she inadvertently influences the weather. As Cocca highlights, this link "positions her as yet another female for whom both emotion and power are control issues."[39] Mutant powers are centered in the body, and when the mutant identity intersects with the female body, these powers often become excessive, as discussed in chapters 2 and 3.

Extremely powerful mutant women or mutant signifiers of femininity eventually become a threat that needs to be destroyed or controlled. The only way Storm can avoid such destruction is to learn control over her powers and gain scientific understanding of weather patterns from Professor Xavier, the powerful white patriarch of the X-Men, which fits into racist narratives claiming that powerful Black (and female) people must be controlled by white men.

Initially, Storm struggles to fit in with the X-Men, until she becomes friends with Jean, who, as Dalbeto and Oliveira point out, becomes a civilizing influence. Jean helps Storm adjust to Western society—for example, she explains to Storm why she cannot swim naked in the public pool.[40] Throughout this period, Storm enacts white stereotypes about behavior and customs in Black Africa and is gently corrected by the white woman in the group, supporting a narrative where the savage needs to be civilized by whiteness. While Jean is the prim and proper white woman, Storm is the Other who is racialized in order to sexualize her for the male audience. Most of the elements used to mark her as a racial Other are the same elements used to make her sexy, such as wanting to swim naked in the pool and her costume. Like the costumes of many other female characters, but unlike that of her female colleague Jean Grey, Storm's costume is sexually titillating and leaves her exposed with little consideration for the practicality required during battle. Cocca admits that Colossus—a fellow male team member—also has a costume that shows a large amount of skin. But, as Cocca emphasizes, the skin is exposed in order to highlight his musculature.[41] While exposed musculature can be read erotically, and certainly will be read that way by several audiences, it mostly works to underline Colossus's power and ability to turn his skin into steel, while Storm's costume is sexualizing and undermines her position as a powerful subject instead of a sexualized object.

In the 1980s, Storm was redesigned and assumed a more punk aesthetic with a Mohawk and leather pants. This style coincided with an exploration of her darker and angrier side, and the comics often portrayed her as a powerful figure, which appealed to an increasing female fan base.[42] Despite this look's popularity and cultural resonance, the 1990s saw Storm redesigned to fit into the bad girl art mold, which was increasingly popular. Alongside the rise of comic book specialty shops, which decreased the diversity of the community through gatekeeping, *Uncanny X-Men* became saturated with semi-naked women who had unrealistic bodily proportions. As Cocca writes, "Increasingly in the 1990s, and into the 2000s, superhero comics niche-marketed to the assumed core audiences of white heterosexual males, and the *X-men* franchise was at the forefront of the trend."[43] While Storm was increasingly dressed in catsuits that completely covered her, the suits were drawn as if she were naked, as is the case for many female (and male) superheroes.

Dalbeto and Oliveira discuss how, even though Storm's characterization is often burdened with stereotypical sexist and racist imagery associated with Black women, such as "Strength, mysticism, sexuality, and exotic and mysterious beauty," in the end, "it is important to stress that she carries traits that correspond to feminist ideals, such as equality between the sexes, women's independence and a multidimensional approach to female characters."[44] However, the comics never explicitly engage with the discrimination she would face as a Black, mutant woman.[45] The intersectionality of Storm's identity is often overlooked in the comics. She is primarily a mutant, and, in the Marvel universe, the mutant community is principally a white minority, used to serve as analogies for race, gender, and sex, but using white, male, and straight characters to dodge real engagement with these issues. This becomes clear through the mutant community's rejection of Storm once her Blackness becomes relevant through her marriage to the Black Panther, T'Challa, especially as depicted in *Civil War: Black Panther* (2007). Initially, when Storm and Black Panther were first created by Marvel, they did not have any kind of relationship. In 1980, Chris Claremont introduced the idea that Storm and T'Challa had briefly met when Storm was twelve years old in *Marvel Team-Up #100*. This became the basis for the retconning of the couple's history in 2006, which made them childhood sweethearts as a prelude to their marriage. As a wedding between a Kenyan princess and an African king, their marriage perpetuates noble savage stereotypes, and the "inevitability" of their union through the childhood sweetheart story line neatly sidesteps any fears of miscegenation that arise out of Storm's previous relationships with white partners, such as Wolverine.

The depiction of Storm's marriage throughout the *Civil War: Black Panther* story line also fits into the cultural view of marriage as consuming the identity of the woman. Historically, in Western society, a wife became her husband's legal property upon marriage, and the married couple was considered to be one body: that of the husband. Throughout her marriage, Storm struggles to reconcile her own identity with the one required of her as Black Panther's wife and queen. When Black Panther is told, on several occasions, to control his wife, neither Storm nor Black Panther explicitly addresses this sexist presumption that the wife represents her husband and needs to be controlled by him. When Storm intervenes in a fight between Black Panther and Dr. Doom, Black Panther is outraged that she did not let him handle the fight alone. In the ensuing panels, instead of engaging with Black Panther's anger at her "overstepping" her bounds, his damaged pride at needing to be rescued by his wife, or his sexist attempt to cut her out of the battle between him and Dr. Doom, Storm simply kisses him and all is forgiven.

In *Civil War*, the Superhero Registration Act (SRA) is introduced at the federal level and requires all superheroes to register their superpowers and civilian identities with the government. This legislation leads to a break in the superhero community when some superheroes decide to comply, seeing legislation as the only way to ensure accountability, and others refuse, believing that registration only leads to government control. Other countries follow America's example, with debates on civil liberties and "the superhero tradition" entering the global stage. When Storm, as the queen of Wakanda, reaches out to the mutant community and asks them to speak out against the SRA, Emma Frost, as the white, female leader of the mutant community, refuses. Storm claims that if she were still a leader in the mutant community, they would challenge the SRA. Emma's refusal to publicly condemn the SRA is poignant as the mutant community has often come under threat by a registration act, which is considered to be the first step in the direction of eventual segregation, followed by genocide. But Emma refuses because of the superhero community's refusal to come to mutants' aid when they were threatened. Emma's refusal to speak out against a nationwide registration act for all superheroes perpetuates the idea that minority communities cannot set aside their own agendas and petty squabbles in favor of solidarity. Furthermore, Storm's marriage to Black Panther and her subsequent stepping down as leader of the X-Men expelled her from the white mutant community and she has lost the right to speak for them. This presents minority communities as made up of individuals who have completely singular identities, making it impossible for people to belong to several communities or for communities to overlap.

Storm's complex identity is always reduced to a single identity, the construction of which depends on context and whatever is convenient for the other people in her life. When she and Black Panther visit the White House during the civil war crisis, Iron Man attempts to force Storm into registering as a mutant and a superhero because she is an American citizen and still subject to American law. Black Panther claims that Storm is now the queen of Wakanda and has diplomatic immunity. He considers the request for registration an affront to Wakandan sovereignty. However, Wakandan officials consider Storm to be an American interloper. Not only are Wakandan elders outraged that T'Challa did not chose a Wakandan bride, but they also believe it is impossible for Storm to become Wakandan because of her American nationality. Both the white, American mutant community and the Black, Wakandan community resist Storm's multiplicity and attempt to frame her as part of one single community. This allows them to either reject or claim ownership over Storm, depending on their personal or community-based agendas. This reduction of her complex identity eventually causes Storm to be rejected by her husband. During the events of *AvX* (2012), the Phoenix Force comes to Earth and possesses several mutants, who attack nonmutant communities, including Wakanda. As a result, Black Panther divorces Storm. Even as Storm points out that she had nothing to do with the destruction of the capital, T'Challa rejects her on the basis of her mutant identity alone. When Wakanda is at war with representatives of the mutant community, Black Panther prioritizes Storm's mutant identity and expels her from the Black community. In Black Wakanda, she is considered a white mutant. In the white mutant community, she is thought of as (Black) Wakandan.

Considering Ghee's concept of the true Black superhero prioritizing the needs of Black culture and community over the conservation of the status quo, it is difficult for Storm to be read as a Black superhero because she is most often placed within a predominantly white community and she has left or been rejected from the Black communities she has belonged to (e.g., Kenyan, Wakandan). By failing to engage with the intersectionality of the discrimination she would face as a Black, mutant woman, the comics usually present Storm as performing whiteness. The collapse of her intersectionality into the singular mutant identity, with its loyalty and ties to the predominantly white mutant community, compromises her representation of the Black superhero, not only because of Ghee's culture-bound superhero but also because it erases the lived experience of Black women. X-Men comics tend to depict only fictional forms of discrimination instead of engaging with actual, real-life examples and situations, which limits their ability to comment on racism. This is very clear in the *Storm* comic (2014–2015).

The narrative takes Storm back to Kenya and touches on her past as a thief, the failed mutant community Utopia, and a struggle against a corrupt American politician. In none of these story lines does the narrative explicitly touch on Storm's identity as a Black woman, although it tries to by incorporating events that would be especially poignant for a Black woman to face and deal with. However, because these events are never explicitly linked to Blackness and are always related to mutant-ness, the comic falls short. In this manner, the comic limits itself to depicting fictional discrimination even as it attempts to serve as an analogy for real-life discrimination. For example, in *Storm #007* (2014), Storm is illegally detained and thinks of her (Black, female) interrogator, "She seems nice enough. But so *typical*... thinking *mutants* are just the sum of their *powers*."[46] In this quote, Storm clearly points out that a common form of discrimination faced by mutants is to be reduced to their abilities, which the comics themselves do by giving all the X-Men names (and identities) based on their superpowers. This echoes forms of discrimination faced by other minorities, including Black people, but because it mentions only mutants, the specificity of Black discrimination is lost. The comics fail to identify white hegemony as the source of discrimination and oppression because the person enacting (fictional) racism against Storm is also Black, which seems especially tone-deaf considering the overpolicing of Black communities, the disproportionate incarceration rates of Black people, and the consistent acts of police brutality against Black people by white police officers, who are often exempt from legal repercussions.[47] Hence, Storm's illegal arrest and detainment is specifically poignant because she is a Black woman. The comic's refusal to explicitly engage with Storm's lived experience being uniquely connected to her Black identity, instead of her mutant one, seems incongruous when looking at other story lines in the comics where Storm attempts to help drought-ridden communities in Kenya and helps a young Mexican student reunite with her family. Additionally, the comic depicts the crowds supporting Storm during her illegal arrest as more Black than white, echoing the makeup of the Black Lives Matter protests.[48] The comic implicitly touches on these issues and, thus, misses the opportunity to say something truly meaningful by accurately engaging with the way that the discrimination faced by Black (mutant) women is intersectional and specific.

The X-Men comics fail to identify white hegemony as the source of institutionalized racism and the destruction of non-white communities *because* they are an analogy and only offer depictions of explicit racism aimed at a fictional minority. The comic also falls into the trap of framing minority groups as inherently self-destructive, which is a stereotype perpetuated by white hegemony in order to normalize its violence against these communities and render them invisible. When surveying the ruins of Utopia, an artificial island constructed to lie in the San Francisco Bay to house all mutants, Storm thinks, "We called it *Utopia* and then we *killed* it. Fighting amongst ourselves. I shouldn't have been surprised. It's what I've seen all my life, wherever I go . . . oppressed people destroying each other instead of their overlords."[49] While Storm's words do imply that there *is* an oppressor, the comic again fails to identify the oppressor as white hegemony, with its strategies of folding in and racial bribes, which encourage minority groups to punch down on each other to gain entry into privileged spaces by reaffirming a racist hierarchy. The comics make a point that there is an oppressor but offer nothing substantial about this oppressor or strategies for resistance, which leaves us only with minority communities as self-destructive and divided. Therefore, *Storm* follows the ideological narrative of most *X-Men* comics, shying away from identifying white hegemony as a destructive, oppressing force that minority communities have to placate or assimilate into for survival.

Comics perpetuate the idea that intersectionality is impossible. Storm's prioritization of her mutant identity over her Black one fits into historical expectations of Black women, who were forced to set aside their Blackness when participating in the women's movement dominated by straight, white women or who "have been expected to place a commitment to the race, as defined by men focused solely on their own enfranchisement, over attention to gender, which is often viewed by those men as a divisive, private matter."[50] Storm is consistently identified as a mutant only, fighting the oppressors of mutants, striving for mutant rights, and working to improve the mutant community. It seems there are no rights that need to be won for Storm as a woman, as a Black person, as a Black, female mutant. At no point do the comics address the intersectionality of the discrimination she would face, or discrimination within the community. By failing to engage with Storm's complex identity and the intersectional nature of the discrimination she would face, the comic dismisses both her Black and her female identities. In this manner, Storm's potential as a progressive and powerful figure remains underutilized.

Two years after Storm debuted in 1975, Marvel published a new titular comic for the white Carol Danvers, known as Ms. Marvel. Carol initially appeared in the *Captain Marvel* comics launched in 1968 and had regular appearances in *The Avengers*, with her titular comic launched in 1977. Ms. Marvel followed the popular trend in the 1940s and 1950s of introducing distaff female characters based on male superheroes, as exemplified by DC's Captain Marvel and Mary Marvel, Superman and Supergirl, and Batman and Batgirl/woman.[51] Initially serving as Captain Marvel's love interest, Carol was re-invented as a superhero in Captain Marvel's image, as Cocca writes: "Ms. Marvel wears the same black undies, black gloves, black boots, yellow Hala star, and a black domino mask framed by blonde hair. But her midriff and back were bare and her legs were bare where all those parts on Captain Marvel were covered, and she wore a long red scarf around her neck that villains would later grab. This sets her up immediately as a distaff and half-clothed version of Captain Marvel."[52] Carol was based on Captain Marvel, capitalizing on his success while drawing in a female readership but still providing eye candy to the male demographic. Cocca documents how these early comics focused on Carol's identity as a woman and how her "woman-ness" is "highlighted in just about every issue," especially as Carol navigates a sexist society.[53] This approach drew mixed responses, and the heavy-handed feminist "preaching" was increasingly downplayed and left behind while her costume was updated to be slightly less revealing by 1974. In 1979, she received a complete costume redesign consisting of a black bathing suit, with a yellow lightning bolt on the chest, a red sash, and thigh-high black boots. This remained Ms. Marvel's costume throughout the 1980s and 1990s, until 2012. These decades cemented some of Carol's basic character traits: "Her inner strength, her high emotion, her hot temper, and increasing amounts of her body are on display, as her stories both showcase her character as well as put her in service to other characters' development."[54] Throughout this period, Carol's story lines sometimes incorporate horrifying misogynistic tropes, including losing and regaining different superpowers in response to trauma. She assumes the moniker Binary (1982–1998) and Warbird (1998–2001), only to return as Ms. Marvel in the early 2000s. Cocca writes how "Ms. Marvel's most powerful adversary in this mid-2000s series—again, by a usually all-male and all-white creative team—is often herself."[55] With limited (usually none) female allies, Carol is often isolated and ends up facing villains who are either a part of herself (split personalities, alternate universes) or evil impersonators, like the villain Moonstone. It was not until 2012, when she was relaunched as Captain Marvel, that Carol became a popular and influential superhero.[56]

Unlike her Black colleague, Sam Wilson, Carol inherited a white male legacy title that set her up to become one of the most prominent superheroes in the Marvel universe. Carol's Captain Marvel costume is modeled on the original Captain Marvel costume, with the Hala Star as a chest chevron. However, the new suit has blue as the dominant color instead of black, which, along with the red paneling, brings Carol's color scheme more in line with the American flag. There are military accents present to underline Carol's past in the air force, and the military collar, boots, and gloves are reminiscent of navy dress uniforms. Her red sash is suggestive of her long-lasting Ms. Marvel costume and establishes a clear, linear evolution between her old Ms. Marvel identity and her new Captain Marvel identity. The use of the Hala Star as a chevron has led to extensive merchandising opportunities, allowing Carol to access a large presence within consumer culture, especially after the *Captain Marvel* (2019) film.[57] As Cocca points out, Carol's redesign included the introduction of a female supporting cast, and "the combination of such relationships with the hero's non-sexualization, heroism, strength, perseverance, caring, hotheadedness, risk-taking, agency, humor, and pathos struck a chord with those who had felt alienated from mainstream superhero comics."[58] The launch provided Carol with a vocal and engaged fan base, who drew art, wrote blog entries and letters, and attended comic conventions.

Carol's inheritance of the Captain Marvel title opened the door for a new Ms. Marvel, and in 2014, the sixteen-year-old Pakistani American Muslim Kamala Khan assumed the title with a titular comic.[59] As Cocca writes about the fan reception of Kamala as Ms. Marvel, "As with *Captain Marvel*, the response was overwhelming before the first issue came out."[60] The writers of *Ms. Marvel*, in part, attributed this success through Kamala's relationship with Carol Danvers. Before becoming a hero, Kamala was a Captain Marvel fan, just like the Captain Marvel readership. Framing Kamala as "one of them," inspired by Captain Marvel to do good, allowed her to step into the role organically, mirroring the way that Carol assumed the Captain Marvel title to honor Mar-Vell (the original Captain Marvel). Her immediate success led to an intense cultural presence, as evidenced by the use of Kamala's image by activists to cover up anti-Islam advertisements in 2015 in San Francisco.[61] As Sarah Gibbons writes, from the very first issue, Kamala's series "resists the idea that she should shed her own identity to adopt the values of other American heroes," and, in fact, "the comic eschews normality in favour of embracing alterity and celebrating hybridity."[62] When the audience first meets Kamala, she is hanging out with her friends, and the comic immediately engages with the ethnic and cultural diversity of her community through her friend, Nakia, who refuses to be called Kiki. Kamala jokingly claims that "Proud Turkish Nakia doesn't need 'Amreeki' nickname."[63] According to J. Ajami, S. Rasmi, and N. Abudabbeth, "Amreeki" is a colloquial Arabic term for "American" and, in this instance, refers to the American-style nicknames immigrants are often forced to adopt in order to assimilate into Western cultures.[64] Addressing both Nakia's pride in her Turkish heritage and the habit of Amreeki nicknames, the comic immediately addresses the realities of the way second-generation immigrants navigate the American cultural landscape as well as their own heritage. Another example of this navigation occurs a few panels later, when a white female character named Zoe asks Nakia about her headscarf.

> ZOE: I mean . . . nobody *pressured* you to start wearing it, right? Your father or somebody? Nobody's going to, like, *honor kill* you? I'm just *concerned*.
>
> NAKIA: Actually, my dad wants me to take it off. He thinks it's a *phase*.[65]

Through this conversation, which occurs on the first few pages of the first issue, *Ms. Marvel* points out the stereotypes surrounding Muslims in post-9/11 American culture, which is characterized by the rise of Islamophobia. Assuming that Nakia's father is forcing her to wear the headscarf incorporates stereotypes about Islam as inherently hostile to women and Muslim men as violent and totalitarian. These stereotypes support the widespread cultural narrative that America needs to liberate Muslim women from Islamic oppression used to justify the wars in Iraq and Afghanistan.[66] Zoe's concerned attitude is less an expression of actual concern and more a patronizing projection of American perceptions of Islam. As Gibbons notes, this is stereotypical of neoliberal society's response to diversity, which presents a flexible willingness to engage with diversity but only on the assimilationist terms of whiteness. She writes, "Zoe demonstrates a willingness to tolerate a degree of difference on the part of her peers, but in so doing, she positions herself as an authoritative cultural arbiter" and the gatekeeper of the levels of different that will be tolerated.[67] Nakia's response negates those stereotypes by pointing out that wearing the headscarf is her choice, against her father's wishes. Her father's hope that it is a phase incorporates American notions of teenage rebellion and rejects the headscarf's stereotypical signification of oppression. Instead, it becomes an expression of religious and cultural freedom, and wearing traditional dress becomes a way to resist American cultural imperialism.

Kamala does not wear a headscarf, but she does follow other tenets of Islam, which causes her to clash with white students in her class or the white hegemony in which her community is situated. When she is invited to a party, her father refuses to let her attend and she sneaks out, during which her inner monologue laments how she often has to deviate from established American norms: "Why am I the only one who gets *signed out of health class*? Why do I have to bring pakoras to school for lunch? Why am I stuck with the *weird holidays*? Everybody else gets to be *normal*. Why can't I?"[68] While the earlier discussion between Zoe and Nakia reveals how adherence to non-American heritage can be a choice, this train of thought points out how growing up in a minority culture in a largely homogenous society can lead to experiencing non-white heritage as abnormal and a burden. Kamala is signed out of health class because of her parents' conservative views on sexual education. Pakoras are traditional foods in Pakistani culture, and her Muslim holidays are not incorporated into the culturally Christian American society and its official holidays. This causes Kamala to feel isolated from the norm and her white classmates, whose identity and culture are privileged via the white hegemony. Despite the fact that Kamala grows up in Muslim and Pakistani communities, she still experiences her family's culture as existing outside the established norm, which is so ubiquitous Kamala has internalized it. At the party, Kamala is tricked into drinking alcohol, demonstrating her peers' clear disrespect for Muslim culture and Kamala's values. Zoe also remarks that Kamala smells like curry, which is obviously racist. After a confrontation with Kamala's friend Bruno, who points out that her parents could not possibly have given her permission to attend the party, Kamala leaves. While walking home, she is enveloped in the Terrigen Mist and experiences a vision in which she speaks to the Avengers, including Captain America and the original Ms. Marvel:

> Captain America: You thought that if you disobeyed your parents—your culture, your religion—your classmates would *accept* you. What happened instead?
>
> Kamala: They—they *laughed* at me. Zoe thought that because I snuck out, it was *okay* for her to make fun of my family. Like, Kamala's finally seen the light and kicked the dumb inferior *brown people* and their rules to the *curb*.[69]

During this conversation, Kamala becomes aware that rejecting her culture and assimilating fully into the American mainstream, acting white, will not automatically lead to increased acceptance. Punching down or ridiculing elements of a minority culture is not a viable strategy to gain access to privileged spaces on anything except a superficial level. It only reinforces the racist hierarchy that allows whiteness to dominate. Instead, it is necessary to display solidarity with her community, family, and culture to resist the discrimination and racist attitudes she will have to face. However, as Kamala points out, she does not feel entirely at home in Pakistani culture because she also feels like an American. Kamala is struggling with the intersectionality of her Pakistani American identity as it involves a crossing of boundaries and categories, which is not tolerated in the binary systems used to construct white America, evidenced by the erasure of intersectionality. Kamala wants to become less complicated and more singular. She wants to be the white and blonde-haired, original Ms. Marvel. When the dream-vision fades, Kamala wakes up in a cocoon, and as she climbs out she realizes she now looks exactly like the original Ms. Marvel.[70]

While Kamala has internalized American white hegemony to such a degree that she identifies the tall, white, and blonde-haired Carol Danvers as the ultimate beauty ideal, transforming into that ideal helps her realize her own worth. Becoming the white Ms. Marvel does not make Kamala more confident or happy. She realizes that embodying the white ideal does nothing to resolve or heal the psychological trauma of internalizing whiteness and the desire to erase your own ethnicity. Slowly, Kamala transforms back into her own body. As Kamala says in a later issue, "It took me a while to figure out that Ms. Marvel could be *me*. That I didn't have to be someone else in order to wear the *lightning bolt*."[71] Kamala realizes that heroism is not confined to the white and blonde-haired. Instead, anyone can be a hero. This narrative clearly taps into the narrative of the American Dream, where hard work always becomes success, but is recast in a diverse framework. Through Kamala, who makes the Ms. Marvel role her own, the Ms. Marvel identity comes to represent a diverse and intersectional superhero identity, which is further exemplified by the way Kamala constructs her Ms. Marvel costume, as seen in figure 4.3.[72] Kamala made her first costume using a burkini, a garment made specifically for Muslim women to exercise and swim in without compromising the modesty they choose to maintain. It is made of lightweight fabric that allows freedom of movement but covers the entire body except for the hands, feet, and face. While most burkinis typically have a hood to cover the hair, Kamala chooses to wear hers without.[73] She also wears a scarf around her neck (a throwback to the original Ms. Marvel costume from the 1960s), a domino mask to cover her face, and a pair of blue boots. The costume's color scheme—blue, red, and yellow—is reminiscent of the American flag and Carol Danvers's Captain Marvel costume, which has a similar color scheme. The lightning bolt on her chest is a reference to the long-lasting 1980s–1990s Ms. Marvel costume. Considering that the superhero is mostly an American phenomenon, Kamala's use of the burkini, signifying her Muslim and Pakistani heritage, symbolizes the American Dream: the immigrant using her cultural history and customs to strengthen and contribute to American society.

Kamala, in both her civilian identity as Kamala Khan and as Ms. Marvel, faces challenges unique to her experience as a young, female Muslim Pakistani American. As discussed previously, Zoe's implication that Muslim women are oppressed by their male family members touches on the unique stereotypes about young Muslim women as oppressed in their community and needing to be saved

Figure 4.3. The burkini costume. *Source*: G. Willow Wilson et al., *Ms. Marvel Infinite #1* (New York: Marvel Comics, 2014). © 2014 Marvel Comics.

by white Western women. This view denies Muslim women the agency to make their own choices regarding their religious practices and assumes that Western religious practices or modes of dress are the only way for women to live liberated lives. Kamala also experiences sexist attitudes from people within her community but demonstrates that these issues need to be addressed by those who are part of the community. For example, in *Ms. Marvel #014* (2014), Kamala is introduced to the son of old family friends, Kamran. Initially, they seem to have much in common and Kamala develops a crush on him. He offers her a ride to school and she accepts, but makes him stop the car and let her out when she realizes he is going the wrong way. When he pulls over, Kamala is zapped by a person named

Kaboom and passes out. When she wakes up and confronts Kamran about how he kidnapped her, Kamran blames her for the situation:

> KAMRAN: I had a feeling you'd change your mind once you saw what we're going to offer you. You just needed a little . . . persuasion.
>
> KAMALA: That is incredibly *gross*. *You* are incredibly gross.
>
> KAMRAN: That's not how you seemed to feel when you snuck out with me the other night.
>
> KAMALA: I never thought anything like this would happen! I thought—I thought it meant something else when we were together—something good—
>
> KAMRAN: Who's gonna believe that? You got in my car of your own free will. As far as anybody knows, you chose to be here. *You* put yourself in this situation.[74]

Kamran insists all Kamala needed was a little "persuasion," which echoes the ways boys are encouraged to force or coerce girls into allowing sexual contact.[75] This dialogue closely mirrors conversations typically held about rape, consent, and victim blaming. It is often the victim's actions that are subject to scrutiny by American mass media and the wider community instead of the attacker's assault. What did she do to encourage him? What was she wearing? Having internalized such attitudes, Kamala initially questions whether she was complicit in her own abduction, but then realizes that she does not have to accept Kamran's victim blaming. By echoing discussions of sexual assault in this dialogue, the comic engages with the sexist attitudes young women routinely face and highlights that this is not unique to the Muslim community. The comic encourages critical examination of victim-blaming and woman-blaming attitudes through this dialogue and the following confrontation between Kamran and Aamir, Kamala's older brother.

Aamir is consistently portrayed as the most devout Muslim character in the comics. He dresses in traditional Pakistani clothing, and the only time the audience sees him in American or Western-style clothing is when he is dressed to attend a job interview. He is often shown praying, attending mosque, and quoting from the Quaran. When Kamala refuses to work with Kamran to take over the world, Kamran decides to recruit Aamir instead because of Aamir's assumed religious belief: "You think some little part of Aamir isn't angry? Looking like he does, *believing* what he does . . . you think he doesn't wish he could live in a world where *he* gets to make the rules?"[76] Kamran explicitly engages with stereotypes surrounding Islam, such as the widespread Islamophobic belief that Muslims are angry totalitarians and that Islam, as a religion, supports the destruction of other religions and communities. Coming from Kamran, who is Pakistani American and from a Muslim community himself, such racist attitudes are especially poignant. On the surface, Kamran appears to be the genuine American success story: a completely integrated and assimilated son of first-generation immigrants who wears designer clothing and has been accepted into early admission for college. But it is this American success story that, when gaining superpowers, reveals himself to be a villain intent on establishing a new superior race that will rule the lesser beings on Earth. Through the contrast between Aamir and Kamran, the devout Muslim and the more secular American, the comic rejects Islamophobia and identifies the performance of whiteness as destructive and complicit in white hegemonic imperialism. Kamran kidnaps Aamir and attempts to use the Terrigen Mists to give Aamir powers. However, Aamir rejects Kamran's offer and, in doing so, rejects imperial whiteness while rebuffing the idea that Islam is fundamentally incompatible with freedom and equality.

> AAMIR: But I don't *want* super-powers.
>
> KAMRAN: What are you talking about? Everybody wants super-powers!
>
> AAMIR: Not *me*. I was happy the way I was.
>
> KAMRAN: How could you possibly have been happy the way you were?! You're a—you're—
>
> AAMIR: I'm a what? A religious freak? An MSA nerd? A salafi? Yeah. I'm all those things. And I'm not ashamed of any of them. And if you think that means you can take advantage of my sister—that I'll blame *her* for whatever happened to you, while *you* sashay off into the sunset 'cause you're a guy and nothing is ever your fault—well, my brother, you are *incorrect*.[77]

In this dialogue, Aamir refutes the stereotypes surrounding Islam as an angry and hateful religion while refusing to engage in victim blaming. He explicitly rejects the discourse surrounding female victims of (sexual) assault and refuses to assign any blame to Kamala just because she is a girl. While Kamran advocates the use of superpowers to establish a new oppressive hegemony, both Kamala and Aamir reject this hierarchy in favor of a more equal discourse. Kamala demonstrates how superpowers should be used for good, with "good" defined as "defense of equality, especially how it pertains to the needs of the community," exemplifying Ghee's concept of the culture-bound superhero.

Whitewashing and the destruction of the racial minority community by the white hegemony becomes a regular theme in the *Ms. Marvel* comics. In 2015, a second *Ms. Marvel* run began publication and focused on Kamala's attempts to balance her civilian and superhero commitments through her increasingly escalating confrontation with the Hope Yards Development/Relocation Association, a business initiative aimed at "cleaning up" Jersey City.[78] This organization pretends to help local residents clean up their neighborhood, but actually brainwashes them into selling their properties, which are turned into upper-middle-class apartments and boutiques that local residents cannot afford. This narrative engages with the debate on gentrification and its displacement of Black, Latino, and other nonwhite urban communities.[79] While Hope Yards actively promotes gentrification, members of the neighborhood, including Nakia, organize protests to resist the whitewashing of their community. In the second issue, we see (white) Hope Yards security agents stopping Tyesha, a Black woman in a burka, for walking down the street, asking why she is in the neighborhood. This directly engages with the racism Black and Muslim people face on a daily basis as their movement is increasingly policed in an attempt to keep them out of middle-class neighborhoods.

During a rally to motivate and brainwash more local residents, a spokesperson for Hope Yards explicitly states that "Soon enough, *all* of Jersey City will be renewed, revived and free of *undesirables*."[80] The comic links gentrification and its exploitation of the working class with whiteness and its racist discourse. The use of the word "undesirables" purposefully connects gentrification and segregation as fascist by invoking language used by Nazi propaganda. The situation is complicated further when Hope Yards uses an image of Ms. Marvel on its billboard to create the illusion that she endorses its work. While Kamala works to promote resistance to gentrification and advocates for her community, the "billboard image captures how such resistance can be co-opted," as Gibbons writes.[81] While it is clear to the reader that Kamala's loyalties lie with her multicultural community, even when that loyalty threatens the status quo or the interest of the white hegemony, the comic also lays bare how powerful corporations are able to mask this resistance and solidarity and divide the community.

Conclusion

It is clear that both Sam Wilson and Luke Cage struggled with constructing a Black masculinity that also functioned as a superhero masculinity capable of competing with powerful white superheroes as they script the masculine audience for their audience. Sam's origin story frames him as a Black body injected with white heroism, and yet this has not allowed him to rise to prominence alongside his white contemporaries. Luke, albeit a popular character in group comics and with a successful Netflix series, has also struggled to articulate a clear and direct message that speaks to the value of Blackness. Both come close to embodying what Ghee refers to as the "real" Black superhero, but fail because of comics' inability to accurately identify the community/culture itself, the means by which they are oppressed, and the steps required to end that oppression. However, considering that oppression *is* the status quo for communities of color and superheroes are often genre bound to protect the status quo from outside threats, is the "real" Black superhero even possible? As Consuela Francis writes: "It is entirely possible that a successful Black American superhero is impossible because it seeks to combine two ideals that are antithetical to each other: superheroes and American racial thinking."[82] Due to white-as-norm culture, Black people are automatically cast as the Other, which prevents them from embodying a masculine and heroic ideal. To challenge whiteness, Black superheroes need to unhook from whiteness, because this adherence automatically places them in a hierarchical status below white superheroes. It is not possible to gain parity or equal masculinity with white superheroes on whiteness' terms, and, at this time, comics have not been able to articulate something new and crucially required: Black masculinity on its own powerful terms.

It is important to acknowledge here that all identities are intersectional, but the dominant cultural narrative encourages us to think of identity in singular terms. This is especially true for those specific aspects of identity that are used to construct a normative frame and are thus rendered invisible. For instance, the human or "universal" experience is often presented as the white, able-bodied, straight, and cisgender man. Cultural narratives often present this view without question and encourage the audience to think of this man as the "man" in "mankind," free of gender, race, or sexual markers right up until the moment that status is challenged. Black superheroes, bisexual superheroes, and black, female superheroes, such as Storm, challenge the white man's status as the universal signifier. Therefore, superheroes of color are placed within white communities to mitigate that threat. For instance, through her identity as a mutant, which is often linked to whiteness, Storm becomes linked with whiteness and is rendered less dangerous or challenging. Storm is required to identify as a singular aspect of her identity and use that singularity to inform her political, cultural, and personal motivation. The comics, her communities, and her universe demand that she do so. Storm, too, is folded in and more palatable and commercially viable to a (white) mainstream audience.

Kamala Khan, the heir to a white legacy, similar to Sam Wilson's Captain America, approaches whiteness' attempts at folding in on her own terms. Unlike her contemporaries, she is not the body of color injected with whiteness or the white character in black/brown face. While Kamala is an Inhuman, which is one of the many white-race-as-racial-analogy groups, her loyalty lies and remains with her family, friends, and community. Her stories explicitly engage with the real-life problems faced by this community, which is also explicitly diverse and unified by a shared commitment to that diversity. The femininity that Kamala displays breaks with traditional norms through her acceptance of her own hybridity and difference. This allows her to maintain ownership of the Ms. Marvel title. In part, this is also because Captain Marvel has clearly moved on from "being Ms. Marvel," while Captain America never really relinquished the title. The sequential and circular nature of comic books, which requires a continuous return to the status quo, means that Sam was only borrowing the Captain American title and the audience knew it. Kamala, however, can take this title and make it her own.

Sam Wilson and Steve Rogers, Luke Cage and Danny Rand, Storm and Professor Xavier, and Kamala Khan and Carol Danvers are all part of a trend that establishes a superhero of color through the blessing, guidance, and mentorship of—or partnership with—an (established) white superhero. Their community of color is either absent or dominated by white people, except for Kamala, who is supported by various members of her diverse community. While Sam Wilson was given his wings by Black Panther, they never really established any solidarity based on any shared Black experiences. Instead, Sam followed in Steve Rogers's footsteps. While Luke Cage served the needs of his Black, Harlem community, his partnership with Danny Rand increasingly took him out of that community. While Storm returned to her roots, or married a Black man, she ultimately remains trapped in her white community. Kamala alone rises above these limitations, with a diverse community, the support of fellow superheroes of color, and her white mentors. Perhaps the real Black superhero is a superhero who is not only culture bound but also lifted up by a visible and present community of color.

Conclusion

THE NEXT STEPS

In 2016, the first issue of the brand-new *Captain America: Steve Rogers* comic series came out. Written by Nick Spencer, the issue revealed that Captain America had actually been a Nazi spy all along. During the publication of the story, Nick Spencer maintained in interviews that it was not fake and Captain America really was a Nazi.[1] Considering that Captain America was created by Jack Kirby and Joe Simon, two Jewish men, and that he had explicitly functioned as an anti-Nazi superhero, many fans felt this change was offensive. While the story line later revealed that Captain America had been the victim of fake, implanted memories, initial speculation among fans focused on a possible standoff between Steve Rogers and Sam Wilson for the title of Captain America. At a time when Captain America can be both a Nazi and a Black man, it is clear that superhero narratives are as bitterly embroiled in American society and the comic book community's increased polarization as any other form of mass media catering to both increasingly conservative and progressive audiences. This results in what is known as "ludonarrative dissonance," meaning that the "message" of the book as communicated through the character's dialogue contradicts the "message" of the book as communicated through narrative development or character design. On the surface, American superhero comic books advocate for tolerance, equality, and justice, but they fail to construct narratives that actively interrogate institutionalized structures of inequality. Because of this failure, the dominant cultural ideology within them reinforces stereotypes surrounding minorities while upholding the white male American hegemony. There may be some space for subversive or challenging readings, but these are often only available to those audiences actively constructing a challenging narrative, and, as discussed, the folding-in mechanism works to render these subversive readings harmless. This reinforces toxic structures surrounding gender and race in American culture as well as perpetuating and constructing such ideology in the comic book community, what is commonly referred to as nerd or geek culture.

As discussed in the introduction, comic books simultaneously contribute to and are influenced by general trends in American culture and hegemonic mass media, where traditional norms and values are dictated by the white heteropatriarchy. Within American society, whiteness is institutionalized as an invisible norm. It constructs itself as race-less and neutral. Through this neutrality, it masks its hierarchical superior position over Blackness and other minorities, as Jane H. Hill argues.[2] This superiority is entrenched in all levels of society, meaning that public and privileged spaces are often accessible to only white people, or to the Exceptional Black or Exceptional Minority whose entrance into privileged spaces is both limited and used to protect the system from accusations of racism. Within the Global North's white supremacist hierarchy, white people are at the top and everyone else is judged on their ability to approximate or perform whiteness, which intersects with performances of gender and sexuality. The sociopolitical system of heteropatriarchy maintains the supremacy of cisgender, straight men, which is maintained through the strict policing of gender and sex performances. In a nutshell, men are the protectors and breadwinners, and women are the meek yet sexual objects they can win or discard. Women are always romantically and sexually drawn to men and vice versa. This is the "normal" and "natural" way for people to be, and the most "normal" and "natural" people are white people. Everyone else is a deviant Other that needs to be rejected from public spaces. white, straight, and cisgender men are privileged in this system, but only so far as they are able to maintain a masculinity that requires them to suppress any emotions associated with femininity, never show any weakness, and adhere to masculine behavior, which is increasingly defined by hypermasculinity.

Increasingly, hypermasculinity is culturally exalted and what is masculine can be more accurately defined as that which is not feminine, while the feminine is everything that is excessive and soft, unmasculine. The construction of the hegemonic masculinity all men should aspire to, as described by Raewyn Connell, is perpetuated in comics and depends on the destruction or denigration of the female. The conceptualization of the audience as masculine, referred to as male-as-norm syndrome, occurs in all mass media, where films aimed at women are "chick flicks" and films aimed at men are simply films. Constructing masculinity by othering femininity is further carried out in language used in technological and scientific discourse. Especially when connected to military endeavors, progress is coded as male conquest of the female and as masculine procreation of the masculine. Technology is culturally understood as males producing males producing masculinity, which is symbolized by the cultural myth of the phallus as a vehicle of virility and reproduction. The male superhero embodies this cultural signification of masculine through this phallic body. Considering comics' prolific use of voyeuristic close-ups intimately depicting male bodies, the body of the superhero is fundamental to the construction of the male superhero as a script for masculinity. This body is hard, powerful, and capable of dominating any environment. This is the ideal masculinity—hard, innate masculinity supported by the technological advances capable of sculpting a white masculine body—promoted in American superhero comic books as evidenced through the analysis of Superman, Captain America, and Iron Man.

White female superheroes tend to tap into dominant cultural narratives surrounding women as weak, helpless, irrational, and excessive in order to neutralize the way they complicate the relationship between weak femininity and the masculine warrior ideal. Female superheroes contain the potential to challenge conservative gender ideology, as evidenced through the analysis of Supergirl and Wonder Woman. However, their eternal youth signifies troubling stereotypes about adult and older women, which contributes to the construction of the female superhero as a doll. It reduces the female body to plastic perfection that cannot be achieved while the biological body, in its excess and fecundity, is obliterated. The cult of the doll leads to objectification and sexualization, which is where the figure of the doll meets the porn star. Ultimately, the porn star and the doll share a similar function in the cultural landscape: they exist to be used or moved by an external (male) force. This image of the woman as a doll or porn star inevitably implies the presence of the subject who can act on (or masturbate to) the object-doll. As discussed in chapter 2, the female combatant is capable of resisting the masculine gaze by accessing strategies typically used by male characters, but these strategies are rarely used for female characters as the comics industry works to fold in any challenges to the dominant white heteropatriarchy in order to simultaneously cater to conservative and progressive audiences. The female body's plasticity is used to undermine and mitigate the threat to established gender roles that powerful women inevitably pose.

What is clear is that superheroes and their bodies, no matter what gender, are increasingly rendered plastic. Both male and female superheroes are confronted with impossible bodily standards symbolized through the doll and the action figure. As discussed through the analysis of Iron Man and Supergirl, it becomes clear that men and women must purchase technology, coded as masculine, to rule over their natural and biological bodies, coded as feminine, to construct appropriate gender identities. While these plastic bodies pressure women into assuming extremely feminine appearances, they put extensive pressure on men to deny the feminine in themselves. The elimination of the feminine is necessary to construct the hard, action figure body required for masculinity. In reality, this means that men must control and deny aspects of their identities that have been classified as feminine, which promotes hypermasculinity as a behavioral pattern and ideology. For example, the common saying "boys don't cry" highlights how men are not allowed to display emotions that are considered weak and feminine, such as fear, sadness, and pain. The only emotions men are allowed to fully experience and express are anger, impatience, and otherwise violent emotions. For example, "pulling pigtails," a phrase used to describe boys bullying young girls as a display of affection, is used to dismiss the boys' violent behavior and the girls' pain. Similarly, "boys will be boys" is used to excuse violent and aggressive behavior in young boys. This teaches young boys that violence is normal, that the only acceptable way to express affection, as men, is through violence, while it teaches young girls to romanticize violence.[3]

The way men are pushed to suppress emotion in order to create masculine identity is known as normative male alexithymia in the field of psychology. It refers to the way "traditional masculine role socialization" causes men to believe that "their masculine identity conflicts with many emotions they feel and what they feel they are 'allowed' to express."[4] Having feelings associated with femininity or a lack of masculinity creates a cognitive dissonance that contributes to a sense of crisis, leading to immediate suppression of the nonmasculine emotion. This contributes to men's inability to verbalize and cater to their own emotional needs. Combined with the image of women as emotional and "natural caretakers," this then forces men to project their feelings onto women and require them to do much or even all of the emotional labor of any interpersonal relationship. The gender roles present in mass media promote this vision of masculinity and, along with the action/superhero, reduce masculinity to violence and power. They also connect this ideal of violence and power to ridiculously fit and powerful bodies. With eating disorders, bodybuilding addiction, and depression on the rise in male demographics, it is clear that the demands of masculinity take an enormous toll on men. However, these requirements still place men in a dominant and privileged position in society. Men's adherence to the cult of the action figure is seen as an accomplishment worthy of praise, as evidenced by the admiration that male actors receive when they transform their bodies, such as Hugh Jackman as Wolverine and Christian Bale as Batman, while women's adherence is taken as a given, standardized to the extent that deviation from the ideal is punished. Their subordinate position to men within the sociocultural hierarchy of the white heteropatriarchy limits their access to professional, social, and cultural spaces and makes them vulnerable to exploitation and violence. However, for white women, the performance of white femininity often, in very real terms, provides a measure of protection from the levels of discrimination faced by women of color. Women who do not perform white, traditional femininity and are considered too fat, too masculine, too Black, too gay, too ambitious, too strong, and so on are rejected from privileged and public spaces altogether.

In superhero comic books, as in most American mass media, heteronormativity renders heterosexuality invisible, which means that homosexuality, as marked and visible, needs to be desexualized and heteronormalized. Homosexual characters are often cast as the strange Other who either participates in homonormativity or must be destroyed. Furthermore, considering Kenneth Ghee's concept of the culture-bound superhero in light of LGBTQIA+ (lesbian, gay, bisexual, transgender, queer, intersex, asexual, and other nonstraight identities) representation, many LGBTQIA+ superheroes fail to be a superhero for LGBTQIA+ audiences.[5] If only true LGBTQIA+ superheroes are superheroes who are culture bound, can resist the status quo, resist heteronormativity, and champion the needs of their communities, LGBTQIA+ representation in superhero comics is lacking, because the community is completely absent. Neither Billy nor Teddy nor Batwoman seems to be part of any LGBTQIA+ community, even while living in large cities. Gay men are often desexualized into the homonormative or domestinormative to reduce their radical potential and present them as nonthreatening. Lesbian characters struggle to belong in the heteronormative, hinting at how lesbianism is less acceptable to straight, white audiences than male homosexuality because of how lesbianism, much like straight women's sexuality, is assumed to serve the white man. Lesbian homonormativity would undo the fetishization of lesbianism and is therefore less acceptable. When not belonging to heteronormativity, the male and female homosexual are both completely Othered, and this Otherness is often conflated with other marginalized, nonhegemonic identities to further reinforce stereotypes used to bar LGBTQIA+ people from straight, white spaces. Being Othered can also lead the narrative to participate in the "bury your gays" trope, which is similar to the way some narratives kill off characters of color in order for the other white characters to experience emotions or learn valuable lessons about racism.

While comics have come a long way in terms of including superheroes of color, it is clear that the simple presence and visibility of those heroes is not enough to construct an antiracist narrative. The Black male superhero is often white-performing or promoting politics of respectability, which inevitably perpetuates white-as-norm culture. The Black female superhero falls into the same trap of having to perform whiteness, which negates any attempts to approach characters intersectionally. Comics continually fail to engage with intersectionality and real-life presentations of racism while sustaining racial stereotypes. In order to be antiracist, comic books must unhook from whiteness by moving away from white characters as an analogy for race, providing characters of color with communities of color, identifying the oppressing hegemony as white and patriarchal, and increasing the diversity of the industry at large.

The way that comics perpetuate traditional American ideas about gender and race means that they indirectly contribute to the violence in society attributed to those ideas. For example, female characters are often drawn in skimpy costumes that sexualize and objectify their bodies. Even taking the inevitable erotic aspect of voyeuristic close-up panels into account, male superheroes are often protected from this objectification through their possession of the phallus, the position of power, and visual codes used to protect them from the gaze, such as active stances and powerful angles. Even when the male body is framed as actively sexual, this often contains the sexual conquest of women and is part of the hypermasculine discourse where sex and violence are conflated. Simultaneously, it is clear that increasingly younger girls are sexualized in American mass media, including comics. Combined with the conflation of sex and violence, this normalizes the sexual assault of young girls, not only by older men but also by their peers. The sexualization of young girls normalizes sexual contact between minors, leading to sexual abuse among young people, where "[overall], 27 percent of girls and 25 percent of boys reported they had experienced verbal or physical sexual harassment or violence."[6] While comic books are not directly responsible for sexual assault among minors, they contribute to an overall culture that normalizes sexual abuse. Another example in which the revealing costumes female superheroes wear can place real people in danger is the stuntwomen who portray female superhero characters in films or on TV. In most cases, these stuntwomen cannot wear enough padding to properly protect themselves because their costume is too revealing for any additional protective gear. The construction of women as plastic dolls and men as violent action heroes also contributes to a cultural narrative where the disproportionate amount of violence women face on the street, in professional situations, and in intimate, interpersonal relationships is considered normal.[7] For comic books, specifically, this has given rise to toxic nerd culture.

Most male participants of nerd culture consider it a space reserved solely for men.[8] Women who participate in nerd culture are often seen as interlopers spoiling male spaces. Male nerds pride themselves on the idea that the masculinity constructed through nerd culture is divorced from hegemonic masculinity, specifically its conquest of women.[9] Nerd culture's narrative on masculinity claims that nerds are unappealing to women because they consume specific kinds of content, such as comics and sci-fi TV shows and films. The very existence of nerd girls reveals that it is not the consumption of "nerdy" material that makes nerd culture or nerd masculinity unattractive, but the toxic masculinity hiding within it. This is epitomized by the attitude that online communities have toward women, gay people, and non-white people.[10] When comics focus on gay, female, or non-white characters, male nerds often perceive this as companies either pandering to progressives or shoehorning them in, reaffirming the attitude that straight white masculinity is the norm because unless it is vital to the story line, incorporating nonstraight, non-white, or nonmasculine identities is propaganda. Hiding behind white-as-norm culture, they consider the inclusion of nonstraight, non-white, nonmasculine identities as a political choice, as if the decision to populate a universe with exclusively straight, white, and male superheroes is not also inherently political. Women in nerd spaces are often labeled as fake geek girls, meaning women who are only interested in nerd content because they want to impress nerd boys. The term delegitimizes their interest and presence in online communities while implying that women's primary focus in life is to impress men. It frames nerd boys as the arbiters of "genuine" interest whose nerd masculinity is secured through the rejection of "fake" nerd girls. Alternatively, some female participants in nerd culture are fetishized as an unattainable ideal. Finding a "real" nerd girl to have sex with is a fantasy that often recurs in these online debates. The girl's pleasure in consuming the nerd content is thus fetishized for the male nerd's sexual pleasure.

Currently, there is a perception in nerd culture and wider popular culture that increasing numbers of women are interested and participating in nerd culture. While the rise of the comic book shop in the 1980s and 1990s created gatekeeping mechanisms that allowed white male nerds to more easily control who purchased and read comics, women do have a historical presence in nerd culture. For example, the Star Trek series, a show stereotyped as enjoyed mainly by male nerds, was predominantly popular with women when it first aired, and the first fanzines, which are considered the foundation of modern fandom or nerd culture, were written by and for women.[11] The currently perceived rise of nerd girls has resulted in an increasingly toxic online environment where male nerds use hostile tactics such as general cyberbullying but also, specifically, doxing and SWATing to bar women from online nerd communities. Doxing is the act of finding and releasing private information, such as the victim's personal address, phone number, and email address, often with the malicious intent of increasingly personalized rape and death threats. SWATing, which is more prominent in the gamer community, refers to the deception of emergency services such as the police, where a fake ongoing crime is reported at the other person's location with the sole purpose of having that person (temporarily) arrested.[12] This disproportionately impacts Black people or other people of color as the disproportionate amount of violence the police use against communities of color renders SWATing a clear and direct threat on their lives.

Additionally, real-life comic spaces, such as comic conventions, are also often unsafe for nerd girls and non-white fans. For example, a fundamental comic-con tradition is cosplay, the act of dressing up as a character using homemade costumes. Cosplayers pride themselves on the skill with which they make their costumes as well as how accurate the costumes are, meaning the degree to which they resemble the characters' costumes. Many female cosplayers experience sexual harassment, and comic-con organizational bodies struggle to police male nerds or even establish protocols for dealing with sexual harassment, as evidenced by the torrent of witness or victim testimonies during the "Cosplay is not Consent" campaign.[13] The skimpy costumes female characters and their cosplayers wear are often used as an excuse for the harassment, echoing debates surrounding slut-shaming and rape in American mass media. People of color often face harassment when cosplaying a white character, while white cosplayers dress up as characters of color without community censure, even when using blackface to achieve the desired effect.[14] When Star Wars introduced the Black English John Boyega to play the main character Fin, there were calls to boycott the film. Nerds of color are also often required to continually prove to white nerds that they are nerdy enough, mirroring the way male nerds police the community against "fake nerd girls."[15] This attitude that, somehow, white male nerds are the arbiters of nerd-ness and have the right, even the moral duty, to gatekeep the community fuels the discrimination that Black people face online and impacts comic book content because it provides further excuses to edit Black people out of comic book content and subsequent merchandising.

As discussed throughout this book, superheroes consistently negotiate the demands of mainstream and conservative gender roles alongside an ethos of equality and antidiscrimination. The push for equality often translates into the creation of more characters of color, whose existence is often mitigated through a lack of relevance to the plotline, appearing as background or side characters, or whose stories are written to support the white-as-norm status quo. I do not, in any way, want to undermine the importance or the positive impact of narratives that present minority superheroes in a positive light. Increasing representation is necessary to undo the burden of representation itself and is a vital first step toward more equalizing narratives. When only a small number of minority characters are visible in mass media, these characters are the single image of an entire minority. A single character cannot fulfill the needs of all the diverse members of a community or dodge the numerous stereotypes the dominant narrative perpetuates. Subsequently, they are blamed for failing to fulfill the need of representation, which should be filled by hundreds and thousands of characters, as they have done for straight, white, and cisgender males. If there were more diverse characters, the fight over representation and stereotypes would not be so fraught or dominating. However, representation alone is incapable of challenging bigoted narratives.

It is important that comics continue to construct not only representative, pro-diversity narratives but also anti-heteronormative, antiracist narratives in order to challenge the white heteropatriarchy. These narratives can only be written by increasing the diversity of the industry itself. By including more people with varied lived experiences of racism, sexism, and homophobia, they can represent instances of real-life discrimination. The reason why *Ms. Marvel* stands out so consistently in its antiracist rhetoric is the diversity of its creative team. The collaboration between diverse people who can distance themselves from the hegemony creates diverse narratives. Importantly, these creator's are also more likely to be well versed in codes of resistance. As discussed in the introduction, audiences are trained to produce dominant readings of any given text, which is coded to support the specific sociocultural and political values of any given society. Readers can and do produce alternative or resistant readings, especially if the media is coded to do so, but this heavily depends on the reader's ability to differentiate between codes of support and codes of resistance, which is influenced by the reader's own sociocultural and political position within the dominant hegemony.[16] People who exist within a subordinate position within the hegemony are often well versed in the codes of discrimination and alienation and are, therefore, able to write codes and modes of resistance into a piece of media. Of course, this remains a difficult and fraught task as the mechanisms of folding in and intra-action work to purge real resistance from these codes or methods and use them to further strengthen the core values already present in the hegemony.

For comics, some progress is being made. For example, Sana Amanat and G. Willow Wilson are currently writing the *Ms. Marvel* comics. In 2015, Margueritte Bennet began writing DC's *Bombshells* title, which features an all-women cast, and Ta-Nehisi Coates's *Black Panther* (2016–ongoing) has inspired the all-Black-characters comic *World of Wakanda* (2016–2017), by Yona Harvey. Alongside the addition of several new gay characters to the DC universe after the New 52 reboot, DC's *Supergirl* TV series (2015–ongoing) has a lesbian main character. In 2017, *Wonder Woman*, directed by Patty Jenkins, was the first female superhero to have her own titular film and received critical acclaim with a box office total of $821.74 million according to *Forbes*.[17] Batwoman regained her titular comic in 2017, and Marvel featured Living Lightning, who came out as gay in 2005, as the main character for the 2018 “No Surrender” storyline in *Avengers*. The blockbuster film *Black Panther* (2018), directed by Ryan Coogler, a Black man, was enormously popular and its impact on the cultural landscape cannot be underestimated. As Damian Garside writes, “The film is at pains to give expression to and represent” not only the power but also “the majesty of Black people” in a way that has not been done before.[18] The film launched Black Panther’s popularity, taking him from a second-tier character who struggled to remain in publication to a superstar phenomenon. The film was an overnight sensation, with the phrase “Wakanda Forever” and the Wakandan crossed-arm salute found everywhere.

Alongside diversifying the industry itself, comics must also step away from assuming their audience is the straight, white cis male and resist the stratification of the merchandising market along gender lines. Especially for young children, the market is divided along strict gender roles where TV shows and cartoons are either for girls or for boys and the merchandising is tailored to what is traditionally considered appropriate for each gender. For example, dolls are for girls but not for boys, and toy cars are marketed to boys instead of girls. Superhero-themed merchandise is often aimed exclusively at boys, to the extent that female characters are withheld from the merchandising. Merchandise of the Avengers’ films of the Marvel Cinematic Universe (MCU) often omits Black Widow, the only female character, from the numerous action figures, lunch boxes, hoodies, and toys. The stratification of the market also impacts superhero content. For instance, *Young Justice* (2010–2013), Warner Bros. Animation’s popular cartoon, which aired on Cartoon Network, was canceled because it was too popular with female fans, as writer and producer Paul Dini admitted in an interview with Kevin Smith, the owner of the *Fatman on Batman* podcast.[19] Dini states that the show was canceled because a female audience means that DC loses the boy market. Apparently, DC and Cartoon Network believed that girls would not purchase the already-produced merchandise, which was aimed at boys, and that, in general, girls do not buy toys.[20] Corporate logic dictates that catering to girls means that (1) boys are not watching the show and (2) toys will not be sold. In 2016, Greg Weisman, one of the show’s developers, revealed that the show was being funded by a line of action figures produced by Mattel. Because not enough action figures were sold, they were cut from production and the show was canceled. Weisman admitted that the toys themselves simply did not cater to the correct demographic, but the damage was already done.[21]

For Marvel, which is now owned by Disney, the stratification of the market along gender lines needs to be maintained to avoid Marvel/Disney competing with itself. Because of its princess collection, Disney can be considered to have a near monopoly in the girls merchandising market; and if Marvel were to produce content that attracts girl audiences, it would lose part of its Disney clientele to Marvel. Subsequently, it would lose out on boys purchasing toys because the Disney princess collection could not possibly appeal to boys.[22] Therefore, the gender imbalance is maintained through the stratification of the merchandising market, which influences content, which also influences the market. Furthermore, because of the lack of Black superheroes, there is a lack of merchandise marketed toward specifically Black audiences and children, except for the MCU Falcon and Black Panther toys. Supposedly, Black children would buy toys with exclusively white superheroes anyway because of white-as-norm culture, but not vice versa. By excluding non-white children from their marketing strategies, both Marvel and DC are missing out on a large and viable demographic. Stepping away from artificially maintaining the superhero merchandising market as a white boys' market and subsequently diversifying their narratives could be an effective strategy for combating traditional gender segregation without compromising these companies' main goal: profit. After all, Warner Bros. Animation renewed its *Young Justice* series for a third season in 2016 following fan appeals, petitions, and persistent online outrage at what amounted to a rejection of a female audience.

However, it is not only a female audience that is hungering for more diverse stories. Large parts of the comic community are open to and even eager for increased diversity, as evidenced by the success of the *Wonder Woman* and *Black Panther* films and the long-running campaign for a *Black Widow* movie.[23] Marvel is also increasingly being held accountable for its lack of diversity by the community, which often points out how the MCU has more white actors named Chris than female or Black main characters. Marvel's TV series, produced by Netflix, tie into the MCU and have also faced some heavy criticism in regard to sexism and racism, especially the *Daredevil* series (2015–2016) in its portrayal of Asian women. In comparison, the Netflix-produced Marvel series *Luke Cage* (2016–2018) has been applauded as portraying insightful and meaningful instances of Black experiences. When Marvel released a statement that it was providing Netflix with the rights to the Iron Fist character, many in the community called for the main character in the comic, Danny Rand, to be played by an Asian American actor instead of a white man to avoid white savior complex stereotypes.[24] Marvel decided to ignore this, similar to the way it ignored calls for an actor of color to play Stephen Strange in the *Doctor Strange* film (2016). These examples demonstrate that, despite the existence of toxic masculinity in nerd culture, there are many diverse people present in the community and industry who are eager to see increased diversity in comics.

Of course, as mentioned in the introduction, there is an increasing backlash against increased representation and against those people campaigning or arguing for increased diversity. For instance, in 2013, Zoe Quinn released *Depression Quest* and received death and rape threats for the lack of violence or skill required in the game, blaming "political intrusion" for ruining gameplay. She documented this harassment and shared this openly with the media, which generated further harassment. In 2014, the situation escalated and became known as Gamergate, solidifying in an actual movement where specific subsets of the gaming community would select targets (female gamers, developers, or people otherwise attempting to discuss the sexism or racism in the community) and create huge pile-on and harassment campaigns. The most prominent of these targets was the feminist media critic Anita Sarkeesian due to her YouTube series *Tropes vs. Women*. While participants in Gamergate attempted to argue that they were only attempting to safeguard ethics in gaming journalism and that those harassing women were not officially affiliated with Gamergate, investigations carried out by those covering Gamergate made it clear that the ethics question was a red herring covering male fans venting their rage and frustration at women for existing in "their" space.[25] Similarly, Comicsgate developed in 2016 as a campaign against the "forced" diversity in American superhero comics, resulting in the harassment of female comic creators, readers, and other participants of the community.[26] In 2018, a fan edited the newly released *Star Wars: The Last Jedi* to remove all the female characters, and, in 2019, another fan did the same thing for the *Avengers: Endgame* film.[27] The fight for who gets to be included, who gets to matter, and who gets to see themselves in mass media is heating up.

Comic audiences, through their support of Kamala Khan and their simultaneous glorification of HYDRA, are a microcosmic example of the larger polarization in American society. Increasingly split along a conservative-liberal ideological dimension, American culture produces mass media that caters to this divide. Comic books are no different and, thus, struggle to present narratives that challenge the hegemony despite their historical explicit stances on diversity and tolerance. As discussed by Carolyn Cocca and Adrienne Resha, this is partly due to the economic demands of the industry; in order to gain new and loyal readership, Marvel and DC are forced to diversify, but not too much to avoid losing the traditional, more conservative, fan base.[28] Comics' inability to challenge the status quo has created an increasingly divided nerd culture, which feeds into both wider American culture and comic book content. While comics maintain deeply rooted conservative attitudes, they have immense potential for the construction of an antihegemonic narrative. Superheroes and comic books can deliver, and we need to demand that they do.

Acknowledgments

I would like to thank Dr. Emma Parker, Dr. Sarah Graham, Dr. Zalfa Feghali, and Professor Jason Dittmer for their expert advice and guidance.

I would also like to thank Rachel Quinney, who helped me make sense of my own thoughts and contributed to the analysis of the visual materials in this book, and Sarah Stevens, who allowed me to use her as a guinea pig with unfailing good humor.

I want to thank my mother, Godelieve Vandenhoven, and my sisters, Ruth and Maria De Dauw, as well as my brother, Dries De Dauw, and his wife, Sarah De Visscher, for their emotional support during the completion of this manuscript.

One last special thanks goes out to my partner, Paul Richards, who kept me sane during endless revision and editing.

Notes

INTRODUCTION

1. As of this writing, the Marvel Cinematic Universe (MCU) consists of the following films, in chronological order: *Iron Man* (2008), *The Incredible Hulk* (2008), *Iron Man 2* (2010), *Thor* (2011), *Captain America: The First Avenger* (2011), *Marvel's The Avengers* (2012), *Iron Man 3* (2013), *Thor: The Dark World* (2013), *Captain America: The Winter Soldier* (2014), *Guardians of the Galaxy* (2014), *Avengers: Age of Ultron* (2015), *Ant-Man* (2015), *Captain America: Civil War* (2016), *Doctor Strange* (2016), *Guardians of the Galaxy Vol. 2* (2017), *Spider-Man: Homecoming* (2017), *Thor: Ragnarok* (2017), *Black Panther* (2018), *Avengers: Infinity War* (2018), *Ant-Man and the Wasp* (2018), *Captain Marvel* (2019), *Avengers: Endgame* (2019), and *Spider-Man: Far from Home* (2019). The Netflix series consists of *Daredevil* (2015–2018), *Jessica Jones* (2015–2019), *Luke Cage* (2016–2018), *Iron Fist* (2017–2018), *The Defenders* (2017), and *The Punisher* (2017–2019). The CW Network series also form a single coherent universe, consisting of *Arrow* (2012–2020), *The Flash* (2014–ongoing), *Supergirl* (2015–ongoing), *DC's Legends of Tomorrow* (2016–ongoing), and *Batwoman* (2019–ongoing).

2. Sarah Whitten, "'Avengers: Endgame' to Be the Highest-Grossing Film of All Time," CNBC, July 20, 2019, https://www.cnbc.com/2019/07/20/avengers-endgame-to-be-the-highest-grossing-film-of-all-time.html#targetText="Avengers%3A%20Endgame"%20is%20poised,Avatar's"%20record%20of%20%242.7897%20billion.

3. For instance, following the casting of Samuel L. Jackson as Nick Fury for the MCU, the comic book also began to draw the originally white Nick Fury as a Black man. Harley Quinn, a famous Batman villain, first appeared in *Batman: The Animated Series* in 1992 before becoming a staple comic book character. There are many more examples.

4. The following discussion is limited to the companies now known as Marvel and DC. For more in-depth discussion of the evolution of the genre and the industry as a whole, see Bradford W. Wright's excellent analysis in *Comic Book Nation: The Transformation of Youth Culture in America* (Baltimore: Johns Hopkins University Press, 2001), as well as Amy Kiste Nyberg's *Seal of Approval: The History of the Comics Code* (Jackson: University Press of Mississippi, 1998) and Aldo J. Regalado's *Bending Steel: Modernity and the American Superhero* (Jackson: University Press of Mississippi, 2015).

5. Orion Ussner Kidder, "Useful Play: Historicization in Alan Moore's *Supreme* and Warren Ellis/John Cassaday's *Planetary*," *Journal of the Fantastic in the Arts* 21, no. 1 (2010): 77.

6. Adrienne Resha, "The Blue Age of Comic Books," *Inks: The Journal of the Comics Studies Society* 4, no. 1 (2020): 66–81.

7. Wright, *Comic Book Nation*, 13.

8. Wright, *Comic Book Nation*, 10.

9. Regalado, *Bending Steel*, 82–83.

10. Wright, *Comic Book Nation*, 10.

11. Regalado, *Bending Steel*, 84.

12. Regalado, *Bending Steel*, 79.

13. "Punching down" refers to the way people from a minority group can reassert their dominance over someone else by highlighting their own privileged characteristic and the other person's minority status. For instance, a popular form of punching down is the pinkwashing of white nationalism, whereby white members of the LGBTQIA+ community can find (temporary) belonging in right-wing spaces by playing up their whiteness and discriminating against Black LGBTQIA+ community members.

14. Regalado, *Bending Steel*, 89.

15. Regalado, *Bending Steel*, 89.

16. Regalado, *Bending Steel*, 142.

17. Miss Fury was initially published as a syndicated strip and subsequently collected in comic book format.

18. Robert Genter, "'With Great Power Comes Great Responsibility': Cold War Culture and the Birth of Marvel Comics," *Journal of Popular Culture* 40, no. 6 (2007): 963.

19. Regalado, *Bending Steel*, 143.

20. Regalado, *Bending Steel*, 147.

21. Relagado, *Bending Steel*, 146.

22. Thomas Hine, *The Rise and Fall of the American Teenager* (London: HarperCollins, 2000), 231–232.

23. Michael Barson and Steven Heller, *Teenage Confidential: An Illustrated History of the American Teen* (San Francisco: Chronicle Books, 1998).

24. Wright, *Comic Book Nation*, 175.

25. Fredric Wertham, *Seduction of the Innocent* (New York: Rinehart, 1954), 192.

26. Wright, *Comic Book Nation*, 175.

27. Nyberg, *Seal of Approval*, 104–128.

28. Regalado, *Bending Steel*, 164.

29. Regalado, *Bending Steel*, 169.

30. Deborah Elizabeth Whaley, *Black Women in Sequence: Re-inking Comics, Graphic Novels and Anime* (Seattle: University of Washington Press, 2015), 75.

31. Nyberg, *Seal of Approval*, 168.

32. Nyberg, *Seal of Approval*, 167.

33. Wright, *Comic Book Nation*, 177.

34. Adilifu Nama, *Super Black: American Pop Culture and Black Superheroes* (Austin: University of Texas Press, 2011), 43.

35. Nama, *Super Black*, 43.

36. Martin Lund, "'Introducing the Sensational Black Panther!' *Fantastic Four* #52–53, the Cold War, and Marvel's Imagined Africa," *The Comics Grid: Journal of Comics Scholarship* 6, no. 1 (2016): 8.

37. Lund, "Introducing the Sensational Back Panther!," 8.

38. Regalado, *Bending Steel*, 171.

39. Regalado, *Bending Steel*, 171.

40. Regalado, *Bending Steel*, 184.

41. Nyberg, *Seal of Approval*, 173.

42. Nyberg, *Seal of Approval*, 174.

43. He first appeared in *Uncanny X-Men* in 1979 and was part of the main cast of the *Alpha Flight* series, which began publication in 1983.

44. Gareth Schott, "From Fan Appropriation to Industry Re-appropriation: The Sexual Identity of Superheroes," *Journal of Graphic Novels and Comics* 1, no. 1 (2010): 23.

45. Derek Lackaff and Michael Sales, "Black Comics and Social Media Economics: New Media, New Production Models," in *Black Comics: Politics of Race and Representation*, ed. Sheena C. Howard and Ronald L. Jackson II (New York: Bloomsbury, 2014), 67–68.

46. Nyberg, *Seal of Approval*, 174.

47. Susan Faludi, *Backlash: The Undeclared War against American Women* (New York: Random House, 1991).

48. Wright, *Comic Book Nation*, 285–295.

49. Regalado, *Bending Steel*, 203.

50. Carolyn Cocca, *Superwomen: Gender, Power, and Representation* (New York: Bloomsbury, 2016), 11.

51. Nyberg, *Seal of Approval*, 178.

52. Nyberg, *Seal of Approval*, 178.

53. Nyberg, *Seal of Approval*, 179.

54. Schott, "From Fan Appropriation to Industry Re-appropriation," 22.

55. Nyberg, *Seal of Approval*, 105.

56. Regalado, *Bending Steel*, 220.

57. Gail Simone, "Who Was the Bisexual Man? Or Is That Off the Table Now That Secret Six Is Done?," *Ape in a Cape: Ask Me Anything, Anything Except That*, October 4, 2011, http://gailsimone.tumblr.com/post/11015369976/who-was-the-bisexual-man-or-is-that-off-the.

58. VashNL, "Save the Date: Marvel Announces Landmark X-Men Marriage," *The Broken Frontier*, May 22, 2012, http://old.brokenfrontier.com/headlines/p/detail/save-the-date-marvel-announces-landmark-x-men-marriage.

59. Dan Jurgens et al., *Superman: The Wedding Album* (New York: DC Comics, 1996).

60. In comparison, Batwoman's planned wedding to her partner, Maggie Sawyer, was prevented in 2013 by DC editors, who rationalized the decision by claiming superheroes in general should not have happy personal lives.

61. Albert S. Fu, "Fear of a Black Spider-Man: Racebending and the Colour-Line in Superhero (Re)casting," *Journal of Graphic Novels and Comics* 6, no. 3 (2015): 271.

62. Cocca, *Superwomen*, 13.

63. Resha, "The Blue Age of Comic Books."

64. Resha, "The Blue Age of Comic Books."

65. Aja Romano, "The Archive of Our Own Just Won a Hugo. That's Huge for Fanfiction," *Vox*, August 19, 2019, https://www.vox.com/2019/4/11/18292419/archive-of-our-own-wins-hugo-award-best-related-work.

66. Cam Tyeson, "MRA Dipshits Cut a Version of *Endgame* with No Brie Larson & 'No Gay Shit,'" Pedestrian, May 13, 2019, https://www.pedestrian.tv/film-tv/mra-fuckwits-avengers-endgame-cutdown/.

67. LGBTQIA+ is an umbrella term that stands for lesbian, gay, bisexual, transgender, queer, intersex, asexual, and other nonstraight identities.

68. Hannah Miodrag, *Comics and Language: Reimagining Critical Discourse on the Form* (Jackson: University Press of Mississippi, 2013), 4–5.

69. Aaron Taylor, "'He's Gotta Be Strong, and He's Gotta Be Fast, and He's Gotta Be Larger Than Life": Investigating the Engendered Superhero Body," *Journal of Popular Culture* 40, no. 2 (2007): 345.

70. Carole A. Stabile, "'Sweetheart, This Ain't Gender Studies': Sexism and Superheroes," *Communication and Critical/Cultural Studies* 6, no. 1 (2009): 87.

71. Ruth J. Beerman, "The Body Unbound: Empowered, Heroism and Body Image," *Journal of Graphic Novels and Comics* 3, no. 2 (2012): 203.

72. Beerman, "The Body Unbound," 203.

73. Mike Madrid, *The Supergirls: Fashion, Feminism, Fantasy, and the History of Comic Book Heroines* (Minneapolis: Exterminating Angel Press, 2009), 291.

74. Consider the Scarlet Witch, who can alter the fabric of reality, compared with Captain America, who can punch people really hard and yet is considered more capable.

75. Madrid, *The Supergirls*, 292.

76. Oskari Kallio and Masood Masoodian, "Featuring Comedy through Ludonarrative Elements of Video Games," *Entertainment Computing* 31 (2019): 1–12.

77. Neil Shyminsky, "Mutant Readers, Reading Mutants: Appropriation, Assimilation and the X-Men," *International Journal of Comic Art* 8, no. 2 (2006): 387.

78. Julianna Aucoin, "The Superhero Diversity Problem," *Harvard Political Review*, October 24, 2014, http://harvardpolitics.com/books-arts/superhero-diversity-problem/.

79. Gail Simone, "Front Page," Women in Refrigerators, March 1999, http://www.lby3.com/wir/index.html.

80. John Bartol, "Dead Men Defrosting," Women in Refrigerators, March 1999, http://www.lby3.com/wir/r-jbartol2.html.

81. The Beat, "Welcome to the Brokeback Pose," *The Beat: The News Blog of Comics Culture*, November 12, 2009, http://www.comicsbeat.com/welcome-to-the-brokeback-pose/; Maurice Mitchell, "A Contortionist Calls the Sexist 'Broke Back' Pose 'Impossible,'" The Geek Twins, April 22, 2013, http://www.thegeektwins.com/2013/04/a-contortionist-calls-sexist-broke-back.html.

82. Carolyn Cocca, "'The BrokeBack Test': A Quantitative and Qualitative Analysis of Portrayals of Women in Mainstream Superhero Comics, 1993–2013," *Journal of Graphic Novels and Comics* 5, no. 4 (2004): 411.

83. "The Hawkeye Initiative," accessed October 13, 2016, http://thehawkeyeinitiative.com/.

84. Cocca, *Superwomen*, 7.

85. Kara Kvaran, "Supergay: Depictions of Homosexuality in Mainstream Superhero Comics," in *Comics as History, Comics as Literature: Roles of the Comic Book in Scholarship, Society and Entertainment*, ed. Annessa Babic (Lanham, MD: Rowman & Littlefield, 2013), 153.

86. Marc Singer, "'Black Skins' and White Masks: Comic Books and the Secret of Race," *African American Review* 36, no. 1 (2002): 110.

87. Singer, "Black Skins' and White Masks," 110.

88. Singer, "Black Skins' and White Masks," 110.

89. Singer, "Black Skins' and White Masks," 112.

90. Singer, "Black Skins' and White Masks," 112.

91. Shyminsky, "Mutant Readers, Reading Mutants," 387.

92. Shyminsky, "Mutant Readers, Reading Mutants," 389.

93. Cocca, *Superwomen*, 11.

94. Nikka Lykke, *Feminist Studies: A Guide to Intersectional Theory, Methodology and Writing* (London: Routledge, 2010), 51.

95. Dawn Heinecken, *The Warrior Women of Television: A Feminist Cultural Analysis of the New Female Body in Popular Media* (New York: Peter Lang, 2003), 5.

96. Casey Brienza, "Producing Comics Culture: A Sociological Approach to the Study of Comics," *Journal of Graphic Novels and Comics* 1, no. 2 (2010): 105–119.

97. Jennifer Stuller, *Ink-Stained Amazons and Cinematic Warriors: Superwomen in Modern Mythology* (London: I. B. Tauris, 2010), 155.

98. Bonnie Dow, *Prime-Time Feminism: Television, Media Culture, and the Women's Movement since 1970* (Philadelphia: University of Pennsylvania Press, 1996), 12.

99. Heinecken, *The Warrior Women of Television*, 17.

100. Judith Butler, *Gender Trouble: Feminism and the Subversion of Identity* (London: Routledge, 2007), 45.

101. Michel Foucault, *The History of Sexuality 1: The Will to Knowledge* (New York: Penguin Books, 1998), 83.

102. Judith Butler, *Undoing Gender* (New York: Routledge, 2004), 50.

103. Judith Butler, *Bodies That Matter: On the Discursive Limits of Sex* (London: Taylor & Francis, 2011), 5.

104. Raewyn Connell, *Masculinities* (Cambridge: Polity Press, 2015), 77.

105. Connell, *Masculinities*, 77.

106. Megan Vokey, Bruce Tefft, and Chris Tysiaczny, "An Analysis of Hyper-Masculinity in Magazine Advertisements," *Sex Roles* 68, no. 9 (2013): 562.

107. Vokey, Tefft, and Tysiaczny, "Hyper-Masculinity in Magazine Advertisements," 562.

108. Vokey, Tefft, and Tysiaczny, "Hyper-Masculinity in Magazine Advertisements," 563.

109. Alex E. Crosby et al., "Suicidal Thoughts and Behaviors among Adults Aged ≥ 18 Years—United States, 2008–2009," *Surveillance Summaries* 60, no. SS13 (2011): 1–22, https://www.cdc.gov/mmwr/preview/mmwrhtml/ss6013a1.htm.

110. Lisa Duggan, "The New Homosexuality: The Sexual Politics of Neoliberalism," in *Materializing Democracy: Toward a Revitalized Cultural Politics*, ed. Russ Castronovo and Dana D. Nelson (Durham, NC: Duke University Press, 2002), 179.

111. Jasbir K. Puar, *Terrorist Assemblages: Homonationalism in Queer Times* (Durham, NC: Duke University Press, 2007), 21.

112. Arwa Mahdawi, "The Troubling Ascent of the LGBT Right Wing," *Guardian*, October 26, 2017, https://www.theguardian.com/commentisfree/2017/oct/26/ascent-lgbt-right-wing-afd.

113. Karla Martin, "Privileging Privilege with the Hope of Accessing Privilege," in *Unhooking from Whiteness: The Key to Dismantling Racism in the United States*, ed. Cleveland Hayes and Nicholas D. Hartlep (Rotterdam: Sense Publishers, 2013), 53.

114. Cleveland Hayes et al., "Toward a Lesser Shade of White: 12 Steps towards More Authentic Race Awareness," in *Unhooking from Whiteness: The Key to Dismantling Racism in the United States*, ed. Cleveland Hayes and Nicholas D. Hartlep (Rotterdam: Sense Publishers, 2013), 6.

115. Heinecken, *The Warrior Women of Television*, 3.

116. This excludes both superheroes who have important historical significance but were originally published in comic strips or other formats and those superheroes who have major gaps in publication history, being out of print for decades, such as *The Phantom*, *Miss Fury*, *Fantomah/Woman in Red*, and others.

117. Schott, "From Fan Appropriation to Industry Re-appropriation," 17–29.

118. At the time of publication, *The Authority* (1999–2010) was owned by WildStorm Publications, which became a publishing imprint of DC in 1999, specifically aiming to reach nontraditional comic audiences.

119. Depending on which definition of superhero you're working with, the very first female superhero was either Fantomah, who first appeared in *Jungle Comics #2* (1940), or *Miss Fury*, who first appeared in a syndicated newspaper strip in 1941.

120. Nolan McCarthy, Keith T. Poole, and Howard Rosenthal, *Polarized America: The Dance of Ideology and Unequal Riches* (Cambridge, MA: MIT Press, 2016).

CHAPTER 1 — WHITE SUPERHEROES AND MASCULINITY

1. Bradford W. Wright, *Comic Book Nation: The Transformation of Youth Culture in America* (Baltimore: Johns Hopkins University Press, 2003), 12–13.

2. Arthur Lawrence, *Journalism as a Profession* (1903; repr., Memphis: General Books, 2013), 1; David H. Weaver and G. Cleveland Wilhoit, *The American Journalist: A Portrait of U.S. News People and Their Work* (Bloomington: Indiana University Press, 1986), 7.

3. Jerry Siegel et al., *Action Comics #1* (New York: DC Comics, 1938), cover.

4. Of course, once you read the story, the cover's meaning changes as it becomes clear that the car Superman is smashing belongs to the bullies and the bad guys who have previously disrespected Clark Kent.

5. Anne Fausto-Sterling, *Sexing the Body: Gender Politics and the Construction of Sexuality* (New York: Basic Books, 2000), 198.

6. Clark Davis, "The Corporate Reconstruction of Middle-Class Manhood," in *The Middling Sorts: Explorations in the History of the American Middle Class*, ed. Burton J. Bledstein and Robert D. Johnston (London: Routledge, 2001), 202–203.

7. Davis, "The Corporate Reconstruction of Middle-Class Manhood," 202–203.

8. Davis, "The Corporate Reconstruction of Middle-Class Manhood," 202–203.

9. Erik Lundegaard, "Truth, Justice and (Fill in the Blank)," *New York Times*, June 30, 2006, http://www.nytimes.com/2006/06/30/opinion/30lundegaard.html?_r=0.

10. Gary Engle, "What Makes Superman So Darned American?," Xavier School I.B. English 2012, July 13, 2010, https://xsibenglish2012.wordpress.com/2010/07/13/what-makes-superman-so-damned-american/.

11. Danny Fingeroth, *Superman on the Couch: What Superheroes Really Tell Us about Ourselves and Our Society* (New York: Bloomsbury, 2004), 56.

12. Lori Maguire, "Supervillains and Cold War Tensions in the 1950s," in *The Ages of Superman: Essays on the Man of Steel in Changing Times*, ed. Joseph J. Darowski (Jefferson, NC: McFarland, 2012), 18.

13. Engle, "What Makes Superman So Darned American?"

14. Aldo J. Regalado, *Bending Steel: Modernity and the American Superhero* (Jackson: University Press of Mississippi, 2015), 166.

15. Regalado, *Bending Steel*, 166.

16. Maguire, "Supervillains and Cold War Tensions in the 1950s."

17. Paul R. Kohl, "The Struggle Within: Superman's Difficult Transition into the Age of Relevance," in Darowski, *The Ages of Superman*, 104.

18. Kohl, "The Struggle Within," 105.

19. Curt Swan et al., *Action Comics #241* (New York: DC Comics, 1958), cover.

20. Jack Weinstein et al., directed by James R. Bagdonas, *Lois & Clark: The New Adventures of Superman*, "Tempus Fugitive," 2:18, aired March 26, 1995, on ABC.

21. Randy Duncan, "Traveling Hopefully in Search of American National Identity: The 'Grounded' Superman as a 21st Century Picaro," in *The Ages of Superman: Essays on the Man of Steel in Changing Times*, ed. Joseph J. Darowski (Jefferson, NC: McFarland, 2012), 223.

22. Scott Snyder et al., *Superman Unchained #5* (New York: DC Comics, 2014).

23. Scott Lobdell et al., *Superman: H'el on Earth* (trade paperback; hereafter TPB) (New York: DC Comics, 2013).

24. TV Tropes, "Underwear of Power," accessed June 26, 2014, http://tvtropes.org/pmwiki/pmwiki.php/Main/UnderwearOfPower.

25. Aaron Taylor, "'He's Gotta Be Strong, and He's Gotta Be Fast, and He's Gotta Be Larger Than Life': Investigating the Engendered Superhero Body," *Journal of Popular Culture* 40, no. 2 (2007): 352.

26. Taylor, "'He's Gotta Be Strong,'" 355.

27. Taylor, "'He's Gotta Be Strong,'" 352.

28. Peter Lehman, *Running Scared: Masculinity and the Representation of the Male Body* (Detroit: Wayne State University Press, 2007), 219.

29. Joshua R. Brown, "No Homo," *Journal of Homosexuality* 58, no. 3 (2011): 300–301.

30. Although the group itself is established as straight, this does not mean that all members of the group are straight. Gay men are often pressured to participate in this behavior in order to avoid ridicule or rejection. Established social groups that consist of gay men only, or individuals who are in a group that considers itself part of the lesbian, gay, bisexual, transgender, queer, intersex, asexual, and other nonstraight identities community, participate in different in-group behavior.

31. Brown, "No Homo," 306.

32. Deborah Cameron, *On Language and Sexual Politics* (London: Routledge, 2006), 66.

33. Cameron, *On Language and Sexual Politics*, 68.

34. Brown, "No Homo," 301.

35. Cameron, *On Language and Sexual Politics*, 68.

36. Lehman, *Running Scared*, 218.

37. Stephen Frosh, *Sexual Difference: Masculinity and Psychoanalysis* (London: Routledge, 2002), 66.

38. The refusal to display the penis must also be considered in light of the age of the target audience. While most readers tend to be teenagers, some readers are children. Any sexual overtones would be scrubbed for such a young audience, which explains why, when there is a bulge in evidence, it is mostly found in more serious comics aimed at young adults.

39. Snyder et al., *Superman Unchained #5*.

40. Susan Bordo, *The Male Body: A New Look at Men in Public and in Private* (New York: Farrar, Straus and Giroux, 2000), 75.

41. In contrast with the chests of obese men, mockingly referred to as "moobs." Likening pectorals to breasts, which are heavy in fat content, is the ultimate insult. This reveals hegemonic masculinity's obsession with hardness and hatred of fat as a symbol for excessive femininity.

42. Jason Dittmer, *Captain America and the Nationalist Superhero: Metaphors, Narratives, and Geopolitics* (Philadelphia: Temple University Press, 2013), 94.

43. As of 2018, this seems, sadly, to no longer be true, as evidenced by the "fans'" outrage over the anti-Nazi politics of the Wolfenstein video game. Tauriq Moosa, "Nazis as the Bad Guys in Videogames? How Is That Controversial?," *Guardian*, October 27, 2017, https://www.theguardian.com/global/commentisfree/2017/oct/27/nazis-videogames-white-grievance-wolfenstein.

44. Aside from the fact that Marvel cannot allow widespread dissemination of the superserum within the comic universe, in order to preserve Captain America's superhero status.

45. This ties into ableist narratives that seek to scapegoat people who struggle with mental illness instead of dealing with the societal forces that create crime and violence.

46. Ed Brubaker et al., *Captain America: Reborn* (TPB) (New York: Marvel Comics, 2011).

47. Christina S. Jarvis, *The Male Body at War: American Masculinity during World War II* (Dekalb: Northern Illinois University Press, 2010), 65–66.

48. Jarvis, *The Male Body at War*, 186.

49. Matthew Cox, "Army Wants New Recruiting Slogan as Powerful as 'Be All You Can Be,'" Military.com, June 26, 2018, https://www.military.com/daily-news/2018/06/26/army-wants-new-recruiting-slogan-powerful-be-all-you-can-be.html.

50. Harrison G. Pope Jr., Katherine A. Phillips, and Roberto Olivardia, *The Adonis Complex: How to Identify, Treat, and Prevent Body Obsession in Men and Boys* (New York: Simon & Schuster, 2002), 30.

51. Yvonne Tasker, *Spectacular Bodies: Gender, Genre and the Action Cinema* (London: Routledge, 1993), 78.

52. Pope, Phillips, and Olivardia, *The Adonis Complex*, 125.

53. Pope, Phillips, and Olivardia, *The Adonis Complex*, 102.

54. Jason Dittmer, "Captain America's Empire: Reflections on Identity, Popular Culture and Post-9/11 Geopolitics," *Annals of the Association of American Geographers* 95, no. 3 (2005): 629–630.

55. Aaron Belkin, *Bring Me Men: Military Masculinity and the Benign Façade of American Empire, 1898–2001* (London: Hurst, 2012), 3.

56. Belkin, *Bring Me Men*, 5.

57. Although, as Belkin points out, this cultural "understanding" is not an accurate reflection of reality.

58. Rick Remender et al., *Captain America #16* (New York: Marvel Comics, 2012).

59. Dittmer, *Captain America and the Nationalist Superhero*, 7.

60. Dittmer, *Captain America and the Nationalist Superhero*, 28.

61. Belkin, *Bring Me Men*, 26.

62. Dittmer, *Captain America and the Nationalist Superhero*, 24–45.

63. Dittmer, *Captain America and the Nationalist Superhero*, 35.

64. Dittmer, *Captain America and the Nationalist Superhero*, 36.

65. Brian Easlea, *Fathering the Unthinkable: Masculinity, Scientists and the Nuclear Arms Race* (London: Pluto Press, 1983).

66. Easlea, *Fathering the Unthinkable*.

67. Easlea, *Fathering the Unthinkable*, 96.

68. For a more in-depth discussion of womb envy, see Karen Horney's *Feminine Psychology* (1922; repr., London: Norton, 1993) as well as Melanie Klein's *Envy and Gratitude: A Study of Unconscious Sources* (1957; repr., London: Routledge, 2013).

69. Rosalind Minsky, *Psychoanalysis and Gender: An Introductory Reader* (London: Routledge, 1996), 100.

70. The elimination of the female in scientific discourse also contributes to the systematic erasure of women's contributions to science.

71. Jacqueline Stevens, "Pregnancy Envy and the Politics of Compensatory Masculinities," *Politics and Gender* 1, no. 2 (2005): 289.

72. Mark Moss, *The Media and the Models of Masculinity* (New York: Lexington Books, 2011), 139.

73. Michael Kimmel, *Manhood in America: A Cultural History* (New York: Oxford University Press, 1998), 20.

74. Robert Genter, "'With Great Power Comes Great Responsibility': Cold War Culture and the Birth of Marvel Comics," *Journal of Popular Culture* 40, no. 6 (2007): 968.

75. Genter, "Cold War Culture and the Birth of Marvel Comics," 968.

76. K. A. Cuordileone, *Manhood and American Political Culture in the Cold War* (London: Routledge, 2005), 23.

77. Moss, *The Media and the Models of Masculinity*, 7.

78. Helen M. Malson, "Anorexic Bodies and the Discursive Production of Feminine Excess," in *Body Talk: The Material and Discursive Regulation of Sexuality, Madness and Reproduction*, ed. Jane M. Ussher (London: Routledge, 1997), 236–237.

79. Even today, moralizing publications often frame children's well-being as the mother's responsibility only and ignores the father.

80. Hans Sebald, *Momism: The Silent Disease of America* (Chicago: Nelson Hall, 1976), 3.

81. Cuordileone, *Manhood and American Political Culture*, 245.

82. Pope, Phillips, and Olivardia, *The Adonis Complex*, 42.

83. Pope, Phillips, and Olivardia, *The Adonis Complex*, 42.

84. Pope, Phillips, and Olivardia, *The Adonis Complex*, 43–44.

85. Pope, Phillips, and Olivardia, *The Andonis Complex*, 50.

86. Warren Ellis et al., *Iron Man: Extremis* (TPB) (New York: Marvel Comics, 2013).

87. Catherine Saunders et al., *Marvel: Year by Year, a Visual Chronicle* (New York: Dorling Kindersley, 2013).

88. Ellis, *Iron Man: Extremis.*

89. Moss, *The Media and the Models of Masculinity*, 143.

90. Moss, *The Media and the Models of Masculinity*, 143.

91. Kimmel, *Manhood in America*, 78.

92. Mike Featherstone, "The Body in Consumer Culture," in *The Body: Social Progress and Cultural Theory*, ed. Mike Featherstone, Mike Hepworth, and Bryan S. Turner (London: SAGE Publications, 1991), 186.

93. Daniel J. Connell, "Presentations of Hypermasculinity in Comic Book Cinema" (paper presented at The Superhero 2, Oxford University, September 9–11, 2016).

94. Connell, "Presentations of Hypermasculinity."

95. Drew Murphy, "Days of Future Past: Queer Identities and the X-Men" (paper presented at The Superhero 2, Oxford University, September 9–11, 2016).

96. Pope, Phillips, and Olivardia, *The Adonis Complex*, 111.

97. *Roosh V*, accessed October 13, 2016, http://www.rooshv.com/; *The Athefist* (blog), accessed October 13, 2016, https://athefist.wordpress.com/.

CHAPTER 2 — THE WHITE FEMALE BODY

1. This would now be referred to as benign sexism.

2. Jill Lepore, *The Secret History of Wonder Woman* (Melbourne: Scribe, 2014), 187.

3. Lepore, *The Secret History of Wonder Woman*, 196.

4. William Moulton Marston and Harry G. Peter, *Sensation Comics #8* (New York: DC Comics, 1942), cover.

5. Charles G. Martignette and Louis K. Meisel, *The Great American Pin-Up* (London: Taschen, 1996), 23.

6. Martignette and Meisel, *The Great American Pin-Up*, 23.

7. Lepore, *The Secret History of Wonder Woman*, 198.

8. Leila J. Rupp, *Mobilizing Women for War: German and American Propaganda, 1939–1945* (Princeton, NJ: Princeton University Press, 1978), 65.

9. Rupp, *Mobilizing Women for War*, 151.

10. M. Michaela Hampf, *Release a Man for Combat: The Women's Army Corps during World War II* (Cologne: Böhlau Verlag, 2010), 147.

11. Hampf, *Release a Man for Combat*, 147.

12. Lepore, *The Secret History of Wonder Woman*, 271.

13. Mitra C. Emad, "Reading Wonder Woman's Body: Mythologies of Gender and Nation," *Journal of Popular Culture* 39, no. 6 (2006): 965.

14. Of course, this is similar to the expansion of Superman's universe, which included a Superboy character, as discussed in chapter 1.

15. Lepore, *The Secret History of Wonder Woman*, 271.

16. Carolyn Cocca, *Superwomen: Gender, Power and Representation* (New York: Bloomsbury, 2016), 30.

17. Lepore, *The Secret History of Wonder Woman*, 271.

18. Kelli E. Stanley, "'Suffering Sappho!' Wonder Woman and the (Re)Invention of the Feminine Ideal," *Helios* 32, no. 2 (2005): 152.

19. Lillian Robinson, *Wonder Women: Feminisms and Superheroes* (London: Routledge, 2004), 81.

20. Yohana Desta, "How Gloria Steinem Saved Wonder Woman," *Vanity Fair*, October 10, 2017, https://www.vanityfair.com/hollywood/2017/10/gloria-steinem-wonder-woman.

21. Susan Faludi, *Backlash: The Undeclared War against American Women* (New York: Random House, 1991).

22. Helen Carreiras and Gerhard Kümmel, "Off Limits: The Cults of the Body and Social Homogeneity as Discursive Weapons in Targeting Gender Integration in the Military," in *Women in the Military and in Armed Conflict*, ed. Helen Carreiras and Gerhard Kümmel (Berlin: Springer, 2008), 31.

23. Carreiras and Kümmel, "Off Limits," 31.

24. Mike Madrid, *The Supergirls: Fashion, Feminism, Fantasy, and the History of Comic Book Heroines* (Minneapolis: Exterminating Angel Press, 2009), 291.

25. Joan Ormrod, "The Goddess, the Iron Maiden and the Sacralisation of Consumerism in Post Crisis Wonder Woman, 1987–1992" (paper presented at Graphic Gothic: The 2016 International Graphic Novel and Comics Conference, Manchester Metropolitan University, July 11–13, 2016).

26. Gerry Conway et al., *Wonder Woman #329* (New York: DC Comics, 1986), cover.

27. Yvonne Tasker, *Spectacular Bodies: Gender, Genre and the Action Cinema* (London: Routledge, 1993), 141.

28. Gail Simone et al., *Wonder Woman: Contagion* (trade paperback; hereafter TPB) (New York: DC Comics, 2010).

29. It is worth pointing out that, like her male colleagues, Wonder Woman seemingly lacks core muscles.

30. Jeffrey A. Brown, "Gender, Sexuality and Toughness: The Bad Girls of Action Film and Comic Books," in *Action Chicks: New Images of Tough Women in Popular Culture*, ed. Sherrie A. Innes (New York: Palgrave Macmillan, 2004), 48.

31. Carole A. Stabile "'Sweetheart, This Ain't Gender Studies': Sexism and Superheroes," *Communication and Critical/Cultural Studies* 6, no. 1 (2009): 87.

32. Mara Wood, "Gender Issues: Wonder Woman's Costume," Talking Comic Books, August 23, 2013, http://talkingcomicbooks.com/2013/08/23/gender-issues-wonder-womans-costume/.

33. Wood, "Gender Issues."

34. Meredith Finch et al., *Wonder Woman #36* (New York: DC Comics, 2011), variant cover.

35. Norman K. Denzin, *The Cinematic Society: The Voyeur's Gaze* (London: SAGE Publications, 1995), 43.

36. Denzin, *The Cinematic Society*, 48.

37. Marita Sturken and Lisa Cartwright, *Practices of Looking: An Introduction to Visual Culture* (New York: Oxford University Press, 2001), 88.

38. Sturken and Cartwright, *Practices of Looking*, 88.

39. Irene Jung Fiala, "Unsung Heroes: Women's Contributions in the Military and Why Their Song Goes Unsung," in *Women in the Military and in Armed Conflict*, ed. Helen Carreiras and Gerhard Kümmel (Berlin: Springer, 2008), 52.

40. Meredith Finch et al., *Wonder Woman #41* (New York: DC Comics, 2015).

41. Michael Barson and Steven Heller, *Teenage Confidential: An Illustrated History of the American Teen* (San Francisco: Chronicle Books, 1998), 12.

42. According to Thomas Hine in *The Rise and Fall of the American Teenager* (London: HarperCollins, 2000), the rise in juvenile crime reported in the papers in the 1930s and 1940s was not substantiated by statistics or corporeal evidence.

43. Barson and Heller, *Teenage Confidential*, 12.

44. Kelley Massoni, *Fashioning Teenagers: A Cultural History of "Seventeen" Magazine* (Walnut Creek, CA: Left Coast Press, 2012), 158.

45. Aldo J. Regalado, *Bending Steel: Modernity and the American Superhero* (Jackson: University Press of Mississippi, 2015), 165.

46. Amy Kiste Nyberg, *Seal of Approval: The History of the Comics Code* (Jackson: University Press of Mississippi, 1998), 168–173.

47. This phrase also appeared in the 1971 version but not in the 1989 one.

48. Nyberg, *Seal of Approval*, 114.

49. Curt Swan et al., *Action Comics #252* (New York: DC Comics, 1959), cover.

50. Swan et al., *Action Comics #252*.

51. Hine, *The Rise and Fall of the American Teenager*, 231–232.

52. Mike Sekowsky, Frank Giacoia, and John Costanza, *Adventure Comics #397* (New York: DC Comics, 1971).

53. Madrid, *The Supergirls*, 84.

54. Orion Ussner Kidder, "Useful Play: Historicization in Alan Moore's *Supreme* and Warren Ellis/John Cassaday's *Planetary*," *Journal of the Fantastic in the Arts* 21, no. 1 (2010): 77.

55. Hine, *The Rise and Fall of the American Teenager*, 4.

56. Hine, *The Rise and Fall of the American Teenager*, 27.

57. Hine, *The Rise and Fall of the American Teenager*, 30.

58. It is significant that almost every incarnation of Super*woman* has been evil and out of control, such as an alternative universe Lois Lane who is part of the Injustice League.

59. Martin Mac an Ghaill and Chris Haywood, *Gender, Culture and Society: Contemporary Femininities and Masculinities* (Basingstoke: Palgrave Macmillan, 2007), 98.

60. Mary F. Rogers, *Barbie Culture* (London: SAGE, 1999), 137.

61. Helen M. Malson, "Anorexic Bodies and the Discursive Production of Feminine Excess," in *Body Talk: The Material and Discursive Regulation of Sexuality, Madness and Reproduction*, ed. Jane M. Ussher (London: Routledge, 1997), 236–237.

62. Jane M. Ussher, *Managing the Monstrous Feminine: Regulating the Reproductive Body* (London: Routledge, 2006), 7.

63. Ussher, *Managing the Monstrous Feminine*, 7.

64. Sandra M. Gilbert and Susan Gubar, *The Madwoman in the Attic: The Woman Writer and the Nineteenth-Century Literary Imagination* (New Haven, CT: Yale University Press, 1980), 5.

65. Rogers, *Barbie Culture*, 33.

66. Mike Featherstone, "The Body in Consumer Culture," in *The Body: Social Progress and Cultural Theory*, ed. Mike Featherstone, Mike Hepworth, and Bryan S. Turner (London: SAGE Publications, 1991), 178.

67. Featherstone, "The Body in Consumer Culture," 178.

68. Mike Johnson et al., *Supergirl, Volume 2: Girl in the World* (TPB) (New York: DC Comics, 2013).

69. Susan Faludi, *The Terror Dream: What 9/11 Revealed about America* (London: Atlantic Books, 2008), 79.

70. Faludi, *The Terror Dream*, 14.

71. Scott Lobdell et al., *Superman: H'el on Earth* (TPB) (New York: DC Comics, 2013).

CHAPTER 3 — GAY CHARACTERS AND SOCIAL PROGRESS

1. Suzanne Danuta Walters, *All the Rage: The Story of Gay Visibility in America* (Chicago: University of Chicago Press, 2001), 12.

2. The original Hawkeye was Clint Barton, who was dead when Kate Bishop first took on the name.

3. Katharine M. Franke, "The Domesticated Liberty of Lawrence v. Texas," *Columbia Law Review* 104 (2004): 1399.

4. Sodomy Laws, "New York Deletes Sodomy from Books," glapn.org, June 20, 2003, https://www.glapn.org/sodomylaws/usa/new_york/nynews009.htm.

5. Lisa Duggan, "The New Homosexuality: The Sexual Politics of Neoliberalism," in *Materializing Democracy: Toward a Revitalized Cultural Politics*, ed. Russ Castronovo and Dana D. Nelson (Durham, NC: Duke University Press, 2002), 181.

6. Duggan, "The The New Homosexuality," 181.

7. Franke, "The Domesticated Liberty," 1411.

8. Franke, "The Domesticated Liberty," 1411.

9. Franke, "The Domesticated Liberty," 1416.

10. Jasbir K. Puar, *Terrorist Assemblages: Homonationalism in Queer Times* (Durham, NC: Duke University Press, 2007).

11. Allan Heinberg et al., *Young Avengers #1* (New York: Marvel Comics, 2005).

12. Heinberg et al., *Young Avengers #1*.

13. Allan Heinberg et al., *Young Avengers #2* (New York: Marvel Comics, 2005).

14. Allan Heinberg et al., *Young Avengers #6* (New York: Marvel Comics, 2005).

15. Gareth Schott, "From Fan Appropriation to Industry Re-appropriation: The Sexual Identity of Comic Superheroes," *Journal of Graphic Novels and Comics* 1, no. 1 (2012): 25.

16. Allan Heinberg quoted by Kara Kvaran, "Supergay: Depictions of Homosexuality in Mainstream Superhero Comics," in *Comics as History, Comics as Literature: Roles of the Comic Book in Scholarship, Society and Entertainment*, ed. Annessa Babic (Lanham, MD: Rowman & Littlefield, 2013), 153.

17. Allan Heinberg et al., *Young Avengers #7* (New York: Marvel Comics, 2005).

18. Allan Heinberg et al., *Avengers: The Children's Crusade* (trade paperback; hereafter TPB) (New York: Marvel Comics, 2012).

19. Mark Moss, *The Media and the Models of Masculinity* (New York: Lexington Books, 2011), 9.

20. The diminutive "ling" also refers to Teddy's age, where "Hulkling" might mean Hulk Jr. As discussed in chapter 2, youth is also inevitably linked to femininity and naïveté.

21. While it may seem obvious to characterize Teddy as a trans character, I am hesitant to do so as Teddy grew up believing he was a cisgender male or mutant and has not expressed a desire to be perceived any differently (at the time of writing).

22. Jane M. Ussher, *Managing the Monstrous Feminine: Regulating the Reproductive Body* (London: Routledge, 2006), 28.

23. Ivor Morrish, *The Dark Twin: A Study of Evil—and Good* (Wappingers Falls, NY: Beekman Books, 1999), 52–62.

24. Ritchie Robertson, "Historicizing Weiniger: The Nineteenth-Century German Image of the Feminized Jew," in *Modernity, Culture and "The Jew,"* ed. Bryan Cheyette and Laura Marcus (Cambridge: Polity Press, 1998), 24.

25. Tim Edwards, *Cultures of Masculinity* (London: Routledge, 2006), 79.

26. Andy Metcalf and Martin Humphries, *The Sexuality of Men* (London: Pluto Press, 1985), 2.

27. Barbara Ehrenreich and Deirdre English, *Witches, Midwives and Nurses: A History of Women Healers* (New York: Feminist Press, 1973), 10.

28. Heinberg et al., *Avengers: The Children's Crusade.*

29. Another example of an out-of-control female mutant superhero is Jean Grey as the phoenix in the Dark Phoenix Saga. Her periodical return from the dead causes characters to continually debate whether she should be killed before she can become the phoenix and threaten to destroy the universe again.

30. Heinberg et al., *Avengers: The Children's Crusade.*

31. Helen M. Malson, "Anorexic Bodies and the Discursive Production of Feminine Excess," in *Body Talk: The Material and Discursive Regulation of Sexuality, Madness and Reproduction*, ed. Jane M. Ussher (London: Routledge, 1997), 238.

32. Mike Madrid, *The Supergirls: Fashion, Feminism, Fantasy, and the History of Comic Book Heroines* (Minneapolis: Exterminating Angel Press, 2009), 292.

33. Barbara Creed, *The Monstrous Feminine: Film, Feminism, Psychoanalysis* (London: Routledge, 1993), 45.

34. It is also telling that Billy seeks to reunite with Wanda but does not attempt to establish a relationship with the Vision when he is returned to life.

35. Hans Sebald, *Momism: The Silent Disease of America* (Chicago: Nelson Hall, 1976), 183.

36. Allan Heinberg et al., *Young Avengers Presents* (TPB) (New York: Marvel Comics, 2008).

37. Heinberg et al., *Avengers: The Children's Crusade.*

38. Kieron Gillen et al., *Young Avengers*, vol. 2, *Alternative Cultures* (TPB) (New York: Marvel Comics, 2014).

39. This destiny is revealed in the 2013–2014 run.

40. To be fair, none of the Young Avengers are as highly sexualized as other superheroes, probably because they are underage in most of the comics. The only character who has a more conventional female superhero costume is Kate Bishop/Hawkeye, who had an exposed midriff until the Brown/McKelvie run redesigned her costume.

41. Cassie Lang/Stature died in a previous storyline, Tommy/Speed is kidnapped at the start of this run and not present for most of it, and Eli/Patriot left the team at the end of *The Children's Crusade* and moved to the Midwest.

42. Gillen et al., *Young Avengers*, vol. 2.

43. Gillen et al., *Young Avengers*, vol. 2.

44. Fredric Wertham, *Seduction of the Innocent* (New York: Rinehart, 1954), 190.

45. Paul Levitz, *The Silver Age of DC Comics: 1956–1970* (Cologne: Taschen Benedikt Verlag Gmbh, 2013).

46. Paul Petrovic, "Queer Resistance, Gender Performance, and 'Coming Out' of the Panel Borders in Greg Rucka and J. H. William III's *Batwoman: Elegy*," *Journal of Graphic Novels and Comics* 2, no. 1 (2011): 68–69.

47. Morrish, *The Dark Twin*, 37.

48. Greg Rucka et al., *Batwoman: Elegy* (TPB) (New York: DC Comics, 2010).

49. Jason Dittmer, *Captain America and the Nationalist Superhero: Metaphors, Narratives, and Geopolitics* (Philadelphia: Temple University Press, 2013), 94; Aaron Belkin, *Bring Me Men: Military Masculinity and the Benign Façade of American Empire, 1898–2001* (London: Hurst, 2012), 3.

50. It is possible to read Kate's performance of the soldier identity as a transgressive depiction of female warrior-hood, but the context of the heteronormative military industrial complex and the potential Freudian origin of her lesbian identity complicate such a reading.

51. Rucka et al., *Batwoman: Elegy.*

52. Rucka et al., *Batwoman: Elegy.*

53. Rucka et al., *Batwoman: Elegy.*

54. Petrovic, "Queer Resistance," 69.

55. Friedrich Weltzien, "Masque-*ulinities*: Changing Dress as a Display of Masculinity in the Superhero Genre," *Fashion Theory* 9, no. 2 (2005): 231.

56. Rucka et al., *Batwoman: Elegy.*

57. Rucka et al., *Batwoman: Elegy.*

58. Rucka et al., *Batwoman: Elegy.*

59. The color scheme used throughout *Batwoman: Elegy* was also foreshadowing. Just like a young Kate wearing black and red so the audience can identify her as Batwoman, Beth always wears pink and white as does Alice.

60. W. Haden Blackman et al., *Batwoman #7* (New York: DC Comics, 2012).

61. W. Haden Blackman et al., *Batwoman #16* (New York: DC Comics, 2013).

62. Rucka et al., *Batwoman: Elegy.*

63. As evidenced by articles such as Tyler Atwood's "11 Celebrity Women Wearing Tuxedos, Because the Red Carpet Needs a Good Shakeup Every Once in a While," Bustle, February 19, 2015, https://www.bustle.com/articles/65069-11-celebrity-women-wearing-tuxedos-because-the-red-carpet-needs-a-good-shakeup-every-once-in, and Natalie Matthews's "Women in Suits: Ladies Who Got It Right, Because Gowns Aren't the Only Look On the Red Carpet," *Elle*, November 6, 2017, https://www.elle.com/fashion/g8897/women-in-suits-menswear/, and the increasing number of fashion houses and high-end stores that offer women's suits, such as Harvey Nichols, Ted Baker, and Harrods.

64. Although, this could be an attempt to reclaim the suit and reframe it as lesbian signification instead of fashionable and playful transgression.

65. Aja Romano, "How DC Comics Lost Its 'Batwoman' Writers—and a Lot of Fans," Dailydot, September 5, 2013, https://www.dailydot.com/parsec/fandom/dc-comics-batwoman-writers-quit-wedding/.

66. Romano, "How DC Comics Lost Its 'Batwoman' Writers."

67. Marc Andreyko et al., *Batwoman #34* (New York: DC Comics, 2014).

68. Barbara Almond, "Monstrous Infants and Vampyric Mothers in Bram Stoker's *Dracula*," *International Journal of Psychoanalysis* 88, no. 1 (2007): 220.

69. Marc Andreyko et al., *Batwoman: Future's End #1* (New York: DC Comics, 2014).

70. Sima Shakeri, "Television Has a 'Bury Your Gays,' Queerbaiting, and LGBTQ Representation Problem," *Huffington Post*, June 30, 2017, http://www.huffingtonpost.ca/2017/06/30/queerbaiting-bury-your-gays-tv_a_23005000/.

71. Riese, "All 211 Dead Lesbian and Bisexual Characters on TV, and How They Died," Autostraddle, March 11, 2016, https://www.autostraddle.com/all-65-dead-lesbian-and-bisexual-characters-on-tv-and-how-they-died-312315/.

CHAPTER 4 — LEGACY, COMMUNITY, AND THE SUPERHERO OF COLOR

1. Kenneth Ghee, "'Will the "Real" Black Superheroes Please Stand Up?!' A Critical Analysis of the Mythological and Cultural Significance of Black Superheroes," in *Black Comics: Politics of Race and Representation*, ed. Sheena C. Howard and Ronald L. Jackson II (New York: Bloomsbury, 2014), 223–238.

2. Aldo J. Regalado, *Bending Steel: Modernity and the American Superhero* (Jackson: University Press of Mississippi, 2015), 200.

3. Regalado, *Bending Steel*, 201.

4. Novotny Lawrence, *Blaxploitation Films of the 1970s: Blackness and Genre* (London: Routledge, 2008), 19.

5. Lawrence, *Blaxploitation Films of the 1970s*, 20.

6. Lawrence, *Blaxploitation Films of the 1970s*, 20.

7. Lawrence identifies the label "blaxploitation" as reductionist because "it fails to assign individual films to their respective genres." There is a tendency to lump all Black-made and Black-character-driven films produced in the 1970s together as blaxploitation. However, the term remains useful in this instance, as it identifies a series of characteristics that span a wide range of genres. Lawrence, *Blaxploitation Films of the 1970s*, 20.

8. Steve Englehart et al., *Captain America and the Falcon #169* (New York: Marvel Comics, 1974).

9. Englehart, *Captain America and the Falcon #169*.

10. Adilifu Nama, *Super Black: American Pop Culture and Black Superheroes* (Austin: University of Texas Press, 2011), 73.

11. Christopher Priest, Joe Bennet, and Jack Jadson, *Captain America and the Falcon #007* (New York: Marvel Comics, 2014).

12. Aside from the initial green-and-orange costume, which was used for only a brief time.

13. There are many superheroes who do not have a chest chevron, such as Thor and the Hulk, but who nevertheless have a logo built out of other, unique character traits (e.g., hammer, oversized fists). However, there is no chest chevron that exclusively belongs to a Black superhero.

14. Chad Barbour, "When Captain America Was an Indian: Heroic Masculinity, National Identity, and Appropriation," *Journal of Popular Culture* 48, no. 2 (2015): 280.

15. Although Sam assumes the title and the shield, he does not receive the supersoldier serum, which has never been successfully replicated, as discussed in chapter 1.

16. Nick Spencer et al., *Captain America: Sam Wilson, Volume 1: Not My Captain America* (trade paperback; hereafter TPB) (New York: Marvel Comics, 2015).

17. Paul Thompson, "Column: Obama Is Not My President," CBS News, November 8, 2008, https://www.cbsnews.com/news/column-obama-is-not-my-president/.

18. Ghee, "'Will the "Real" Black Superheroes Please Stand Up?!,'" 223.

19. Ghee's theory frames culture bound as a prerequisite to Blackness itself, which further generates the idea that the non-culture-bound Black superhero is not truly Black. It implies that Blackness can only be portrayed and experienced in a singular capacity—that is, culture bound. This limits the ability of "culture bound" as a lens to discuss or analyze the ability of Black superheroes to function as politically relevant representation while simultaneously burdening the Black superhero with the responsibility of politically relevant representation, which results in the Black superhero being held to a higher standard than their peers.

20. Kevin M. Kruse, *White Flight: Atlanta and the Making of Modern Conservatism* (Princeton, NJ: Princeton University Press, 2013), 263–265.

21. Lisa Duggan, "The New Homonormativity: The Sexual Politics of Neoliberalism," in *Materializing Democracy: Toward a Revitalized Cultural Politics*, ed. Russ Castronovo and Dana D. Nelson (Durham, NC: Duke University Press, 2002), 175–194.

22. Daniel Geary, *Beyond Civil Rights: The Moynihan Report and Its Legacy* (Philadelphia: University of Pennsylvania Press, 2015), 172–205.

23. Archie Goodwin et al., *Luke Cage, Hero for Hire #1* (New York: Marvel Comics, 1972).

24. Don McGregor et al., *Luke Cage, Power Man #28* (New York: Marvel Comics, 1975).

25. Don McGregor et al., *Luke Cage, Power Man #32* (New York: Marvel Comics, 1976).

26. Kruse, *White Flight*, 264.

27. Richard Reynolds, *Superheroes: A Modern Mythology* (Jackson: University Press of Mississippi, 1994).

28. Nama, *Super Black*, 53–55.

29. Ronald L. Jackson II, *Scripting the Black Masculine Body: Identity, Discourse and Racial Politics in Popular Media* (Albany: State University of New York Press, 2006), 41–45.

30. Jackson, *Scripting the Black Masculine Body*, 41.

31. Blaire Davis, "Bare Chests, Silver Tiaras, and Removable Afros: The Visual Design of Black Comic Book Superheroes," in *The Blacker the Ink: Constructions of Black Identity in Comics and Sequential Art*, ed. Francis Gateward and John Jennings (New Brunswick, NJ: Rutgers University Press, 2015), 198.

32. Lucas do Carmo Dalbeto and Ana Paula Oliveira, "Oh My Goddess: Anthropological Thoughts on the Representation of Marvel's Storm and the Legacy of Black Women in Comics," *The Comics Grid: Journal of Comics Scholarship* 5, no. 7 (2015): 2.

33. Carolyn Cocca, *Superwomen: Gender, Power and Representation* (New York: Bloomsbury, 2016), 123.

34. Cocca, *Superwomen*, 125.

35. Ghee, "'Will the "Real" Black Superheroes Please Stand Up?!,'" 232.

36. Len Wein et al., *Giant-Size X-Men #1* (New York: Marvel Comics, 1975).

37. Wein, *Giant-Size X-Men #1*.

38. Jeffrey A. Brown, *Beyond Bombshells: The New Action Heroine in Popular Culture* (Jackson: University Press of Mississippi, 2015), 134.

39. Cocca, *Superwomen*, 125.

40. Dalbeto and Oliveira, "Oh My Goddess," 3.

41. Cocca, *Superwomen*, 125.

42. Cocca, *Superwomen*, 125–137.

43. Cocca, *Superwomen*, 137.

44. Dalbeto and Oliveira, "Oh My Goddess," 5.

45. Dalbeto and Oliveira, "Oh My Goddess," 5.

46. Greg Pak et al., *Storm #007* (New York: Marvel Comics, 2014).

47. Michelle Alexander, *The New Jim Crow: Mass Incarceration in the Age of Colorblindness* (London: New Press, 2010).

48. Greg Pak et al., *Storm #008* (New York: Marvel Comics, 2014).

49. Pak et al., *Storm #007*.

50. Tamara Beauboeuf-Lafontant, *Behind the Mask of the Strong Black Woman: Voice and the Embodiment of a Costly Performance* (Philadelphia: Temple University Press, 2009), 35.

51. Both DC and Marvel have characters called Captain Marvel. DC's Captain Marvel is Billy Batson and Marvel's Captain Marvel is Carol Danvers.

52. Cocca, *Superwomen*, 185.
53. Cocca, *Superwomen*, 186.
54. Cocca, *Superwomen*, 191.
55. Cocca, *Superwomen*, 197.
56. Tara Butters et al., *Captain Marvel #1* (New York: Marvel Comics, 2016).
57. This design is also the foundation for Carol's costume in the *Captain Marvel* film.
58. Cocca, *Superwomen*, 203.
59. Kamala is not the first woman of color to tie into the Marvel names and legacy. Monica Rambeau, an African American superhero, who later became known as Photon, Pulsar, and Spectrum, initially assumed the Captain Marvel name from 1982 to 1996, although not through a connection with the original male Captain Marvel.
60. Cocca, *Superwomen*, 210.
61. NBC News, "Comic Heroine Ms. Marvel Saves San Francisco from Anti-Islam Ads," January 27, 2015, https://www.nbcnews.com/news/asian-america/comic-heroine-ms-marvel-saves-san-francisco-anti-islam-ads-n294751.
62. Sarah Gibbons, "'I Don't Exactly Have Quiet, Pretty Powers': Flexibility and Alterity in *Ms. Marvel*," *Journal of Graphic Novels and Comics* 8, no. 5 (2017): 451.
63. G. Willow Wilson et al., *Ms. Marvel #001*, vol. 3 (New York: Marvel Comics, 2014).
64. J. Ajami, S. Rasmi, and N. Abudabbeth, "Marriage and Family: Traditions and Practices throughout the Family Life Cycle," in *Handbook of Arab American Psychology*, ed. Mona M. Amer and Germine H. Awad (London: Routledge, 2015), 112.
65. Wilson et al., *Ms. Marvel #001*.
66. Susan Faludi, *The Terror Dream: What 9/11 Revealed about America* (London: Atlantic Books, 2008).
67. Gibbons, "'I Don't Exactly Have Quiet, Pretty Powers,'" 455.
68. Wilson et al., *Ms. Marvel #001*.
69. Wilson et al., *Ms. Marvel #001*.
70. Wilson et al., *Ms. Marvel #001*.
71. G. Willow Wilson et al., *Ms. Marvel #007*, vol. 3 (New York: Marvel Comics, 2014).
72. G. Willow Wilson et al., *Ms. Marvel Infinite #1* (New York: Marvel Comics, 2014).
73. Ahiida, Burqini swimwear, accessed October 21, 2016, https://ahiida.com/.
74. G. Willow Wilson et al., *Ms. Marvel #014*, vol. 3 (New York: Marvel Comics, 2015).
75. Wilson et al., *Ms. Marvel #014*.
76. G. Willow Wilson et al., *Ms. Marvel #016*, vol. 3 (New York: Marvel Comics, 2015).
77. Wilson et al., *Ms. Marvel #016*.
78. The abbreviation for Hope Yards Development/Relocation Association forms HYDRA, a well-known Nazi and terrorist organization within the Marvel universe.
79. Melissa Archer Alvaré, "Gentrification and Resistance: Racial Projects in the Neoliberal Order," *Social Justice* 44, nos. 2–3 (2017): 113–136.
80. G. Willow Wilson et al., *Ms. Marvel #003*, vol. 4 (New York: Marvel Comics, 2016).
81. Gibbons, "'I Don't Exactly Have Quiet, Pretty Powers,'" 459.
82. Consuela Francis, "American Truths: Blackness and the American Superhero," in Gateward and Jennings, *The Blacker the Ink*, 138.

CONCLUSION

1. Christian Holub, "Captain America a Hydra Plant: Marvel's Nick Spencer, Tom Brevoort Talk New Comic," *Entertainment Weekly Online*, May 25, 2016, http://ew.com/article/2016/05/25/captain-america-villain-hydra-nick-spencer-tom-brevoort/?xid=entertainment-weekly_socialflow_twitter.

2. Jane H. Hill, *The Everyday Language of White Racism* (Chichester: Wiley-Blackwell, 2008), 23.

3. As evidenced by the popularity of Stephanie Meyers's *Twilight* series, first published in 2005, where the relationship between the main protagonists, Bella and Edward, has eight of the ten warning signs for abusive relationships as defined by the Women's Aid Organisation. Women's Aid Organisation, "Am I in an Abusive Relationship?," accessed January 6, 2017, https://www.womensaid.org.uk/the-survivors-handbook/am-i-in-an-abusive-relationship/.

4. Greg Henriques, "Why Is It So Hard for Some Men to Share Their Feelings?," *Psychology Today*, November 13, 2014, https://www.psychologytoday.com/blog/theory-knowledge/201411/why-is-it-so-hard-some-men-share-their-feelings.

5. Kenneth Ghee, "'Will the "Real" Black Superheroes Please Stand Up?!' A Critical Analysis of the Mythological and Cultural Significance of Black Superheroes," in *Black Comics: Politics of Race and Representation*, ed. Sheena C. Howard and Ronald L. Jackson II (New York: Bloomsbury, 2014), 230–231.

6. Allie Bidwell, "Study: Sexual Harassment Frequent among Middle School Students," *U.S. News & World Report*, April 6, 2014, http://www.usnews.com/news/articles/2014/04/06/study-sexual-harassment-frequent-among-middle-school-students.

7. "According to the 2010 National Intimate Partner and Sexual Violence Survey (NISVS), 35.6% of women in the United States reported experiencing rape, physical violence, or stalking by a current or former partner or spouse ("intimate partner") in their lifetime. . . . According to the NISVS, approximately one in four women in the United States has experienced severe physical violence by an intimate partner in their lifetime, and approximately one in seven were injured as a result of such violence that included rape, physical violence and/or stalking." Social Institutions and Gender Index, "United States of America," GenderIndex.org, accessed January 16, 2017, https://www.genderindex.org/wp-content/uploads/files/datasheets/US.pdf.

8. Carly Lane, "The Mary Sue Interview: Her Universe Founder Ashley Eckstein," The Mary Sue, December 3, 2015, http://www.themarysue.com/the-mary-sue-interviews-ashley-eckstein/.

9. Tessa Fisher, "Toxic Masculinity and Nerd Culture: Out of the Frying Pan and into the Fire," Some Nerd Girl, September 8, 2015, https://somenerdgirl.com/2015/09/08/toxic-masculinity-and-nerd-culture-out-of-the-frying-pan-and-into-the-fire/.

10. Fisher, "Toxic Masculinity and Nerd Culture."

11. Victoria McNally, "Women Who Love 'Star Trek' Are the Reason That Modern Fandom Exists," Revelist, September 8, 2016, http://www.revelist.com/tv/star-trek-fandom-50th/4643.

12. SWATing is not necessarily restrained by gender and appears to be used predominantly against a player who is outperforming the caller during an online gaming session, but there is not yet any research published on how frequently and in what conditions SWATing is most often used as a harassment tactic.

13. Lauren Barbato, "'Geeks for CONsent' Petition Comic-Con to Just Adopt Anti–Sex Harassment Policies Already," Bustle, July 28, 2014, https://www.bustle.com/articles/33470-geeks-for-consent-petition-comic-con-to-just-adopt-anti-sex-harassment-policies-already.

14. Dela Doll, "Blackface Is Ugly, and I'm Being Harassed: A Tale of Cosplay and Cosplayers Gone Wrong," *Huffpost*, September 7, 2016, https://www.huffpost.com/entry/blackface-is-ugly-and-im-being-harassed-a-tale-of_b_57d00f10e4b0273330ab68aa.

15. Adam Hubrig, "Racism and Misogyny in Nerd Culture: When Your Local Public Is 'Riggety, Riggety Wrecked,'" *Watershed* (blog), October 24, 2017, http://www.watershedblog.com/single-post/2017/10/26/Racism-and-Misogyny-in-Nerd-Culture-When-Your-Local-Public-is-%E2%80%9CRiggety-Riggety-Wrecked%E2%80%9D.

16. Bonnie Dow, *Prime-Time Feminism: Television, Media Culture, and the Women's Movement since 1970* (Philadelphia: University of Pennsylvania Press, 1996), 12.

17. Mark Hughes, "'Wonder Woman' Is Officially the Highest-Grossing Superhero Origin Film," *Forbes*, November 2, 2017, https://www.forbes.com/sites/markhughes/2017/11/02/wonder-woman-is-officially-the-highest-grossing-superhero-origin-film/#22d81acdebd9.

18. Damian Garside, "Ryan Coogler's Film Black Panther," *South African Review of Sociology* 49, no. 2 (2018): 107.

19. Jill Pantozzi, "Warner Bros. Animation Takes Issue with Girls Watching Their Programs," The Mary Sue, December 20, 2013, http://www.themarysue.com/warner-bros-animation-girl-market/.

20. Pantozzi, "Warner Bros. Animation Takes Issue."

21. Eric Francisco, "'Young Justice' Needs a Hero, Says Creator Greg Weisman," Inverse, April 1, 2016, https://www.inverse.com/article/13681-young-justice-needs-a-hero.

22. Monika Bartyzel, "Disney Spent $15 Billion to Limit Their Audience," *Forbes*, May 13, 2015, http://www.forbes.com/sites/monikabartyzel/2015/05/13/disney-spent-15-billion-to-limit-their-audience/#425d39bdea37.

23. Which was finally successful, once the MCU killed the character.

24. Andrew Wheeler, "Why Iron Fist Needs to Be an Asian American Hero, Not Another White Savior Cliché," *Comics Alliance*, December 15, 2015, http://comicsalliance.com/iron-fist-asian-american-or-white-savior/.

25. Jay Hathaway, "What Is Gamergate, and Why? An Explainer for Non-Geeks," Gawker, October 10, 2014, https://gawker.com/what-is-gamergate-and-why-an-explainer-for-non-geeks-1642909080.

26. Leonard Pitts Jr., "Comicsgate: Alt-Right Fan Boys Go After Women in World of Comics," *Miami Herald*, December 28, 2018, https://www.miamiherald.com/opinion/opn-columns-blogs/leonard-pitts-jr/article223686400.html.

27. Martin Belam, "Star Wars Actors Mock Fan Who Recut Film to Remove Women," *Guardian*, January 17, 2018, https://www.theguardian.com/film/2018/jan/17/star-wars-actors-mock-fan-recut-film-remove-women; Cam Tyeson, "MRA Dipshits Cut a Version of 'Endgame' with No Brie Larson & 'No Gay Shit,'" Pedestrian, May 13, 2019, https://www.pedestrian.tv/film-tv/mra-fuckwits-avengers-endgame-cutdown/.

28. Carolyn Cocca, *Superwomen: Gender, Power and Representation* (New York: Bloomsbury, 2016); Adrienne Resha, "The Blue Age of Comic Books," *Inks: The Journal of the Comics Studies Society* 4, no. 1 (2020): 66–81.

Bibliography

Ahiida. Burqini swimwear. Accessed October 21, 2016. https://ahiida.com/.

Ajami, J., S. Rasmi, and N. Abudabbeth. "Marriage and Family: Traditions and Practices throughout the Family Life Cycle." In *Handbook of Arab American Psychology*, edited by Mona M. Amer and Germine H. Awad, 103–116. London: Routledge, 2015.

Alexander, Michelle. *The New Jim Crow: Mass Incarceration in the Age of Colorblindness*. London: New Press, 2010.

Almond, Barbara. "Monstrous Infants and Vampyric Mothers in Bram Stoker's *Dracula*." *International Journal of Psychoanalysis* 88, no. 1 (2007): 219–235.

Alvaré, Melissa Archer. "Gentrification and Resistance: Racial Projects in the Neoliberal Order." *Social Justice* 44, nos. 2–3 (2017): 113–136.

Andreyko, Marc, Rafael Albuquerque, Jason Masters, Guy Major, Mark Doyle, Todd Klein, Rachel Gluckstern, Dave Wielglosz, and Bobbie Chase. *Batwoman: Future's End #1*. New York: DC Comics, 2014.

Andreyko, Marc, Jeremy Haun, Rafael Albuquerque, Moritat, Pia Guerra, Guy Major, Todd Klein, Mark Doyle, Rachel Gluckstern, Dave Wielgosz, and Bobbie Chase. *Batwoman #34*. New York: DC Comics, 2014.

The Athefist (blog). Accessed October 13, 2016. https://athefist.wordpress.com.

Atwood, Tyler. "11 Celebrity Women Wearing Tuxedos, Because the Red Carpet Needs a Good Shakeup Every Once in a While." Bustle, February 19, 2015. https://www.bustle.com/articles/65069-11-celebrity-women-wearing-tuxedos-because-the-red-carpet-needs-a-good-shakeup-every-once-in.

Aucoin, Julianna. "The Superhero Diversity Problem." *Harvard Political Review*, October 24, 2014. http://harvardpolitics.com/books-arts/superhero-diversity-problem/.

Barbato, Lauren. "'Geeks for CONsent' Petition Comic-Con to Just Adopt Anti–Sex Harassment Policies Already." Bustle, July 28, 2014. https://www.bustle.com/articles/33470-geeks-for-consent-petition-comic-con-to-just-adopt-anti-sex-harassment-policies-already.

Barbour, Chad. "When Captain America Was an Indian: Heroic Masculinity, National Identity, and Appropriation." *Journal of Popular Culture* 48, no. 2 (2015): 269–284.

Barson, Michael, and Steven Heller. *Teenage Confidential: An Illustrated History of the American Teen*. San Francisco: Chronicle Books, 1998.

Bartol, John. "Dead Men Defrosting." Women in Refrigerators, March 1999. http://www.lby3.com/wir/r-jbartol2.html.

Bartyzel, Monika. "Disney Spent $15 Billion to Limit Their Audience." *Forbes*, May 13, 2015. http://www.forbes.com/sites/monikabartyzel/2015/05/13/disney-spent-15-billion-to-limit-their-audience/#425d39bdea37.

The Beat. "Welcome to the Brokeback Pose." *The Beat: The News Blog of Comics Culture*, November 12, 2009. http://www.comicsbeat.com/welcome-to-the-brokeback-pose/.

Beauboeuf-Lafontant, Tamara. *Behind the Mask of the Strong Black Woman: Voice and the Embodiment of a Costly Performance*. Philadelphia: Temple University Press, 2009.

Beerman, Ruth J. "The Body Unbound: Empowered, Heroism and Body Image." *Journal of Graphic Novels and Comics* 3, no. 2 (2012): 201–213.

Belam, Martin. "Star Wars Actors Mock Fan Who Recut Film to Remove Women." *Guardian*, January 17, 2018. https://www.theguardian.com/film/2018/jan/17/star-wars-actors-mock-fan-recut-film-remove-women.

Belkin, Aaron. *Bring Me Men: Military Masculinity and the Benign Façade of American Empire, 1898–2001*. London: Hurst, 2012.

Beydoun, Khaled A. "Colin Kaepernick: Mix of Racism, Anti-Islam Rhetoric Are Increasingly Toxic." The Undefeated, September 2, 2016. https://theundefeated.com/features/colin-kaepernick-mix-of-racism-anti-islam-rhetoric-are-increasingly-toxic/.

Bidwell, Allie. "Study: Sexual Harassment Frequent among Middle School Students." *U.S. News & World Report*, April 6, 2014. http://www.usnews.com/news/articles/2014/04/06/study-sexual-harassment-frequent-among-middle-school-students.

Blackman, W. Haden, J. H. Williams III, Amy Reeder Hadley, Guy Major, Rob Hunter, Todd Klein, Mike Marts, Harvey Richards, Rickey Purdin, and Eddie Berganza. *Batwoman #7*. New York: DC Comics, 2012.

Blackman, W. Haden, J. H. Williams III, Dave Stewart, Todd Klein, Rickey Purdin, Harvey Richards, Mike Marts, and Bobbie Chase. *Batwoman #16*. New York: DC Comics, 2013.

Bordo, Susan. *The Male Body: A New Look at Men in Public and in Private*. New York: Farrar, Straus and Giroux, 2000.

Brienza, Casey. "Producing Comics Culture: A Sociological Approach to the Study of Comics." *Journal of Graphic Novels and Comics* 1, no. 2 (2010): 105–119.

Brown, Jeffrey A. *Beyond Bombshells: The New Action Heroine in Popular Culture*. Jackson: University Press of Mississippi, 2015.

Brown, Jeffrey A. "Gender, Sexuality and Toughness: The Bad Girls of Action Film and Comic Books." In *Action Chicks: New Images of Tough Women in Popular Culture*, edited by Sherrie A. Innes, 47–74. New York: Palgrave Macmillan, 2004.

Brown, Joshua R. "No Homo." *Journal of Homosexuality* 58, no. 3 (2011): 299–314.

Brubaker, Ed, Bryan Hitch, Butch Guice, Paul Mounts, John Cassaday, Laura Martin, Leinil Francis Yu, Joe Kubert, Alex Ross, Joe Quesada, Danny Miki, Richard Isanove, Joe Caramagna, Tom Brevoort, Jeanine Schaefer, and Lauren Sankovitch. *Captain America: Reborn* (trade paperback; hereafter TPB). New York: Marvel Comics, 2011.

Butler, Judith. *Bodies That Matter: On the Discursive Limits of Sex*. London: Taylor & Francis, 2011.

Butler, Judith. *Gender Trouble: Feminism and the Subversion of Identity*. London: Routledge, 2007.

Butler, Judith. *Undoing Gender*. London: Routledge, 2004.

Butters, Tara, Michele Fazekis, Kris Anka, Matthew Wilson, Joe Caramagna, Sana Amanat, Charles Beacham, and Axel Alonso. *Captain Marvel #1*. New York: Marvel Comics, 2016.

Cameron, Deborah. *On Language and Sexual Politics*. London: Routledge, 2006.

Carreiras, Helen, and Gerhard Kümmel. "Off Limits: The Cults of the Body and Social Homogeneity as Discursive Weapons in Targeting Gender Integration in the Military." In *Women in the Military and in Armed Conflict*, edited by Helen Carreiras and Gerhard Kümmel, 29–48. Berlin: Springer, 2008.

Cocca, Carolyn. "'The Brokeback Test': A Quantitative and Qualitative Analysis of Portrayals of Women in Mainstream Superhero Comics, 1993–2013." *Journal of Graphic Novels and Comics* 5, no. 4 (2004): 411–428.

Cocca, Carolyn. *Superwomen: Gender, Power and Representation*. New York: Bloomsbury, 2016.

Connell, Daniel J. "Presentations of Hypermasculinity in Comic Book Cinema." Paper presented at The Superhero 2, Oxford University, September 9–11, 2016.

Connell, Raewyn. *Masculinities*. Cambridge: Polity Press, 2015.

Conway, Gerry, Don Heck, José Luis García-López, Nansi Hoolahan, Helen Vesik, Alan Gold, and Dick Giordano. *Wonder Woman #329*. New York: DC Comics, 1986.

Cox, Matthew. "Army Wants New Recruiting Slogan as Powerful as 'Be All You Can Be.'" Military.com, June 26, 2018. https://www.military.com/daily-news/2018/06/26/army-wants-new-recruiting-slogan-powerful-be-all-you-can-be.html.

Creed, Barbara. *The Monstrous Feminine: Film, Feminism, Psychoanalysis*. London: Routledge, 1993.

Crosby, Alex E., Beth Han, LaVonne A. G. Ortega, Sharyn E. Parks, and Joseph Gfroerer. "Suicidal Thoughts and Behaviors among Adults Aged ≥ 18 Years—United States, 2008–2009." *Surveillance Summaries* 60, no. SS13 (2011): 1–22. https://www.cdc.gov/mmwr/preview/mmwrhtml/ss6013a1.htm.

Cuordileone, K. A. *Manhood and American Political Culture in the Cold War*. London: Routledge, 2005.

Dalbeto, Lucas do Carmo, and Ana Paula Oliveira. "Oh My Goddess: Anthropological Thoughts on the Representation of Marvel's Storm and the Legacy of Black Women in Comics." *Comics Grid: Journal of Comics Scholarship* 5, no. 7 (2015): 1–5.

Davis, Blaire. "Bare Chests, Silver Tiaras, and Removable Afros: The Visual Design of Black Comic Book Superheroes." In *The Blacker the Ink: Constructions of Black Identity in Comics and Sequential Art*, edited by Francis Gateward and John Jennings, 193–212. New Brunswick, NJ: Rutgers University Press, 2015.

Davis, Clark. "The Corporate Reconstruction of Middle-Class Manhood." In *The Middling Sorts: Explorations in the History of the American Middle Class*, edited by Burton J. Bledstein and Robert D. Johnston, 201–216. London: Routledge, 2001.

Delgado, Richard, Jean Stefancic, and Ernesto Leindo. *Critical Race Theory: An Introduction*. New York: New York University Press, 2012.

Denzin, Norman K. *The Cinematic Society: The Voyeur's Gaze*. London: SAGE Publications, 1995.

Desta, Yohana. "How Gloria Steinem Saved Wonder Woman." *Vanity Fair*, October 10, 2017. https://www.vanityfair.com/hollywood/2017/10/gloria-steinem-wonder-woman.

Dittmer, Jason. *Captain America and the Nationalist Superhero: Metaphor, Narrative, and Geopolitics*. Philadelphia: Temple University Press, 2013.

Dittmer, Jason. "Captain America's Empire: Reflections on Identity, Popular Culture and Post-9/11 Geopolitics." *Annals of the Association of American Geographers* 95, no. 3 (2005): 626–643.

Doll, Dela. "Blackface Is Ugly, and I'm Being Harassed: A Tale of Cosplay and Cosplayers Gone Wrong." *Huffpost*, September 7, 2016. https://www.huffpost.com/entry/blackface-is-ugly-and-im-being-harassed-a-tale-of_b_57d00f10e4b0273330ab68aa.

Dow, Bonnie. *Prime-Time Feminism: Television, Media Culture, and the Women's Movement since 1970*. Philadelphia: University of Pennsylvania Press, 1996.

Duggan, Lisa. "The New Homosexuality: The Sexual Politics of Neoliberalism." In *Materializing Democracy: Toward a Revitalized Cultural Politics*, edited by Russ Castronovo and Dana D. Nelson, 175–194. Durham, NC: Duke University Press, 2002.

Duncan, Randy. "Traveling Hopefully in Search of American National Identity: The 'Grounded' Superman as a 21st Century Picaro." In *The Ages of Superman: Essays on the Man of Steel in Changing Times*, edited by Joseph J. Darowski, 218–230. Jefferson, NC: McFarland, 2012.

Easlea, Brian. *Fathering the Unthinkable: Masculinity, Scientists and the Nuclear Arms Race*. London: Pluto Press, 1983.

Edwards, Tim. *Cultures of Masculinity*. London: Routledge, 2006.

Ehrenreich, Barbara, and Deirdre English. *Witches, Midwives and Nurses: A History of Women Healers*. New York: Feminist Press, 1973.

Ellis, Warren, Adi Granov, Randy Gentile, Tom Brevoort, Molly Lazer, Andy Schmidt, and Nicole Wiley. *Iron Man: Extremis* (TPB). New York: Marvel Comics, 2013.

Emad, Mitra C. "Reading Wonder Woman's Body: Mythologies of Gender and Nation." *Journal of Popular Culture* 39, no. 6 (2006): 954–984.

Engle, Gary. "What Makes Superman So Darned American?" Xavier School I.B. English, July 13, 2010. https://xsibenglish2012.wordpress.com/2010/07/13/what-makes-superman-so-damned-american/.

Englehart, Steve, Mike Friedrich, Sal Buscema, Frank McLaughlin, Petra Goldberg, Gaspar Saladino, Charlotte Jetter, Roy Thoms, and John Costanza. *Captain America and the Falcon #169*. New York: Marvel Comics, 1974.

Faludi, Susan. *Backlash: The Undeclared War against American Women*. New York: Random House, 1991.

Faludi, Susan. *The Terror Dream: What 9/11 Revealed about America*. London: Atlantic Books, Limited, 2008.

Fausto-Sterling, Anne. *Sexing the Body: Gender Politics and the Construction of Sexuality*. New York: Basic Books, 2000.

Featherstone, Mike. "The Body in Consumer Culture." In *The Body: Social Progress and Cultural Theory*, edited by Mike Featherstone, Mike Hepworth, and Bryan S. Turner, 170–196. London: SAGE Publications, 1991.

Fiala, Irene Jung. "Unsung Heroes: Women's Contributions in the Military and Why Their Song Goes Unsung." In *Women in the Military and in Armed Conflict*, edited by Helen Carreiras and Gerhard Kümmel, 49–62. Berlin: Springer, 2008.

Finch, Meredith, David Finch, Richard Friend, Sonia Oback, Sal Cipriano, David Pina, Matt Idelson, and Bobbie Chase. *Wonder Woman #36*. New York: DC Comics, 2011.

Finch, Meredith, David Finch, Jonathan Glapion, Brad Anderson, Johnny Desjardins, Rob Leigh, Paul Kaminski, Mike Cotton, Eddie Berganza, and Bobbie Chase. *Wonder Woman #41*. New York: DC Comics, 2015.

Fingeroth, Danny. *Superman on the Couch: What Superheroes Really Tell Us about Ourselves and Our Society*. New York: Bloomsbury, 2004.

Fisher, Tessa. "Toxic Masculinity and Nerd Culture: Out of the Frying Pan and into the Fire." Some Nerd Girl, September 8, 2015. https://somenerdgirl.com/2015/09/08/toxic-masculinity-and-nerd-culture-out-of-the-frying-pan-and-into-the-fire/.

Foucault, Michel. *The History of Sexuality 1: The Will to Knowledge*. London: Penguin Books, 1998.

Francis, Consuela. "American Truths: Blackness and the American Superhero." In *The Blacker the Ink: Constructions of Black Identity in Comics and Sequential Art*, edited by Frances Gateward and John Jennings, 137–152. New Brunswick, NJ: Rutgers University Press, 2015.

Francisco, Eric. "'Young Justice' Needs a Hero, Says Creator Greg Weisman." Inverse, April 1, 2016. https://www.inverse.com/article/13681-young-justice-needs-a-hero.

Franke, Katharine M. "The Domesticated Liberty of Lawrence v. Texas." *Columbia Law Review* 104 (2004): 1399–1426.

Frosh, Stephen. *Sexual Difference: Masculinity and Psychoanalysis*. London: Routledge, 2002.

Fu, Albert S. "Fear of a Black Spider-Man: Racebending and the Colour-Line in Superhero (Re)Casting." *Journal of Graphic Novels and Comics* 6, no. 3 (2015): 269–283.

Garside, Damian. "Ryan Coogler's Film Black Panther." *South African Review of Sociology* 49, no. 2 (2018): 107–110.

Geary, Daniel. *Beyond Civil Rights: The Moynihan Report and Its Legacy*. Philadelphia: University of Pennsylvania Press, 2015.

Genter, Robert. "'With Great Power Comes Great Responsibility': Cold War Culture and the Birth of Marvel Comics." *Journal of Popular Culture* 40, no. 6 (2007): 953–978.

Ghee, Kenneth. "'Will the "Real" Black Superheroes Please Stand Up?!' A Critical Analysis of the Mythological and Cultural Significance of Black Superheroes." In *Black Comics: Politics of Race and Representation*, edited by Sheena C. Howard and Ronald L. Jackson II, 223–238. New York: Bloomsbury, 2014.

Gibbons, Sarah. "'I Don't Exactly Have Quiet, Pretty Powers': Flexibility and Alterity in *Ms. Marvel*." *Journal of Graphic Novels and Comics* 8, no. 5 (2017): 450–463.

Gilbert, Sandra M., and Susan Gubar. *The Madwoman in the Attic: The Woman Writer and the Nineteenth-Century Literary Imagination*. New Haven, CT: Yale University Press, 1980.

Gillen, Kieron, Jamie McKelvie, Katie Brown, Emma Viecelli, Christian Ward, Annie Wu, Matthew Wilson, Lee Loughridge, Jordie Bellaire, Clayton Cowles, Lauren Sankovitch, Jon Moisan, Becky Cloonan, Ming Doyle, Joe Quinones, Maris Wicks, Mike Norton, Stephen Thompson, Kris Anka, Joe Quesada, and Axel Alonso. *Young Avengers*, vol. 2, *Alternative Cultures* (TPB). New York: Marvel Comics, 2014.

Goodwin, Archie, George Tuska, Billy Graham, Skip Kohloff, Stan Lee, and John Romita Sr. *Luke Cage, Hero for Hire #1*. New York: Marvel Comics, 1972.

Hampf, M. Michaela. *Release a Man for Combat: The Women's Army Corps during World War II*. Cologne: Böhlau Verlag, 2010.

Hathaway, Jay. "What Is Gamergate, and Why? An Explainer for Non-Geeks." Gawker, October 10, 2014. https://gawker.com/what-is-gamergate-and-why-an-explainer-for-non-geeks-1642909080.

The Hawkeye Initiative. Accessed October 13, 2016. http://thehawkeyeinitiative.com/.

Hayes, Cleveland, Brenda G. Juárez, Matthew T. Witt, and Nicholas D. Hartlep. "Toward a Lesser Shade of White: 12 Steps towards More Authentic Race Awareness." In *Unhooking from Whiteness: The Key to Dismantling Racism in the United States*, edited by Cleveland Hayes and Nicholas D. Hartlep, 1–16. Rotterdam: Sense Publishers, 2013.

Heinberg, Allan, Jim Cheung, John Dell, Justin Ponsor, Cory Petit, and Tom Brevoort. *Young Avengers #1*. New York: Marvel Comics, 2005.

Heinberg, Allan, Jim Cheung, John Dell, Justin Ponsor, Cory Petit, and Tom Brevoort. *Young Avengers #2*. New York: Marvel Comics, 2005.

Heinberg, Allan, Jim Cheung, John Dell, Justin Ponsor, Cory Petit, and Tom Brevoort. *Young Avengers #6*. New York: Marvel Comics, 2005.

Heinberg, Allan, Jim Cheung, Matt Fraction, Kevin Grevioux, Paul Cornell, Roberto Aguirre-Sacasa, Brian Reed, Harvey Talibao, Ed Brubaker, Juan Vlasco, Paco Medina, Alina Urusov, Cory Petit, Mark Brooks, Mitch Breitweiser, Brian Reber, Alan Davis, Mark Farmer, Paul Mounts, and Chris Eliopoulos. *Young Avengers Presents* (TPB). New York: Marvel Comics, 2008.

Heinberg, Allan, Jim Cheung, Dave Meikis, John Dell, Justin Ponsor, Cory Petit, Matt Fraction, Ed Brubaker, Brian Reed, Roberto Aguirre-Sacasa, Paul Cornell, and Tom Brevoort. *Young Avengers #9*. New York: Marvel Comics, 2005.

Heinberg, Allan, Jim Cheung, Mark Morales, Justin Ponsor, Cory Petit, Lauren Sankovitch, Tom Brevoort, Joe Quesada, and Jelena Djurdjevic. *Avengers: The Children's Crusade* (TPB). New York: Marvel Comics, 2012.

Heinberg, Allan, Andrea DiVito, Drew Hennessey, Justin Ponsor, Cory Petit, and Tom Brevoort. *Young Avengers #7*. New York: Marvel Comics, 2005.

Heinecken, Dawn. *The Warrior Women of Television: A Feminist Cultural Analysis of the New Female Body in Popular Media*. New York: Peter Lang, 2003.

Henriques, Greg. "Why Is It So Hard for Some Men to Share Their Feelings?" *Psychology Today*, November 13, 2014. https://www.psychologytoday.com/blog/theory-knowledge/201411/why-is-it-so-hard-some-men-share-their-feelings.

Hill, Jane H. *The Everyday Language of White Racism*. Chichester: Wiley-Blackwell, 2008.

Hine, Thomas. *The Rise and Fall of the American Teenager*. London: Harper Collins, 2000.

Holub, Christian. "Captain America a Hydra Plant: Marvel's Nick Spencer, Tom Brevoort Talk New Comic." *Entertainment Weekly Online*, updated May 25, 2016. http://ew.com/article/2016/05/25/captain-america-villain-hydra-nick-spencer-tom-brevoort/?xid=entertainment-weekly_socialflow_twitter.

Horney, Karen. *Feminine Psychology*. 1922. Reprint, London: Norton, 1993.

Hubrig, Adam. "Racism and Misogyny in Nerd Culture: When Your Local Public Is 'Riggety, Riggety Wrecked.'" *Watershed* (blog), October 24, 2017. http://www.watershedblog.com/single-post/2017/10/26/Racism-and-Misogyny-in-Nerd-Culture-When-Your-Local-Public-is-%E2%80%9CRiggety-Riggety-Wrecked%E2%80%9D.

Hughes, Mark. "'Wonder Woman' Is Officially the Highest-Grossing Superhero Origin Film." *Forbes*, November 2, 2017. https://www.forbes.com/sites/markhughes/2017/11/02/wonder-woman-is-officially-the-highest-grossing-superhero-origin-film/#22d81acdebd9.

Jackson, Ronald L. II. *Scripting the Black Masculine Body: Identity, Discourse and Racial Politics in Popular Media*. Albany: State University of New York Press, 2006.

Jarvis, Christina S. *The Male Body at War: American Masculinity during World War II*. Dekalb: Northern Illinois University Press, 2010.

Johnson, Mike, Michael Green, Mahmud Asrar, Dave McCaig, Dan Green, John J. Hill, Will Moss, Matt Idolson, Bill Reinhold, Paul Mounts, Rob Leigh, and Eddie Berganza. *Supergirl, Volume 2: Girl in the World* (TPB). New York: DC Comics, 2013.

Jurgens, Dan, John Byrne, Terry Austin, Glenn Whitmore, Karl Kesel, David Michelinie, Louise Simonson, and Roger Stern. *Superman: The Wedding Album*. New York: DC Comics, 1996.

Kallio, Oskari, and Masood Masoodian. "Featuring Comedy through Ludonarrative Elements of Video Games." *Entertainment Computing* 31 (2019): 1–12.

Kidder, Orion Ussner. "Useful Play: Historicization in Alan Moore's *Supreme* and Warren Ellis/John Cassaday's *Planetary*." *Journal of the Fantastic in the Arts* 21, no. 1 (2010): 77–96.

Kimmel, Michael. *Manhood in America: A Cultural History.* New York: Oxford University Press, 1998.

Klein, Melanie. *Envy and Gratitude: A Study of Unconscious Sources.* 1957. Reprint, London: Routledge, 2013.

Kohl, Paul R. "The Struggle Within: Superman's Difficult Transition into the Age of Relevance." In *The Ages of Superman: Essays on the Man of Steel in Changing Times*, edited by Joseph J. Darowski, 103–114. London: McFarland, 2012.

Kruse, Kevin M. *White Flight: Atlanta and the Making of Modern Conservatism.* Princeton, NJ: Princeton University Press, 2013.

Kvaran, Kara. "Supergay: Depictions of Homosexuality in Mainstream Superhero Comics." In *Comics as History, Comics as Literature: Roles of the Comic Book in Scholarship, Society and Entertainment*, edited by Annessa Babic, 141–156. Lanham, MD: Rowman & Littlefield, 2013.

Lackaff, Derek, and Michael Sales. "Black Comics and Social Media Economics: New Media, New Production Models." In *Black Comics: Politics of Race and Representation*, edited by Sheena C. Howard and Ronald L. Jackson II, 65–78. New York: Bloomsbury, 2014.

Lane, Carly. "The Mary Sue Interview: Her Universe Founder Ashley Eckstein." The Mary Sue, December 3, 2015. http://www.themarysue.com/the-mary-sue-interviews-ashley-eckstein/.

Lawrence, Arthur. *Journalism as a Profession.* 1903. Reprint, Memphis: General Books, 2013.

Lawrence, Novotny. *Blaxploitation Films of the 1970s: Blackness and Genre.* London: Routledge, 2008.

Lehman, Peter. *Running Scared: Masculinity and the Representation of the Male Body.* Detroit: Wayne State University Press, 2007.

Lepore, Jill. *The Secret History of Wonder Woman.* Melbourne: Scribe, 2014.

Levitz, Paul. *The Golden Age of DC Comics: 1935–1956.* Cologne: Taschen Benedikt Verlag Gmbh, 2013.

Levitz, Paul. *The Silver Age of DC Comics: 1956–1970.* Cologne: Taschen Benedikt Verlag Gmbh, 2013.

Lobdell, Scott, Tom DeFalco, Mike Johnson, Kenneth Rocafort, R. B. Silva, Rob Lean, and Mahmud A. Asrar. *Superman: H'el on Earth* (TPB). New York: DC Comics, 2013.

Lund, Martin. "'Introducing the Sensational Black Panther!' *Fantastic Four* #52–53, the Cold War, and Marvel's Imagined Africa." *The Comics Grid: Journal of Comics Scholarship* 6, no. 1 (2016): 1–21.

Lundegaard, Erik. "Truth, Justice and (Fill in the Blank)." *New York Times*, June 30, 2006. http://www.nytimes.com/2006/06/30/opinion/30lundegaard.html?_r=0.

Lykke, Nikka. *Feminist Studies: A Guide to Intersectional Theory, Methodology and Writing.* London: Routledge, 2010.

Mac an Ghaill, Martin, and Chris Haywood. *Gender, Culture and Society: Contemporary Femininities and Masculinities.* Hampshire: Palgrave Macmillan, 2007.

Madrid, Mike. *The Supergirls: Fashion, Feminism, Fantasy, and the History of Comic Book Heroines.* Minneapolis: Exterminating Angel Press, 2009.

Maguire, Lori. "Supervillains and Cold War Tensions in the 1950s." In *The Ages of Superman: Essays on the Man of Steel in Changing Times*, edited by Joseph J. Darowski, 16–28. London: McFarland, 2012.

Mahdawi, Arwa. "The Troubling Ascent of the LGBT Right Wing." *Guardian*, October 26, 2017. https://www.theguardian.com/commentisfree/2017/oct/26/ascent-lgbt-right-wing-afd.

Malson, Helen M. "Anorexic Bodies and the Discursive Production of Feminine Excess." In *Body Talk: The Material and Discursive Regulation of Sexuality, Madness and Reproduction*, edited by Jane M. Ussher, 223–245. London: Routledge, 1997.

Marston, William Moulton, and Harry G. Peter. *Sensation Comics #8*. New York: DC Comics, 1942.

Martignette, Charles G., and Louis K. Meisel. *The Great American Pin-Up*. London: Taschen, 1996.

Martin, Karla. "Privileging Privilege with the Hope of Accessing Privilege." In *Unhooking from Whiteness: The Key to Dismantling Racism in the United States*, edited by Cleveland Hayes and Nicholas D. Hartlep, 53–56. Rotterdam: Sense Publishers, 2013.

Massoni, Kelley. *Fashioning Teenagers: A Cultural History of "Seventeen" Magazine*. Walnut Creek, CA: Left Coast Press, 2012.

Matthews, Natalie. "Women in Suits: Ladies Who Got It Right, Because Gowns Aren't the Only Look On the Red Carpet." *Elle*, November 6, 2017. http://www.elle.com/fashion/g8897/women-in-suits-menswear/.

McCarthy, Nolan, Keith T. Poole, and Howard Rosenthal. *Polarized America: The Dance of Ideology and Unequal Riches*. Cambridge, MA: MIT Press, 2016.

McGregor, Don, Frank Robbins, Vince Colletta, Janice Cohen, Karen Mantlo, Marv Wolfman, Ron Wilson, and Joe Sinnott. *Luke Cage, Power Man #32*. New York: Marvel Comics, 1976.

McGregor, Don, George Tuska, Vince Colletta, Petra Goldberg, Dave Hunt, Marv Wolfman, Fil Kane, and Frank Giacoia. *Luke Cage, Power Man #28*. New York: Marvel Comics, 1975.

McNally, Victoria. "Women Who Love 'Star Trek' Are the Reason That Modern Fandom Exists." Revelist, September 8, 2016. http://www.revelist.com/tv/star-trek-fandom-50th/4643.

Mercer, Kobena. *Welcome to the Jungle: New Positions in Black Cultural Studies*. New York: Routledge, 2013.

Metcalf, Andy, and Martin Humphries. *The Sexuality of Men*. London: Pluto Press, 1985.

Minsky, Rosalind. *Psychoanalysis and Gender: An Introductory Reader*. London: Routledge, 1996.

Miodrag, Hannah. *Comics and Language: Reimagining Critical Discourse on the Form*. Jackson: University Press of Mississippi, 2013.

Mitchell, Maurice. "A Contortionist Calls the Sexist 'Broke Back' Pose 'Impossible.'" The Geek Twins, April 22, 2013. http://www.thegeektwins.com/2013/04/a-contortionist-calls-sexist-broke-back.html.

Moosa, Tauriq. "Nazis as the Bad Guys in Videogames? How Is That Controversial?" *Guardian*, October 27, 2017. https://www.theguardian.com/global/commentisfree/2017/oct/27/nazis-videogames-white-grievance-wolfenstein.

Morrish, Ivor. *The Dark Twin: A Study of Evil—and Good*. Wappingers Falls, NY: Beekman Books, 1999.

Moss, Mark. *The Media and the Models of Masculinity*. New York: Lexington Books, 2011.

Murphy, Drew. "Days of Future Past: Queer Identities and the X-Men." Paper presented at The Superhero 2, Oxford University, September 9–11, 2016.

Nama, Adilifu. *Super Black: American Pop Culture and Black Superheroes*. Austin: University of Texas Press, 2011.

NBC News. "Comic Heroine Ms. Marvel Saves San Francisco from Anti-Islam Ads." January 27, 2015. https://www.nbcnews.com/news/asian-america/comic-heroine-ms-marvel-saves-san-francisco-anti-islam-ads-n294751.

Nyberg, Amy Kiste. *Seal of Approval: The History of the Comics Code*. Jackson: University Press of Mississippi, 1998.

Ormrod, Joan. "The Goddess, the Iron Maiden and the Sacralisation of Consumerism in Post Crisis Wonder Woman, 1987–1992." Paper presented at Graphic Gothic: The 2016 International Graphic Novel and Comics Conference, Manchester Metropolitan University, July 11–13, 2016.

Pak, Greg, Al Barrionuevo, Tom Palmer, Ruth Redmond, Cory Petit, and Daniel Ketchum. *Storm #007*. New York: Marvel Comics, 2014.

Pak Greg, Stephanie Hans, Al Barrioneuvo, Tom Palmer, Ed Tadeo, Ruth Redmond, Cory Petit, and Daniel Ketchum. *Storm #008*. New York: Marvel Comics, 2015.

Pantozzi, Jill. "Warner Bros. Animation Takes Issue with Girls Watching Their Programs." The Mary Sue, December 20, 2013. http://www.themarysue.com/warner-bros-animation-girl-market/.

Petrovic, Paul. "Queer Resistance, Gender Performance and 'Coming Out' of the Panel Borders in Greg Rucka and J. H. William III's *Batwoman: Elegy*." *Journal of Graphic Novels and Comics* 2, no. 1 (2011): 67–76.

Pitts, Leonard, Jr. "Comicsgate: Alt-Right Fan Boys Go After Women in World of Comics." *Miami Herald*, December 28, 2018. https://www.miamiherald.com/opinion/opn-columns-blogs/leonard-pitts-jr/article223686400.html.

Pope, Harrison G., Jr., Katherine A. Phillips, and Roberto Olivardia. *The Adonis Complex: How to Identify, Treat and Prevent Body Obsession in Men and Boys*. New York: Simon & Schuster, 2002.

Priest, Christopher, Joe Bennet, and Jack Jadson. *Captain America and the Falcon #007*. New York: Marvel Comics, 2014.

Puar, Jasbir K. *Terrorist Assemblages: Homonationalism in Queer Times*. Durham, NC: Duke University Press, 2007.

Regalado, Aldo J. *Bending Steel: Modernity and the American Superhero*. Jackson: University Press of Mississippi, 2015.

Remender, Rick, Cullen Bunn, Scot Eaton, Steve Epting, and Axel Alonso. *Captain America #16*. New York: Marvel Comics, 2012.

Resha, Adrienne. "The Blue Age of Comic Books." *Inks: The Journal of the Comics Studies Society* 4, no. 1 (2020): 66–81.

Reynolds, Richard. *Superheroes: A Modern Mythology*. Jackson: University Press of Mississippi, 1994.

Riese. "All 211 Dead Lesbian and Bisexual Characters on TV, and How They Died." Autostraddle, March 11, 2016. https://www.autostraddle.com/all-65-dead-lesbian-and-bisexual-characters-on-tv-and-how-they-died-312315/.

Robertson, Ritchie. "Historicizing Weiniger: The Nineteenth-Century German Image of the Feminized Jew." In *Modernity, Culture and "The Jew,"* edited by Bryan Cheyette and Laura Marcus, 23–29. Cambridge: Polity Press, 1998.

Robinson, Lillian. *Wonder Women: Feminisms and Superheroes*. London: Routledge, 2004.

Rogers, Mary F. *Barbie Culture*. London: SAGE Publications, 1999.

Romano, Aja. "The Archive of Our Own Just Won a Hugo. That's Huge for Fanfiction." *Vox*, updated August 19, 2019. https://www.vox.com/2019/4/11/18292419/archive-of-our-own-wins-hugo-award-best-related-work.

Romano, Aja. "How DC Comics Lost Its 'Batwoman' Writers—and a Lot of Fans." Dailydot, September 5, 2013. https://www.dailydot.com/parsec/fandom/dc-comics-batwoman-writers-quit-wedding/.

Roosh V. Accessed October 13, 2016. http://www.rooshv.com.

Rucka, Greg, Dave Stewart, Adam Hughes, J. H. Williams III, Jock, Alex Ross, J. G. Jones, and Todd Klein. *Batwoman: Elegy* (TPB). New York: DC Comics, 2010.

Rupp, Leila J. *Mobilizing Women for War: German and American Propaganda, 1939–1945*. Princeton, NJ: Princeton University Press, 1978.

Saunders, Catherine, Stan Lee, Joe Quesada, Heather Scott, Julia March, Alastair Dougall, and Dorling Kindersley publishing staff. *Marvel: Year by Year, a Visual Chronicle*. New York: Dorling Kindersley, 2013.

Schott, Gareth. "From Fan Appropriation to Industry Re-appropriation: The Sexual Identity of Superheroes." *Journal of Graphic Novels and Comics* 1, no. 1 (2010): 17–29.

Sebald, Hans. *Momism: The Silent Disease of America*. Chicago: Nelson Hall, 1976.

Sekowsky, Mike, Frank Giacoia, and John Costanza. *Adventure Comics #397*. New York: DC Comics, 1971.

Shakeri, Sima. "Television Has a 'Bury Your Gays,' Queerbaiting, and LGBTQ Representation Problem." *Huffington Post*, June 30, 2017. http://www.huffingtonpost.ca/2017/06/30/queerbaiting-bury-your-gays-tv_a_23005000/.

Shyminsky, Neil. "Mutant Readers, Reading Mutants: Appropriation, Assimilation and the X-Men." *International Journal of Comic Art* 8, no. 2 (2006): 387–405.

Siegel, Jerry, Joe Shuster, Vincent Sullivan, and Jack Adler. *Action Comics #1*. New York: DC Comics, 1938.

Simone, Gail. "Front Page." Women in Refrigerators, March 1999. http://www.lby3.com/wir/index.html.

Simone, Gail. "Who Was the Bisexual Man? Or Is That Off the Table Now That Secret Six Is Done?" *Ape in a Cape: Ask Me Anything, Anything Except That*, October 4, 2011. http://gailsimone.tumblr.com/post/11015369976/who-was-the-bisexual-man-or-is-that-off-the.

Simone, Gail, Brad Anderson, Hi-Fi, Nicola Scott, Aaron Lopresti, Matt Ryan, BIT, Doug Hazlewood, Raúl Fernández, Wayne Faucher, John Dell, Travis Lanham, Fernando Dagnino, Travis Moore, and Chris Batista. *Wonder Woman: Contagion* (TPB). New York: DC Comics, 2010.

Singer, Marc. "'Black Skins' and White Masks: Comic Books and the Secret of Race." *African American Review* 36, no. 1 (2002): 107–119.

Snyder, Scott, Jim Lee, Dustin Nguyen, Scott Williams, Alex Sinclair, John Kalisz, Sal Cipriano, Matt Idelson, and Chris Conroy. *Superman Unchained #5*. New York: DC Comics, 2014.

Social Institutions and Gender Index. "United States of America." GenderIndex.org. Accessed January 16, 2017. https://www.genderindex.org/wp-content/uploads/files/datasheets/US.pdf.

Sodomy Laws. "New York Deletes Sodomy from Books." Glapn.org, June 20, 2003. https://www.glapn.org/sodomylaws/usa/new_york/nynews009.htm.

Spencer, Nick, Daniel Acuna, Joe Caramagna, Mike Choi, Romulo Fajardo Jr., Joe Bennett, Belardino Brabo, Tom Brevoort, Katie Kubert, Alanna Smith, Paul Renaud, Jeff Youngquist, and Axel Alonso. *Captain America: Sam Wilson, Volume 1: Not My Captain America* (TPB). New York: Marvel Comics, 2015.

Stabile, Carole A. "'Sweetheart, This Ain't Gender Studies': Sexism and Superheroes." *Communication and Critical/Cultural Studies* 6, no. 1 (2009): 86–92.

Stanley, Kelli E. "'Suffering Sappho!' Wonder Woman and the (Re)Invention of the Feminine Ideal." *Helios* 32, no. 2 (2005): 143–171.

Stevens, Jacqueline. "Pregnancy Envy and the Politics of Compensatory Masculinities." *Politics and Gender* 1, no. 2 (2005): 265–296.

Stuller, Jennifer. *Ink-Stained Amazons and Cinematic Warriors: Superwomen in Modern Mythology*. London: I. B. Tauris, 2010.

Sturken, Marita, and Lisa Cartwright. *Practices of Looking: An Introduction to Visual Culture*. New York: Oxford University Press, 2001.

Swan, Curt, Stan Kaye, Robert Bernstein, Al Plastino, and Otto Binder. *Action Comics #252*. New York: DC Comics, 1959.

Swan, Curt, Stan Kaye, Wayne Boring, Mort Weisinger, and Jerry Coleman. *Action Comics #241*. New York: DC Comics, 1958.

Tasker, Yvonne. *Spectacular Bodies: Gender, Genre and the Action Cinema*. London: Routledge, 1993.

Taylor, Aaron. "'He's Gotta Be Strong, and He's Gotta Be Fast, and He's Gotta Be Larger Than Life': Investigating the Engendered Superhero Body." *Journal of Popular Culture* 40, no. 2 (2007): 344–360.

Thompson, Paul. "Column: Obama Is Not My President." CBS News, November 8, 2008. https://www.cbsnews.com/news/column-obama-is-not-my-president/.

TV Tropes. "Underwear of Power." Accessed June 26, 2014. http://tvtropes.org/pmwiki/pmwiki.php/Main/UnderwearOfPower.

Tyeson, Cam. "MRA Dipshits Cut a Version of 'Endgame' with No Brie Larson & 'No Gay Shit.'" Pedestrian, May 13, 2019. https://www.pedestrian.tv/film-tv/mra-fuckwits-avengers-endgame-cutdown/.

Ussher, Jane M. *Managing the Monstrous Feminine: Regulating the Reproductive Body*. London: Routledge, 2006.

VashNL. "Save the Date: Marvel Announces Landmark X-Men Marriage." The Broken Frontier, May 22, 2012. http://old.brokenfrontier.com/headlines/p/detail/save-the-date-marvel-announces-landmark-x-men-marriage.

Vokey, Megan, Bruce Tefft, and Chris Tysiaczny. "An Analysis of Hyper-Masculinity in Magazine Advertisements." *Sex Roles* 68, no. 9 (2013): 562–576.

Walters, Suzanne Danuta. *All the Rage: The Story of Gay Visibility in America*. Chicago: University of Chicago Press, 2001.

Weaver, David H., and G. Cleveland Wilhoit. *The American Journalist: A Portrait of U.S. News People and Their Work*. Bloomington: Indiana University Press, 1986.

Wein, Len, Dave Cockrum, Peter Iro, Glynis Wein, John Costanza, Roy Thomas, Werner Roth, John Verpoorten, Artie Simek, Stan Lee, Arnold Drake, Joe Rosen, Linda Fite, Sam Grainger, Marv Woflman, Gil Kane, and Dany Crespi. *Giant-Size X-Men #1*. New York: Marvel Comics, 1975.

Weinstein, Jack, Lee Hutson, Deborah Joy LeVine, Joe Shuster, and Jerry Siegel. Directed by James R. Bagdonas. *Lois & Clark: The New Adventures of Superman*. "Tempus Fugitive." 2:18. Aired March 26, 1995, on ABC.

Weltzien, Friedrich. "Masque-*ulinities*: Changing Dress as a Display of Masculinity in the Superhero Genre." *Fashion Theory* 9, no. 2 (2005): 229–250.

Wertham, Fredric. *Seduction of the Innocent*. New York: Rinehart, 1954.

Whaley, Deborah Elizabeth. *Black Women in Sequence: Re-inking Comics, Graphic Novels and Anime*. Seattle: University of Washington Press, 2015.

Wheeler, Andrew. "Why Iron Fist Needs to Be an Asian American Hero, Not Another White Savior Cliché." Comics Alliance, December 15, 2015. http://comicsalliance.com/iron-fist-asian-american-or-white-savior/.

Whitten, Sarah. "'Avengers: Endgame' to Be the Highest-Grossing Film of All Time." CNBC, July 20, 2019. https://www.cnbc.com/2019/07/20/avengers-endgame-to-be-the-highest

-grossing-film-of-all-time.html#targetText="Avengers%3A%20Endgame"%20is%20 poised,Avatar's"%20record%20of%20%242.7897%20billion.

Wilson, G. Willow, Adrian Alphona, Kris Anka, Ian Herring, Joe Caramagna, Sana Amanat, and Charles Beacham. *Ms. Marvel #016*, vol. 3. New York: Marvel Comics, 2015.

Wilson, G. Willow, Adrien Alphona, Ian Herring, Joe Caramagna, Sana Amanat, Stephen Wacker. *Ms. Marvel Infinite #1*. New York: Marvel Comics, 2014.

Wilson, G. Willow, Adrian Alphona, Takeshi Miyazawa, Cliff Chiang, Ian Herring, Joe Caramagna, Sana Amanat, and Charles Beacham. *Ms. Marvel #003*, vol. 4. New York: Marvel Comics, 2016.

Wilson, G. Willow, Takeshi Miyazawa, Jake Wyatt, Ian Herring, Joe Caramagna, Sana Amanat, Nick Lowe, and Charles Beacham. *Ms. Marvel #014*, vol. 3. New York: Marvel Comics, 2015.

Wilson, G. Willow, Sara Pichelli, Ian Herring, Joe Caramagna, Sana Amanat, Devin Lewis, Stephen Wacker, and Adrian Alphona. *Ms. Marvel #001*, vol. 3. New York: Marvel Comics, 2014.

Wilson, G. Willow, Jake Wyatt, Ian Herring, Joe Caramagna, Sana Amanat, and Jamie McKelvie. *Ms. Marvel #007*, vol. 3. New York: Marvel Comics, 2014.

Women's Aid Organisation. "Am I in an Abusive Relationship?" Accessed January 6, 2017. https://www.womensaid.org.uk/the-survivors-handbook/am-i-in-an-abusive-relationship/.

Wood, Mara. "Gender Issues: Wonder Woman's Costume." Talking Comics Books, August 23, 2013. http://talkingcomicbooks.com/2013/08/23/gender-issues-wonder-womans-costume/.

Wright, Bradford W. *Comic Book Nation: The Transformation of Youth Culture in America*. Baltimore: Johns Hopkins University Press, 2001.

Index

Note: Page numbers in *italics* indicate figures.

About the Author

Esther De Dauw is a comics scholar who completed her PhD at the University of Leicester. Her research focuses on superheroes, gender, and race.